Exposing America:
Photographs from August 1, 1864 through July 31, 1866

David Horton

Edited by N. C. Knight

soundhole publishing company

EXPOSING AMERICA:
PHOTOGRAPHS FROM AUGUST 1, 1864 TO JULY 31, 1866

Published by

soundhole publishing
P. O. Box 2003
Tucker, Georgia 30085

www.soundholepublishing.com

Copyright 2006 © by David Horton

All rights reserved. Except for use in a review, the reproduction or utilization of this work in whole or in part in any form by any electronic, mechanical, or other means, now known or hereafter invented, including xerography, photocopying and recording, or in any information storage or retrieval system is forbidden without the written permission of the publisher .

Every attempt has been made to include accurate information in this book. Any errors or omissions are solely those of the author. However there may be technical inaccuracies or typographical errors. soundhole publishing, inc. assumes no liability for errors or omissions in this book, or for the use o the information contained herein. Information may be changed or updated without written notice.

Book Designed By: David Horton and N. C. Knight
Cover Designed By: David Horton and N. C. Knight
David Horton Photograph By N. C. Knight

Dust Jacket Front: St. Louis Post Office, c. 1864, Hoelke & Benecke
Dust Jacket Back: unknown by W. A. Smith, Plymouth, OH.
Dust Jacket Front Flap: Pulaski Monument, Perry & Loveridge, Savannah, GA

ISBN 0-9768760-6-X
Printed in China

Special Dedication

To my wife Nancy Henry Horton for the patience not to choke the life from me when I desperately needed it. (And, I needed it often.)

Dedication

This book is dedicated to the photographers whose images are used in this book. Without those pioneers, our knowledge of that era would be limited to handed-down tales, history books, letters, artists sketches and news articles. With the advent of photography, visual evidence came into existence. No longer were we bound by the written or spoken description of an event or person or place.

From the earliest inception of photography with Daguerre in France to the Father of American Photography, Samuel F. B. Morse, to today's sophisticated digital camera, we are indebted to photographers everywhere for preserving history for future generations.

We cannot forget to thank the people who preserved these images. Without them, such wonderful evidence of a lifestyle gone by would not exist. Without them, collecting photographs would be less rich, less challenging, and less exciting.

Acknowledgements

Special thanks to: Michael Griffith for Historical Editing
    Maureen Hardegree, copy editor

Also thanks to Michael Welch, Bruce Baryla, Eric Jackson, Michael Scarfman, Udo Minglesdorf, Dick Lyons, The Hart Brothers, David Wynn Vaughan and Little David, George Whiteley, III, Dr. Roger Rowell, Peggy Mitchell and hundreds of acquaintances from whom invaluable help in sharing information, aid seeking and acquiring the images used in this book and a willingness to contribute to this project have proven the fraternal nature of friends, collectors and dealers.

Exposing America: Photographs From August 1, 1864 through July 31, 1866

Introduction

Among of the first evidence of the industrial revolution was the availability of photographs to the common man. A complicated distribution and manufacturing scenario provided images of famous people, loved ones, familiar locales, exotic places from around the world and copies of art to the discriminator at fees from less than ten cents per image.

Large companies, such as E & H. T. Anthony of New York, provided plates and chemicals to photographers from the Daguerreian era through the ambrotype era and into the era of albumen photographs and tin-types. Photographers already had sources of chemicals and hardware for re-sale to photo artists. When America was caught by carte-o-mania, the fad of collecting photographs, in the early 1860s, it was a natural step up from small to large quantities of the products needed.

Photographers needed card stock to mount photos and a printed imprint that would serve as an advertiser. The photographers must acquire the necessities and still be competitive and inexpensive enough that a large percentage of the population could afford their work. This was accomplished largely by the competitiveness of the suppliers who bought goods in large enough quantities and operated at margins that would insure continued sources of materials and chemicals.

The Carte de Visite or CDV was the mainstay of the business for the small operator. CDVs were uniform in size, 2 1/2" X 4 1/8", hence the CDV album, a convenient place to store images of family, friends, politicians, Civil War leaders and heroes. These albums did such a good job of preservation that many images survive in pristine condition today.

Other formats were also used. From images as large as 20 ½" X 17 ½" to as small as ½" X ½" tin-type gems, from ambrotype to stereo views and various processes and formats in between, today's collector is challenged only by his imagination as to format and process of the next tax-stamped images or sun fixing as it was called.

The Civil War was quite expensive in terms of life, property and cash. Property was given voluntarily in the South to support the war effort by means of bonds. In the North, the war was prosecuted by implementing a tax system to fund it. Tax laws enacted in 1862 taxed everything from canned beans to documents and included income taxation. By 1863 new taxes were needed to help with the mounting war debt. The dollar was losing value, and the war could be lost by an economic collapse. Photography, a luxury item, was added to the list of taxed items in 1864 to provide additional revenue. The photographers mounted opposition in the press and found support in their trade magazines, and in 1866 the law requiring a tax stamp on photographs was repealed. Afterwards the Photographers were allowed to pay taxes based on their incomes.

For this two year period, we have an opportunity to view America through its own eyes. Almost all aspects of life were recorded on the photographs of this period, and we have a snapshot of the time. Take time to enjoy, as this generation did, the views and interpretations of the end of the Civil War and the beginning of the photographic recording of American history.

Author's Notes

For the purposes of this book, the photographs are not only valued for the images, but also for the stamp used to pay the tax on the picture, the photographer who took the picture, for the backmark and for the cancellation on the reverse of the image. The reverse side of an image, in some instances, is much more valuable than the front in terms of information and historical value.

Much has been written concerning early photographic methods. The primary types of photography done during the tax period are the albumen print, the tin-type or ferrotype and the ambrotype. The latter two are one of a kind images while the albumen refers to the negative. Due to the use of albumized negatives, many prints, as in the case of E & H. T. Anthony, up to 50,000 images could be printed from one negative. 3600 could be manufactured in one day. The usual number of copy images sold to a patron was six or twelve.

Tin-types are found in multiples but their existence in multiples is due to the apparatus known as Wing's camera. The camera was built to accommodate multiple lenses, three, four, six and twelve. The photographer could then expose as much or as little of the tin-type plate as needed. Because the images were taken simultaneously, they are from slightly different perspectives. The images can be recombined and viewed in stereo. It is possible to build stereo views from apparent duplicate tin-types. True tin-type stereo views, two views on one piece of tin, are rare. Those that are known to exist do not have a tax stamp on the reverse.

The tin-type was popular because it resembled the earlier, more expensive ambrotype when placed in a case. It was less expensive to produce and it eliminated a step, the conversion from the negative to the positive. Both ambrotype and the tin-type are negatives placed on a dark background. This process makes them appear as positives.

The ambrotype was the next step of photography from the Daguerreotype. Instead of an image chemically fixed on a highly polished silver-plated copper plate, the photographer fixed an image on a piece of glass. The ambrotype, being superior in view ability and cost, succeeded the Daguerreotype in the mid 1850s. Ambrotypes are always placed in a case. The case was manufactured to protect the image and give the image a suitable presentation. The chemical side was turned in toward the cases to protect the emulsion, unlike the Daguerreotype which was turned out, and a protective glass plate was installed to protect the image

For both Daguerreotypes and ambrotypes, paper tape held the image. A gold-colored brass mat framed the subject. These one of a kind images, by the tax period, could be copied onto albumized negatives and sold. The ambrotype is seldom encountered with tax stamps affixed, and the Daguerreotype is scarce during the tax period.

The photographs which follow belong to my collection. I prize each image for reasons particular to that image which I will explain in greater detail with examples of the photographs. I hope that readers will enjoy the photographs and information presented here.

Sincerely,

David Horton

Exposing America: Photographs from August 1, 1864 through July 31, 1866

Table of Contents:

Chapter One: Photography: Processes, Formats and Pioneers — 1

Tin-type	1
Albumen	4
Cased Images	5
Daguerreotype and Oreo	6
Ambrotype	7
Stereo Views	8
Large Format Tin-types	12
Albumen	13
Cabinet Cards, Jewelry	16
Sir Rowland Hill	17
Samuel Finley Breese Morse	18
George S. Boutwell	20

Chapter Two: The Images — 21

Portrait Types	22
Tinted Photographs	24
Trick and Mirrored Photography	28

Topical Listing

Actors and Actresses	32
Animals	35
Barnum's Museum	38
The Disabled	41
Ethnic	44
"Freaks" and Other Circus Performers	47
Interiors	49
Machines	50
Masonic Orders	52
Military	54
Musical	65
Occupational	69

Outdoor Scenes	74
Mount Vernon	91
Patriotic Children	93
Personalities	94
Postmortem	96
Statuary and Works of Art	98
Stereo Viewers	105
Toys	107
Weddings	110

Chapter Three:
Photography, The Stamp Law and the Stamps — 112

The Revenue Stamps	114
The Stamps	115
Scarcity Charts and Graphs	128
Fancy Cancels and Punch Cancels	134

Chapter Four:
The Photographer's Art — 138

Mounted Tin-Types	138
Burgeoning Era of Victorian Women	140
Group Images	142
Fancy Vignettes	147
Famous Photographers	150
Strip Labels	153
Studio Succession	155
Fancy Backs	156
Southern Photographers	168
Western Photographers	176
Image within an Image	178
Projection Views	181

Appendices — 183

Verified Photographers Working During the Tax Period	183
Stamps Used on Photographs	220
Bibliography	222
Glossary	224
Afterward	226

Index — 228

Chapter One

Photography: Processes, Formats and Pioneers

A photograph represents a physical manifestation of a moment in time. For the collector and historians, the examination of those images provides a form of education, a glimpse into another era and the satisfaction of knowing history is preserved for generations to come.

Tin-type of a hesitant youth. The image, once in a case as evidence by the oval mark, is now loose.

Tax paid by Dual Frank, a pair of one cent red Proprietary stamps and a three cent green Proprietary stamp paying the five cent rate.

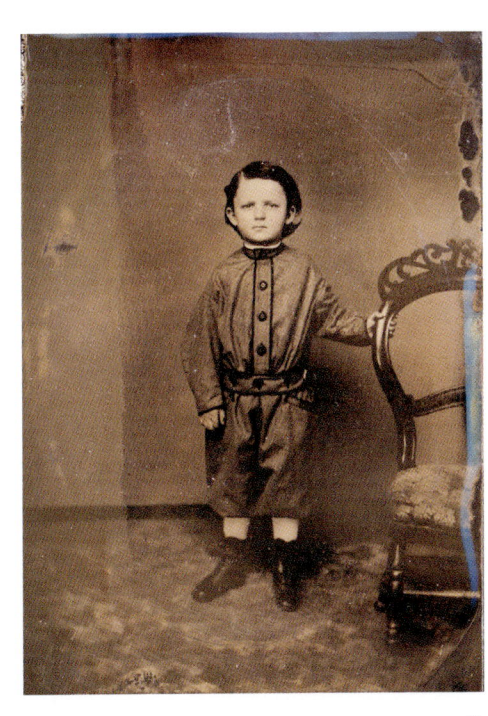

It is doubtful whether the person who carefully placed these photographs into albums one hundred and forty years ago realized the importance of that gesture. Rather, he or she probably intended to put the images into a book that would provide easy access for family and visitors to their homes. Life existed at a much slower paced and was far less complicated then. Today, looking at a photograph album might seem to be a bit tame for an afternoon's diversion.

People sought diversions from the war. What with receiving news almost daily about the deaths of family members, friends and acquaintances, sitting and looking at a photo album seemed to be a pleasant way to spend some time. It also served as a way of remembering family members near and far, those who had passed on, and a lifestyle that existed no more.

The scarcity of photographs for the emerging middle class made them more valuable. Each photograph must have been treasured. The evidence for that is obvious from the way people dressed when they knew they were going to be photographed. Today, when photography is readily available, and people can snap a picture with a camera in their cell phones, the value is greatly diminished in my eyes.

The approximate conversion of today's dollars to that of the end of the Civil War is 66 to 1. In that largely agrarian society, people worked ten hours a day, six days a week to earn $460. per year. In today's more service-oriented society, with a work week of forty hours, $30,000. is approximately equivalent to that apparently meager income at the end of the Civil War. Converting that to the cost of twelve images at $2.50, a person would work one day to pay the cost of the images and one hour to pay the tax of twenty-four cents at two cents per image, or simply put, one hour for the tax alone. It is a small wonder that the images were highly prized and preserved.

Some insights are deduced from the ratio of photographers to the populace, the rate of tax charged, and the style of clothes worn. From this analysis, prosperity of a geographic area can be ascertained. Other details of daily life can also be observed. For the serious collector, the historian, the antiques dealer, or for anybody interested in the past, these photographs are invaluable.

The image below is a quarter plate **tin-type** of a husband and wife with three well-dressed children.

The stamp is pre-cancelled by Thomas Shaw, Chagrin Falls, OH. Paying the five cent rate is a red Inland Exchange stamp. This photograph probably came in a case, and the five cents paid for the case and for the photograph.

PHOTOGRAPHED BY J. Q. A. TRESIZE, ZANESVILLE, OHIO.

This large format **albumen** depicts the site of the recently buried Abraham Lincoln, image by J. Q. A. Tresize of Zaneville, Ohio. Note the ropes to discourage visitors from coming closer to the two armed honor guards. Actual image size is 5 1/2" x 7 7/8." Overall mat size is 9 5/8" x 12." The stamp on the verso, a three cent green Proprietary, is correctly cancelled by Tresize.

4

Tin-type 1/6th plate **cased image** in a gutta percha case. The portrait is typical. The stamps are a pair of Internal Revenue two cent orange, one of which has been bisected diagonally to pay the three cent rate.

Only known **Daguerreotype** with tax stamps. The stamps were found in the 1/2 leather-covered case and not attached to the photograph. According to tax law, the entire item was taxed as a unit, and, at the photographer's discretion, he would affix the stamps either to the back of the photograph or to the inside of the case.

Open "**oreo**" in a gutta percha case.

Partial three cent green Foreign Exchange stamp on the back of the tin-type.

1/4 plate **ambrotype** in case, ten cent rate paid by the use of a block of five two cent blue Proprietary stamps.

Stereo Views

Before photography, artists with knowledge of perspective and visual depth perception, drew side by side perspective images with slightly different horizontal perspectives. This exercise could then be viewed and thereby produced a stereo view, an image with depth. This principle was quickly adapted to photography early in the Daguerreian era. The quite expensive views, vistas and landscapes, architecture or personalities, were viewed in three dimensions for amusement.

Photographic methods changed quickly. Stereo views, similar to the carte de visites, were now produced inexpensively. Because technology advanced to the ability to transfer images from a negative inexpensively, large numbers of middle class citizens suddenly had access to a new form of entertainment only their rich cousins could afford prior to this technology jump.

Stereo views were available from local photographers and retailers on a large variety of topics. Views of the homeland, current events, famous people, the wonders of the world, and any subject the photographer might consider commercial, became available.

This large emerging market not only captured the imagination of hundreds of photographers who made their living in the studio, the populace who could now be entertained by firelight with favorite images but also the government who taxed the new product under the photographic tax laws. The tax laws were applied to stereo views similarly to other formats of photography. Most stereos are found with the two cent rate. Most of the views were a commercial venture intended to be sold by the photographer, agent or distributor. Occasionally a photographer would be commissioned to do family or group portraiture. The rate found on this type of portraiture is normally five cents indicating a sale price up to one dollar.

The firm of Edward and H.T. Anthony was the largest producer of stereo views. They purchased images from various photographers. Among their popular views are those from the Civil War. The common cancellation of the Anthony firm was a cross produced by lining out sheets of stamps.

The uncommon two cent orange Proprietary stamp is commonly found on the Anthony views. The firm purchased the remaining stock of over a half million stamps because they liked the way the orange stamp looked on their yellow mount. The Anthony firm also sold finished views, paper, chemicals, cameras, accessories and stamps. A number of New York photographers used the two cent orange Proprietary stamp in larger numbers than other locales.

The fondness of Americans for stereo views was not dampened by the tax. Stereo views have remained popular into the twenty-first century.

Stereo tissue sold by London Stereograph and Photographic Co., NY. Image is pin pricked for the illusion of candles when held to light. View is in the Vatican. Stereo tissues are rarely found with a tax stamp.

Stamp is a three cent green Proprietary with a circular date cancel. The stamp was trimmed to fit the mount.

Albumen stereoview of the bones of unburied in Ireland due to the famine caused by the potato blight, c. 1840s. View is by an unknown photographer, sold by E & H. T. Anthony, NY, with an orange two cent Proprietary stamp. Note the cross cancellation. E & H. T. Anthony had an employee whose job it was to line out sheets of stamps.

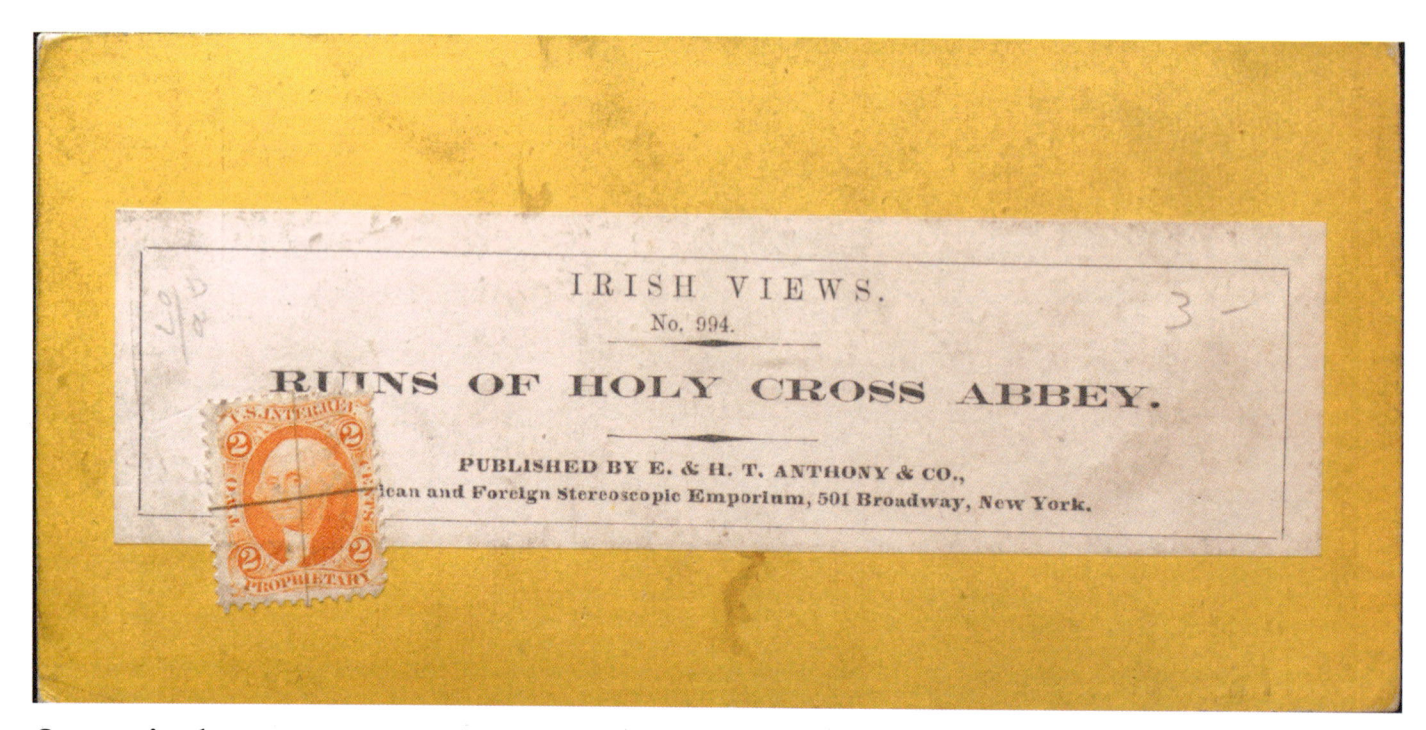

Stamp is the two cent orange Proprietary. Crossed ink strokes cancel the stamp.

10

Albumen stereo view of R. M. Linn sitting below Umbrella Rock adjacent to his photography studio, Lookout Mountain, TN.

Three cent green Proprietary stamp used to pay taxes.

11

Large Formats
Tin-Type

Full plate tin-type in a mat. The tinted gold emblem on hat and buttons indicated military service. The box on the right in the photograph was used to view CDVs. By turning the handle, a roll of images would pass the viewing window.

The largest rate known to date on a photograph is a cancelled one dollar red Probate of Will, cancelled August 30, 1864. The stamp probably paid for the image, mat and frame.

Albumen

Large albumen image of the side wheeler *Itasca* taken by an Ilion, NY photographer. Note the two cent orange Bank Check stamps paying the four cents tax, a rate not mandated. The rate charged was probably inclusive of the image and frame.

A large re-touched albumen image of Abraham Lincoln by Alexander Gardner done in Washington, 1863. Note the cancellation on the two five cent, red Proprietary stamps of the Gardner Studio paying the ten cent rate. The cancel indicates the re-touch was done in the studio of the original photographer.

Albumen print of thirteen military men and one small boy. The two cent orange Internal Revenue stamp was used on photographs from about 1865 to 1866. Why taxes were paid after the tax had expired can only be conjecture.

Cabinet Card

Albumen portrait of Ralph Waldo Emerson by an unknown photographer on a cabinet card size board. Cabinet cards were not used until 1866. The larger size and closer portraits slowly replaced the CDV. It is rare to find cabinet cards with tax stamps. A pair of two cent blue Proprietary stamps with half of one stamp torn away pays the three cent rate.

Ralph Waldo Emerson, abolitionist, essayist, poet, and orator is well remembered as a member of the "academic races" of New England.

Jewelry

Ambrotype image of a gentleman encased in a brooch with a three cent stamp used to pay the tax. This is the only piece of jewelry known with tax stamps.

SIR ROWLAND HILL
(December 3, 1795- August 27, 1879)

This image is of the inventor of the postage stamp, Sir Rowland Hill. Sir Rowland Hill not only invented the postage stamp but also the uniform postage rates based on weight instead of distance.

At age thirty-eight Hill became Secretary of the South Australia Commission, an association which helped the colonization from his native England to Australia. He became interested in postal reform and published a pamphlet entitled "Post Office Reform: It's Importance and Practicability." He proposed that letters be charged by weight, and that the sender should pay the postage. The proposal went before Parliament and was given Royal Assent in 1839. On January 10, 1840 the first adhesive type postage stamp, the Penny Black, came into use. From the position of schoolmaster he ascended to Secretary of the Post Office. During this tenure, he was knighted in 1860 for inventing the postage stamp.

His invention, a small bit of paper with an assessed value, is still use today. The stamp played an integral role in the collection of revenue for the United States in the form of Revenue stamps.

Sir Rowland Hill probably autographed this carte. He holds a pen in the photo. He was well known for his contribution to postal history as the inventor of the postage stamp.

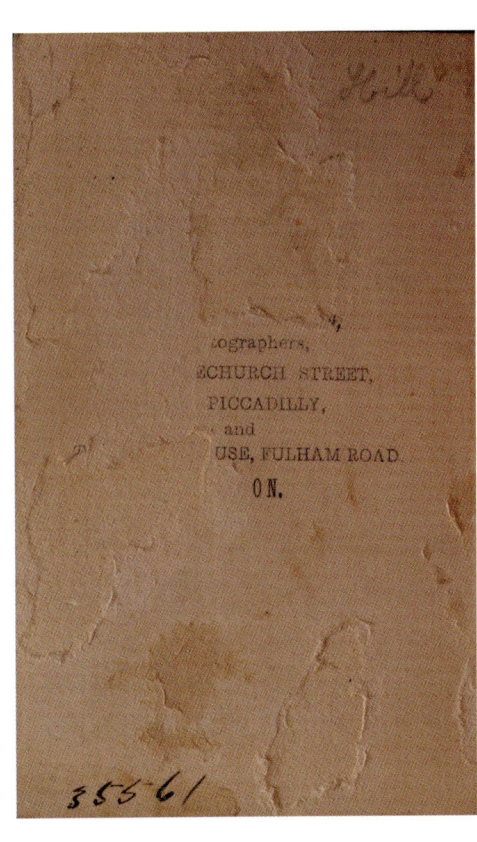

SAMUEL FINLEY BREESE MORSE
(APRIL 27, 1791-APRIL 2, 1871)

Samuel Morse, well known as the inventor of the Morse Code and the telegraph, has another moniker, Father of American Photography. He taught some of America's finest photographers the art of the Daguerreotype, named after the inventor of the process M. Daguerre of France. In the spring of 1839, Morse traveled to Paris to secure a patent for his telegraph apparatus. While there, he heard of the experiments of Daguerre. Being keen on the subject and having done some unsuccessful experiments with photography in America, he was anxious to meet the man who could paint with sunbeams.

"I do not like to go home without first seeing Daguerre's results," Morse confided in the American Consul, Robert Walsh. Walsh suggested that Morse invite Daguerre to see his telegraphic apparatus. Morse was invited to Daguerre's laboratory where he viewed fine image specimens of the Louvre, Notre Dame, interiors, still life and other works of art. Daguerre had been unsuccessful at the human portrait and revealed to Morse that "he doubted it could be done".

The next day at noon, Daguerre went to visit Morse and to witness the operation of his telegraph. The visit lasted over an hour. During Daguerre's absence, his exhibit and laboratory burned. All was destroyed. Morse wrote about the new process. The article was published May 1839 in *The Democratic Review* where he describes the Daguerreotypes as "Rembrandt perfected."

Morse was the first American to receive the process details directly from Daguerre. He was able to construct the first Daguerrian apparatus and possibly took the first image in America. From the back window of New York University on a playing card size plate an image of the Church of the Messiah was obtained. Morse, inspired by Daguerre, enlisted his two brothers, Sidney and Richard to assist in removing the roof of their six story building and covering it with a skylight. Equipping it with cameras it became the first "tabernacle for the sun."

John W. Draper, a chemist, and Morse were the first to do human portraiture. Depending upon weather conditions it would take a painful ten to twenty minutes of the sitter being still for the chemicals to react to the light. Some of the leading photographers of the age began as Morse's students: Samuel Broadbent, Jerimiah Gurney, Mathew Brady and Albert Sands Southworth.

The father of American photography is pictured with awards in science and for the invention of the telegraph.

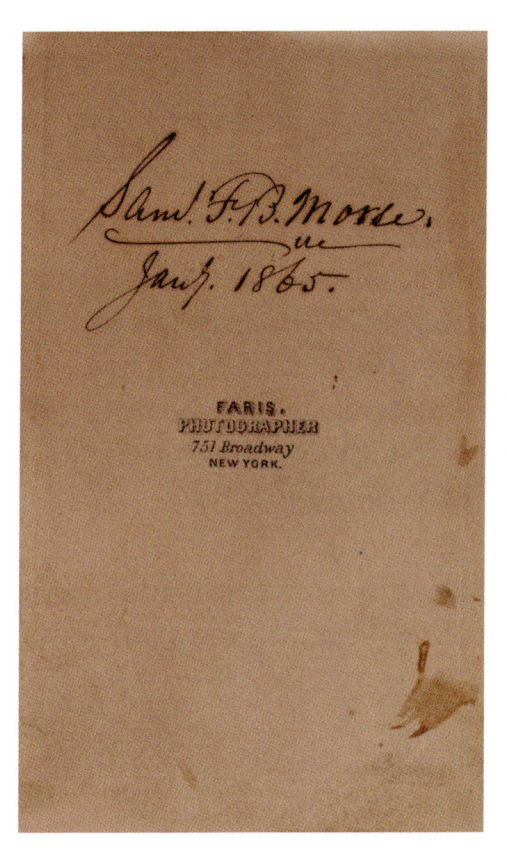

Samuel F. B. Morse, "Father of Photography," autographed and dated in the tax period. Note the medals he proudly wears. Most were give for his contribution, the telegraph.

Cabinet card of George S. Boutwell done in the reknowned Brady Studios.

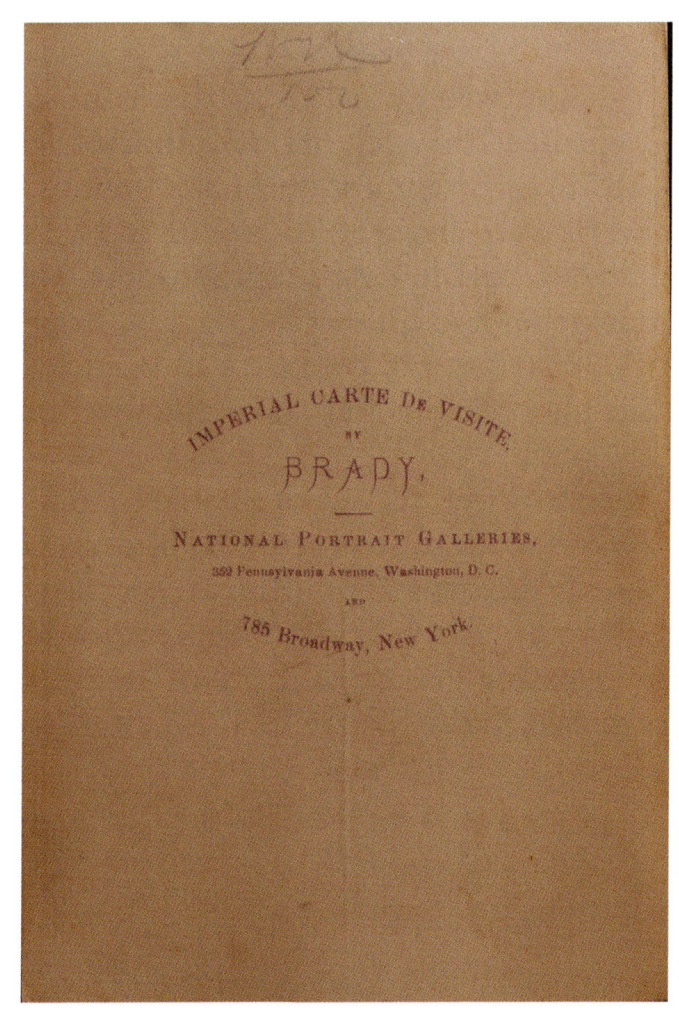

GEORGE S. BOUTWELL
(January 28, 1818 - February 27, 1905)

Boutwell was the first Commissioner of the Internal Revenue (July 17, 1862-March 4, 1863). As noted in the letter from Salmon P. Chase, George Boutwell, the former Governor of Massachusetts, is recommended for the job: "The important duties devolved on this office demand the highest obtainable ability and integrity. Having carefully considered all the names suggested, I find no one whose bearer unites the qualities in higher degree." (Letter from Salmon P. Chase to President Abraham Lincoln, The Abraham Lincoln Papers, Library of Congress.)

As commissioner, Boutwell was responsible for operating a new program, designed as a revenue-raising measure to help pay for the Civil War, signed into law by Abraham Lincoln.

This new law levied a three percent tax on incomes between $600 and $10,000 and a five percent tax on incomes of more than $10,000. In 1867 due to public opposition to the income tax, rates were reduced and in 1872 income tax was repealed. According to Internal Revenue records, from 1868 to 1913, 90 percent of all revenue to the United States came from taxes on liquor, beer, wine and tobacco.

Boutwell awarded the first contract to produce revenue stamps to Butler and Carpenter, Philadelphia, PA. Today, these stamps are known as The First Issue (1862 - 1871) of revenue stamps. The stamps, of various color, denomination, perforation and title are attached to articles in two categories, proprietary in nature such as matches, perfume, photographs, etc. and banking instruments such as checks, mortgages and bills of lading, etc. Boutwell approved stamp design, color, face value, title, distribution, contracts and articles to be taxed. It was not until August 1, 1864 that photographs fell under the taxation laws.

Boutwell served as a congressman from 1863-1869 and was appointed by Ulysses S. Grant to the office of Secretary of the Treasury from 1869 to 1873. Shortly after his appointment, speculators tried to corner the gold market on what is known as "Black Friday," September 23, 1869. He successfully blocked the scheme by releasing great quantities of Treasury gold and flooded the market. Boutwell returned to the Senate in 1873 after leaving the Treasury.

Chapter Two

The Images

Full Standing, three quarter seated, three quarter standing, bust and bust vignette are the most common portrait types of this period. The optics of the first generation of lenses dictated the image size relative to the reproduced image size. The result was an image that suited the mount size of the carte de visite and was easily produced. After the introduction of the second generation of lenses, a new format was born, the Cabinet Card. The advantage was a larger, closer image of the sitter. The cabinet card began a climb in popularity in 1866 and is scarcely found with tax stamps. Although the carte de visite lasted into the 20th century, the cabinet card became the favored format by the 1880s.

Portrait Types

Standing

A head stand was necessary to maintain the pose long enough to properly expose the negatives.

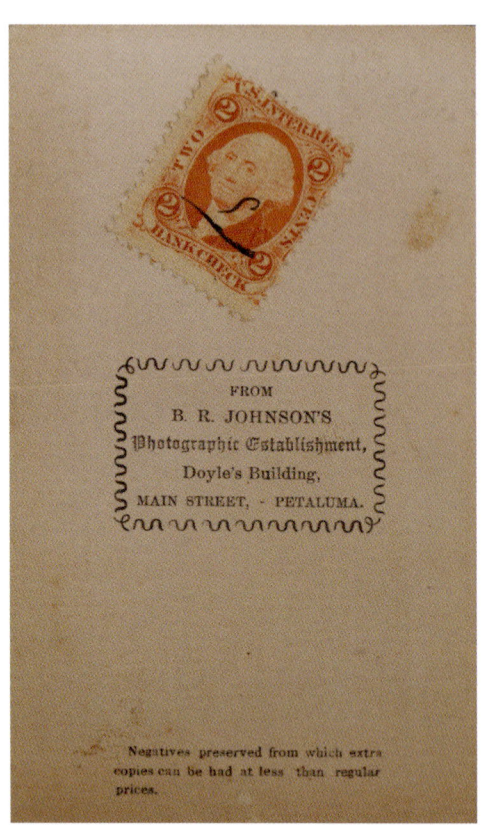

Albumen CDV of a California military bugler. Note the head stand visible at his feet. The stamp is a two cent orange Bank Check used to pay the tax.

Three-quarter Seated

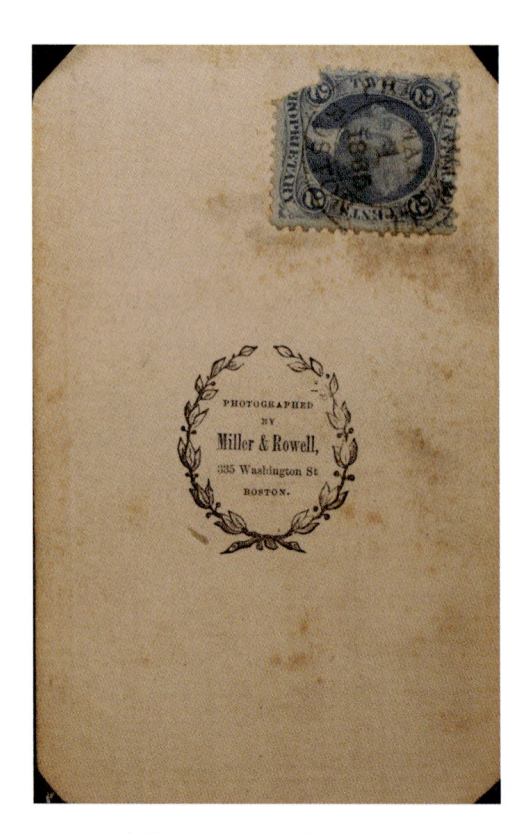

CDV of unknown actress in this seated portrait.

Two cent blue Proprietary stamp cancelled by Miller & Rowell with circular date cancel.

Three-quarter Standing

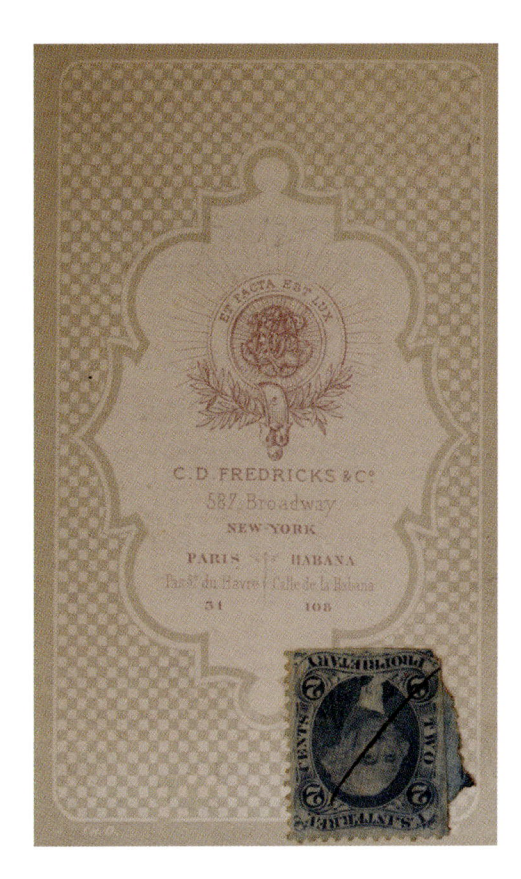

Unknown actress by C. D. Fredricks in a three-quarter standing orientation.

Note ink cancelled two cent Proprietary blue stamp.

Bust Vignette

Unknown tinted vignette of a man wearing a star suspended from a medal hanger.

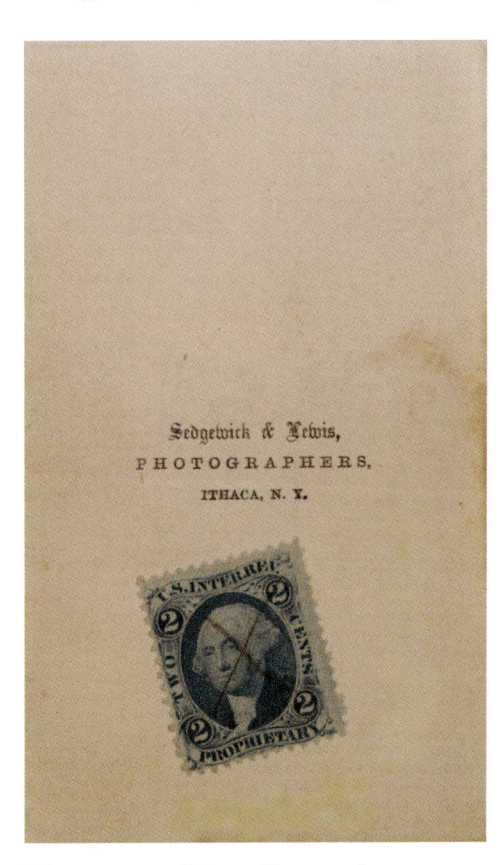

Two cent blue Proprietary stamp cancelled with an "X."

Tinted Photographs

It has long been alleged by photography historians that photography replaced the artists who painted miniature portraits. These skilled artists found they had been replaced by a mechanical device. A drawback to securing a photograph was that it could only be produced in black and white and with a full range of grays. Work soon became available for the artist to perform the chore of tinting images. Some early Daguerreotypes are very skillfully tinted, but the task of tinting historically fell upon the photographer and the photographer's wife. Most photographers and photographer's wives were not trained artists, but many attained skills suitable to tinting photographs.

During the tax period, tinting was an added expense and is sometimes reflected in the tax rate collected with the exception of Southern photographers who needed to give their customers a little extra to encourage business. Typically, Southern photographers added vignetting and tinting at no additional cost.

The following group of three albumen CDVs is finely tinted. Note the use of glasses added to cancel the stamp of the first CDV.

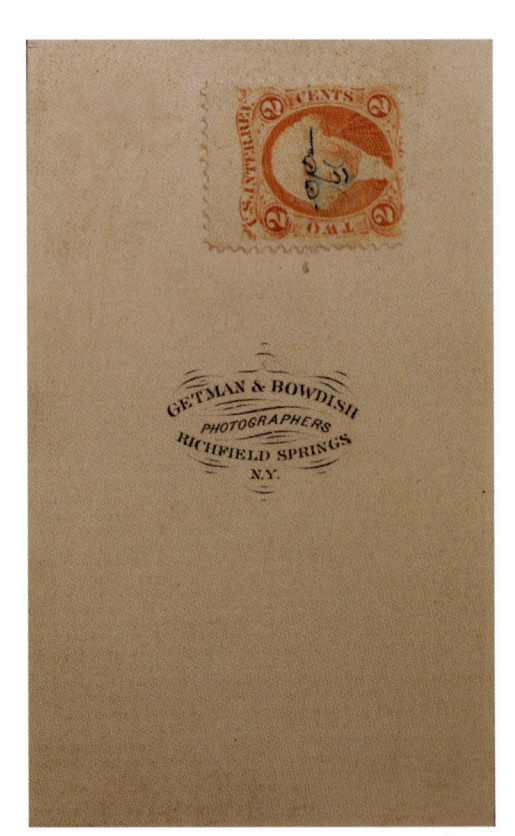

24

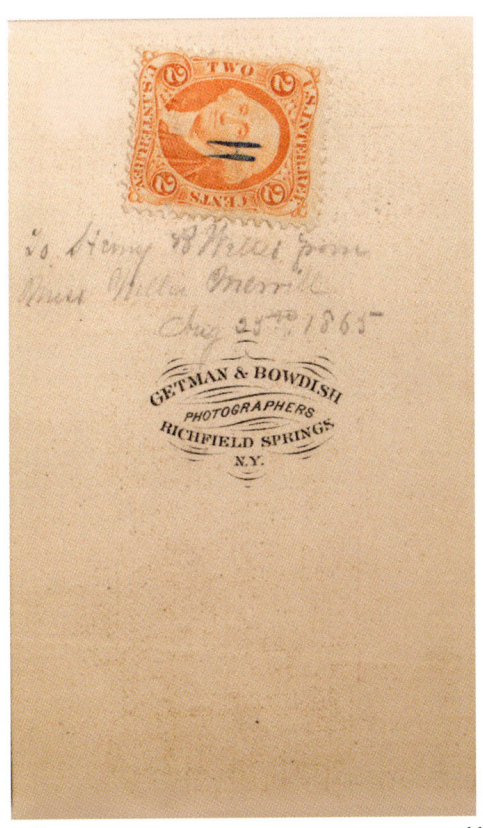

These two stamps are cancelled with simple pen strokes on the Internal Revenue two cent orange stamps. The images appear to be of people dressed for some type of pageant.

25

Albumen CDV of a young boy dressed in Scottish togs. This is another finely tinted example. Note the double stroke cancellation on the two cent orange Proprietary stamp.

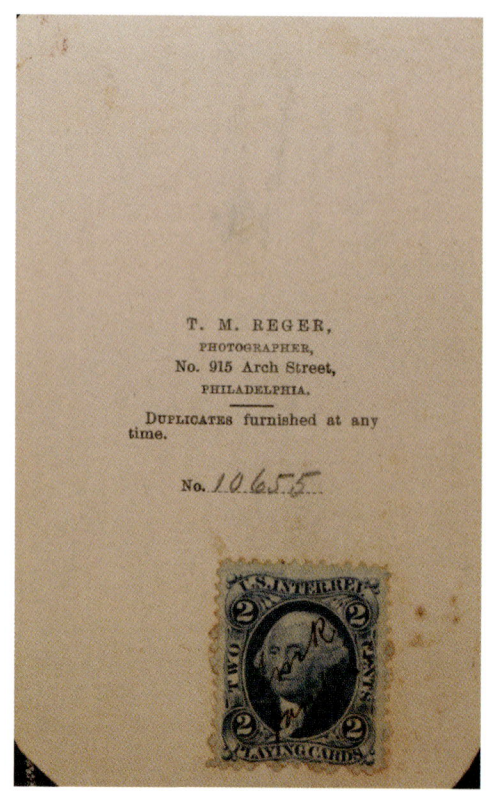

Finely tinted example of a woman in winter apparel. The two cent blue Playing Cards stamp used to pay the taxes on the photograph is cancelled by the photographer T. M. Reger with his initials.

Two cent blue Proprietary stamp cancelled with an "X" mark.

Augusta Walby attired in Scottish regalia on a tinted CDV.

Two cent blue Proprietary stamp. Note the extra row of perforations vertically on the stamp.

Very finely tinted image of a dancer. Image by the prestigious studio of C. D. Fredricks, NY.

27

Trick and Mirrored Photography

People of the 19th century found amusement in the result of technical manipulation of the negative. The sitter would pose, anticipating another person in the view, while the photographer would adjust the camera so as to put the sitter left or right of center of the negative. With the negative masked on the other half an exposure would be made. The photographer would then mask the exposed half of the negative and prepare to expose the second half. The sitter would move to the second position and the second exposure would be made. The image produced would then show the sitter in two different positions on the image. A weakness in the portrait is usually seen in the middle of the image where it had been exposed twice or over-exposed. The additional work done is sometimes reflected in the tax rate.

Note the ghosting of the overlapping dresses at the bottom of the photograph.

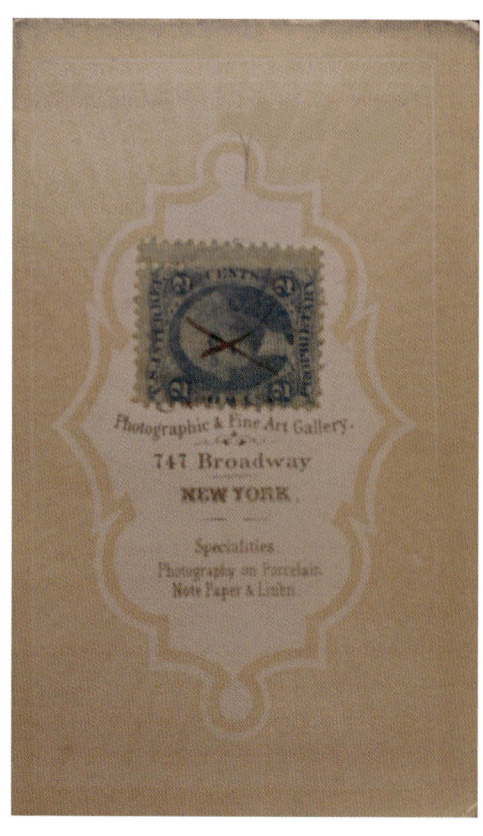

Two cent blue Proprietary stamp. Note three extra perforations upper right of stamp.

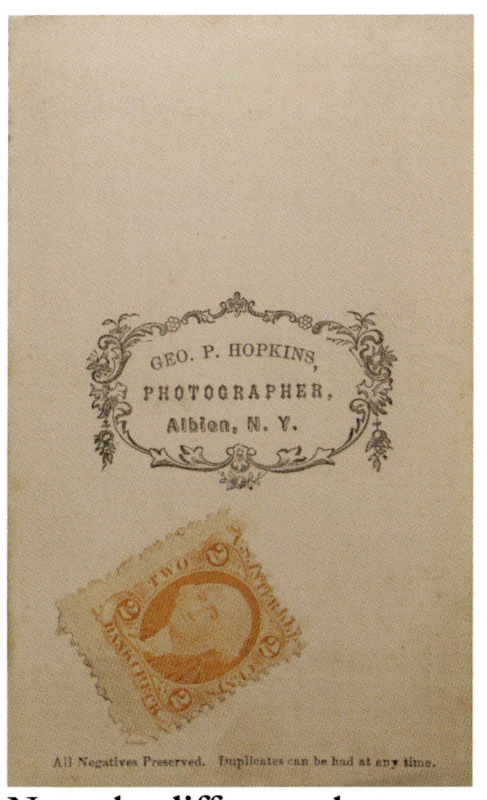

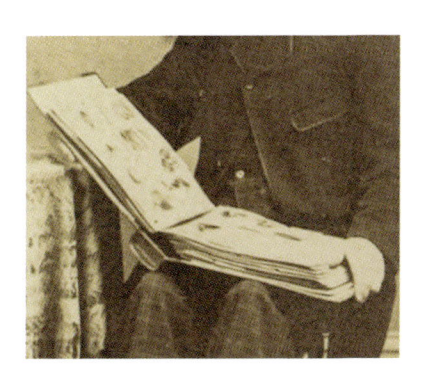

Note the difference between this George P. Hopkins backmark and the one on the following page. Two cent orange Bank Check stamp is not cancelled.

Double exposure of bearded man looking through a photo album.

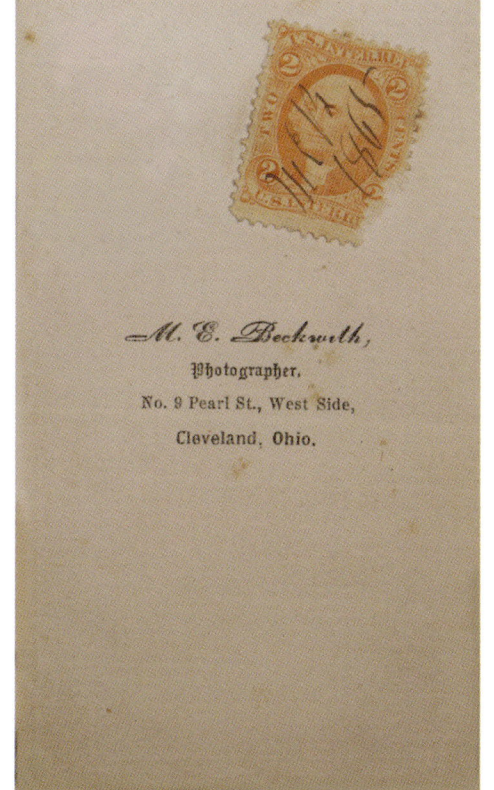

Two cent orange Internal Revenue stamp cancelled with the photographer's initials and year.

Trick photo. Double exposure, probably the photographer with his chemicals being assisted by himself.

29

Trick photo of reverse over-the-shoulder horn player being conducted by himself.

Note the intricate details on the backmark of George P. Hopkins, photographer. An allegorical scene is depicted.

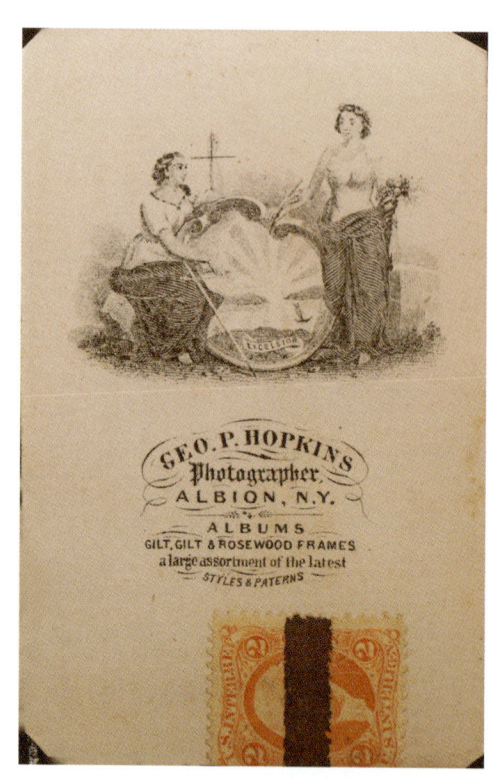

Two cent orange Internal Revenue stamp cancelled with a black bar.

Trick photo of three people. The people changed positions in the second exposure.

Three cent green Proprietary stamp used was cancelled with a date stamp.

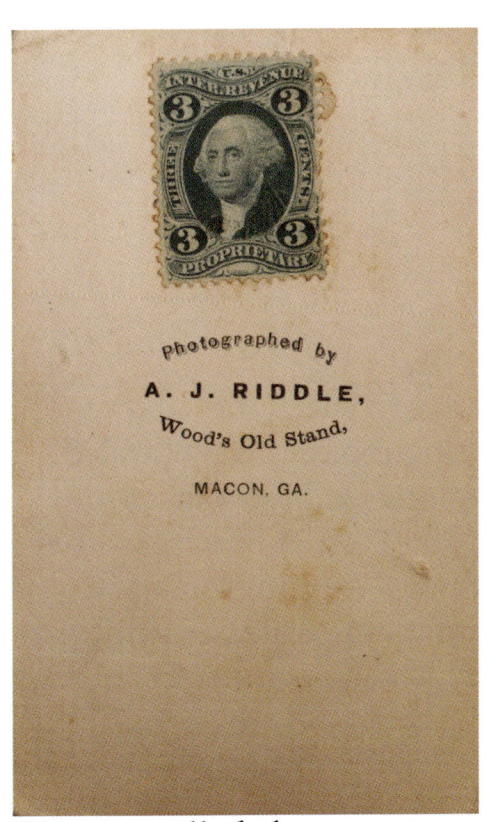

Non-cancelled three cent green Proprietary stamp used to pay tax on the photo.

Mirrored photo of a southern woman showing her hair style. Photo by A. J. Riddle, the only photographer officially hired by the Confederacy during the Civil War.

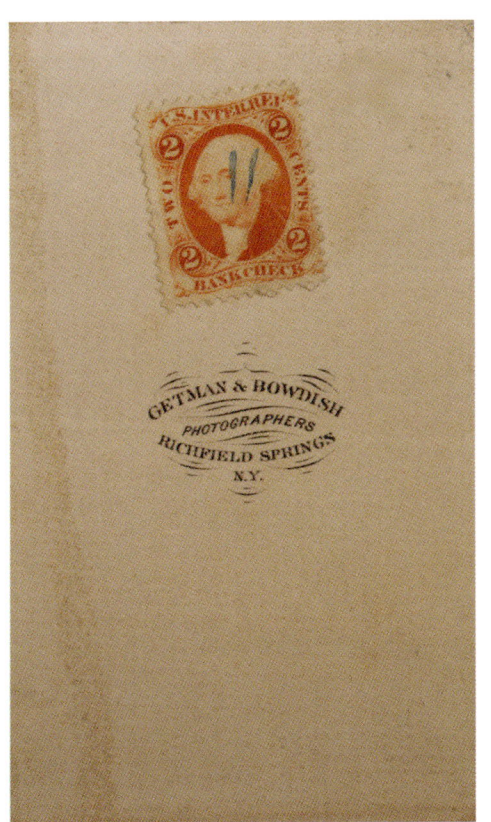

The two cent orange Bank Check stamp was used for the tax on the photo and cancelled with two straight marks.

Another mirrored photo. This one shows the woman's face in the mirror, a difficult task with the shallow depth of field produced by early lenses.

Actors and Actresses

The proud traditions of the playwright were carried forward to the actors and actresses here portrayed. Many small communities had acting troupes who carried the traditions of Shakespeare's England to America. A common subject during the Civil War was the revolutionary patriotism which formed the United States. In the cities of New York, Philadelphia, Baltimore, New Orleans and Washington, D. C., plays were enacted following the traditions of the day. Actors and actresses achieved fame and a following. Depicted is Maggie Mitchell, whom Abraham Lincoln watched perform in many roles.

Maggie Mitchell (Margaret Julia Mitchell) portrait. She performed at Ford's Theatre for President Lincoln many times before he was assassinated. She was most often seen in "Fanchon, The Cricket."

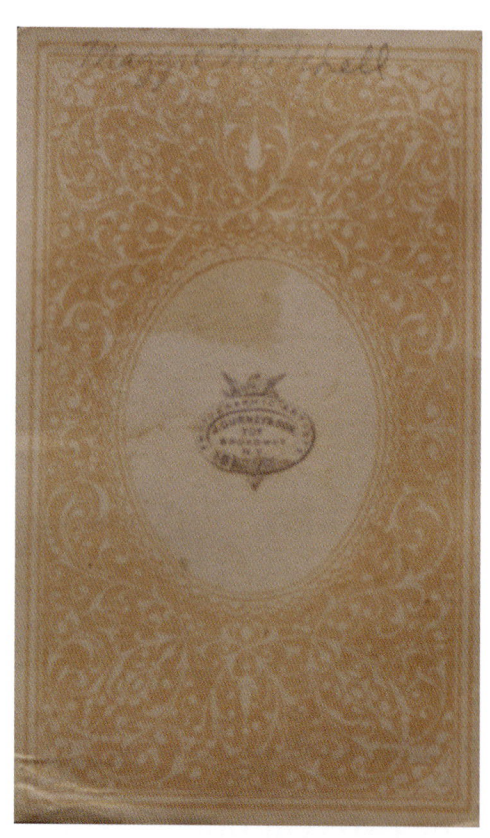

It appears that there was a tax stamp affixed, now removed.

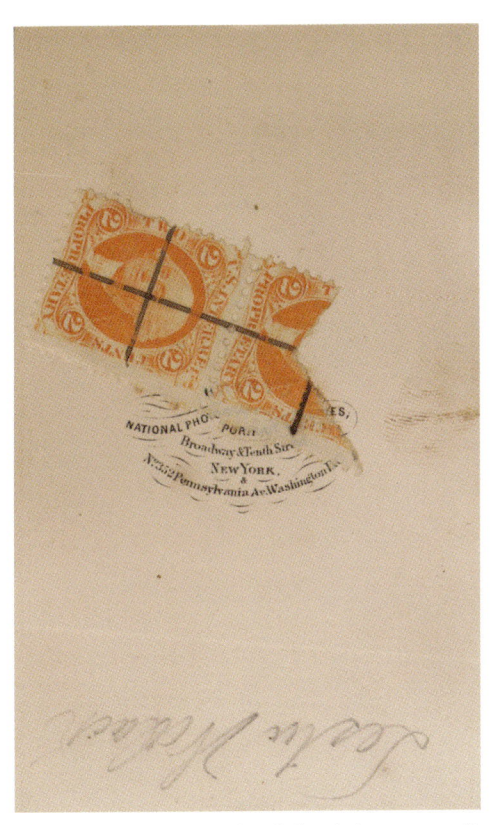

This is a probable bisect of a two cent orange Proprietary stamp.

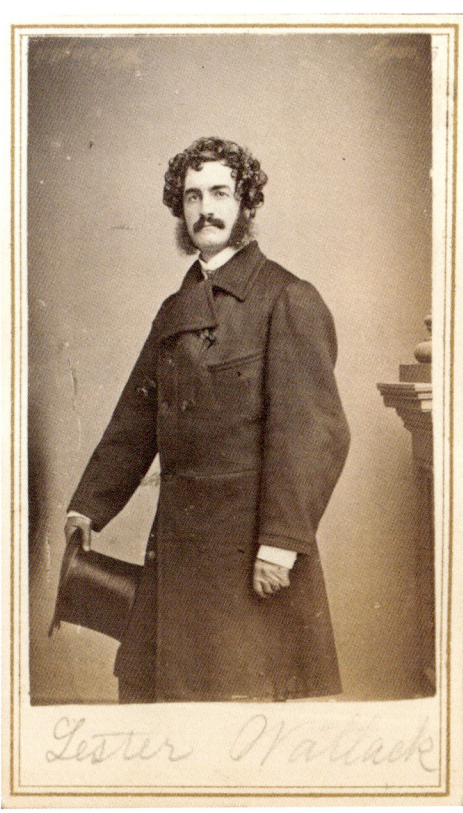

Lester Wallach owned one of New York's largest and most prestigious theatres.

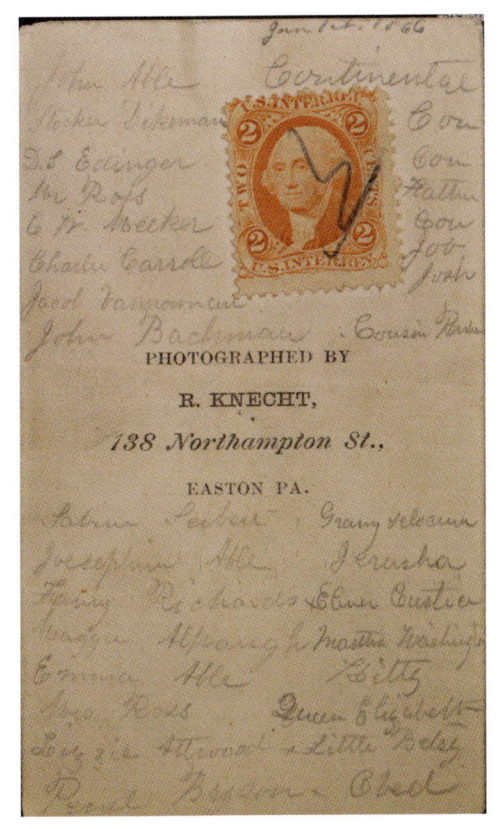

The tax stamp is a two cent orange Internal Revenue cancelled in pen.

Large group of theatre people dressed in Revolutionary War costumes. Note the identification of the individuals on the reverse.

33

Mademoiselle Ravel, a noted tightrope walker and actress.

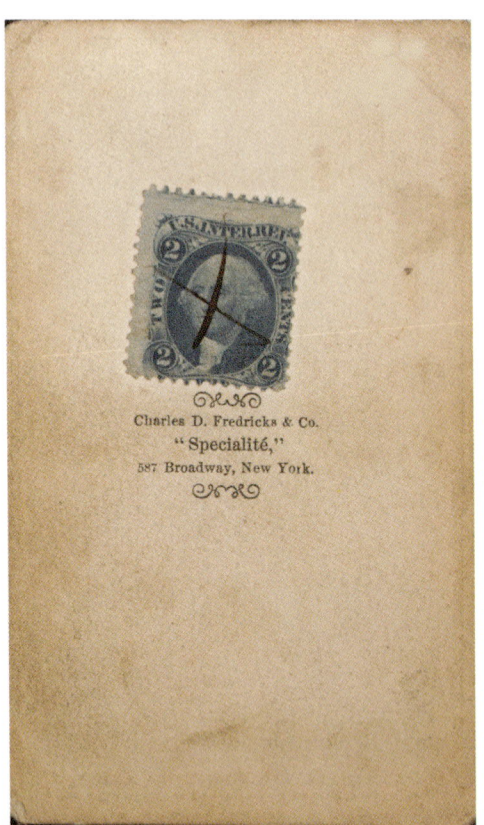

The tax on the photograph was paid by this two cent blue stamp, title unknown.

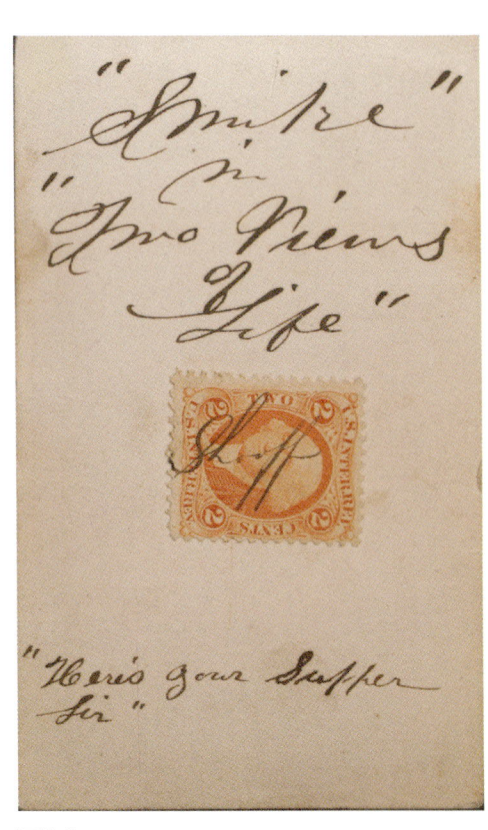

An actor described by his stage name, the play, and the line portrayed.

This two cent orange Internal Revenue was hand-signed by Shoaff.

Animals

Photography of animals in the 1860s was very difficult, due to the unpredictability of the animal. The length of time needed to make a usable exposure was ten to thirty seconds depending on lighting conditions (bright sun or cloudy). Photographers even had difficulty with people holding still for this length of time as is evident in the stands sometimes visible in the photographic image at the feet of the sitter which were designed to hold the head and body still. If an animal could be brought into the studio, the photographer had a better chance of success than if the animal was outdoors. There were other unpredictable circumstances such as weather conditions and distractions with which to contend outdoors. It is therefore understandable that, while images with animals in the studio are scarce, images of animals outdoors are even more rare.

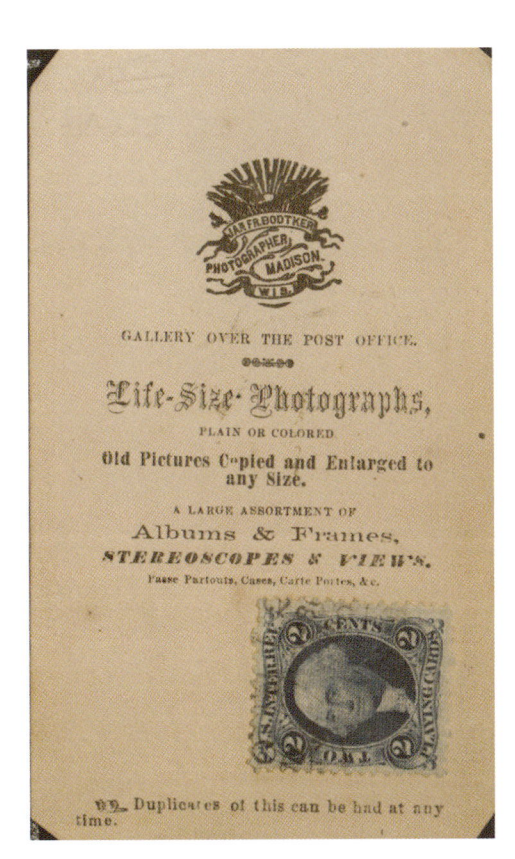

The two cent blue Playing Cards stamp is affixed to the ornate back of "Old Abe" by James Fr. Bodtker, Madison, WI.

Old Abe was caught by a Chippewa Indian named Big Sky and sold for a bushel of corn. He eventually became the mascot for the 8th Wisconsin Infantry Regiment. It is said that Old Abe, named for Abraham Lincoln, gave fierce battle cries when the 8th Wisconsin engaged the enemy. Old Abe was involved in several battles, including the Battle of Atlanta. He lived out his later years in the State Capitol of Wisconsin and died in a fire in 1881.

Landscape oriented image of a man and trained spotted pony.

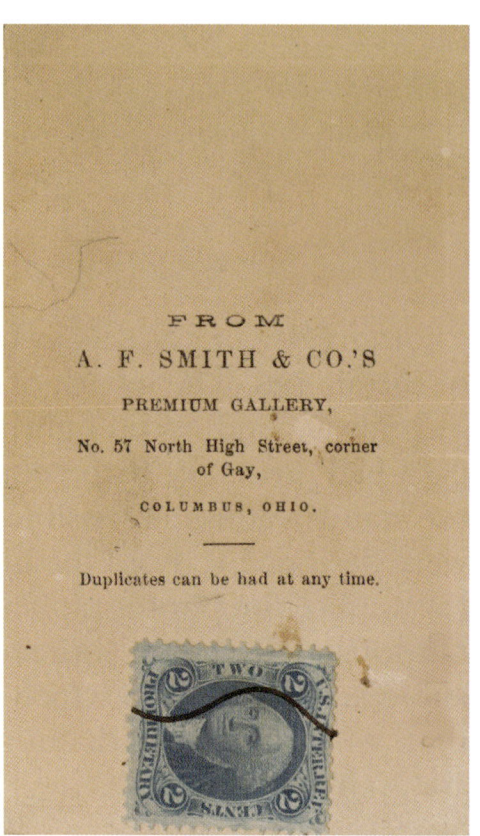

Two cent blue Proprietary stamp used to pay taxes.

A Union Civil War soldier holds the bridles of two well-groomed Thoroughbreds.

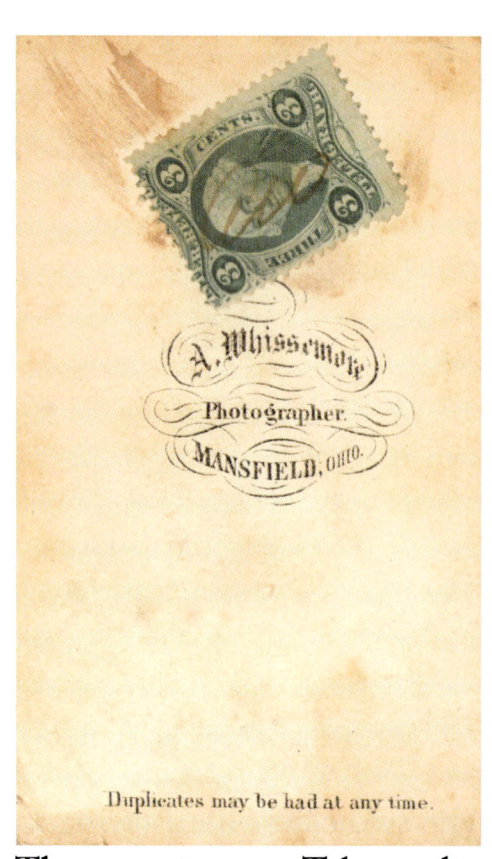

Three cent green Telegraph stamp paid the taxes on this photograph.

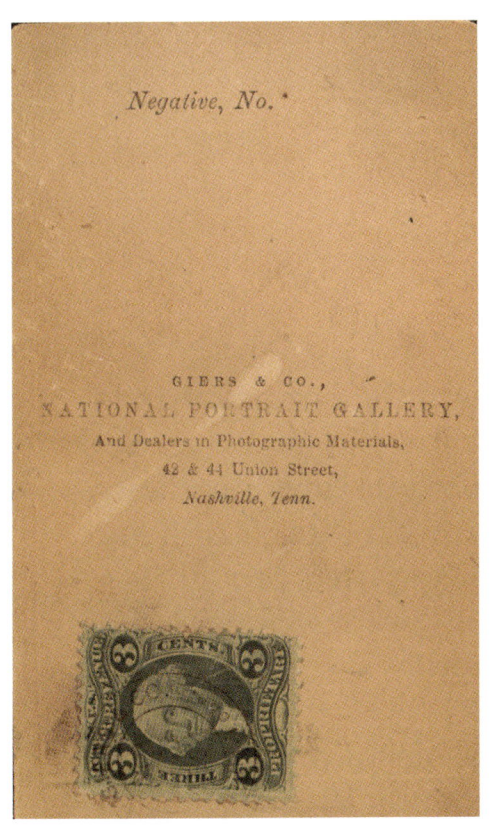

This three cent Green Proprietary stamp was used to pay taxes on this photograph.

Photograph of a Nashville, TN youth and a parrot.

Two cent orange Bank Check stamp used for taxes.

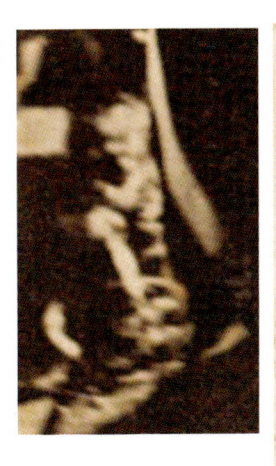

Man training a bear cub. Note the doll's head on a spring in the enlarged area of the image for the bear. Also visible are two black youths peering over the fence.

37

Barnum's Museum

Come one, come all! Look at the Victorian attitude toward the unnatural and deformed! The uncanny ability of people to look their fellow human beings and feel sorrow, superiority, wonder and callousness all at the same time is common even today. Complicated stories were told about the land where freaks of nature were common, of how primitive cultures and clandestine meetings brought these evolutionary sideshows to light. Most of the "freaks" were well paid actors brought from poverty to the stage by a clever, self promoting agent and employer.

While there are many cases where the performer was not mentally capable of understanding his plight, there are many more instances of the actors being far better off than they would have been without the circus or side show.

James Murphy was one of Barnum's circus giants. This photograph was originally sold at the Barnum Museum, which can be inferred from the Barnum cancellation on the stamp.

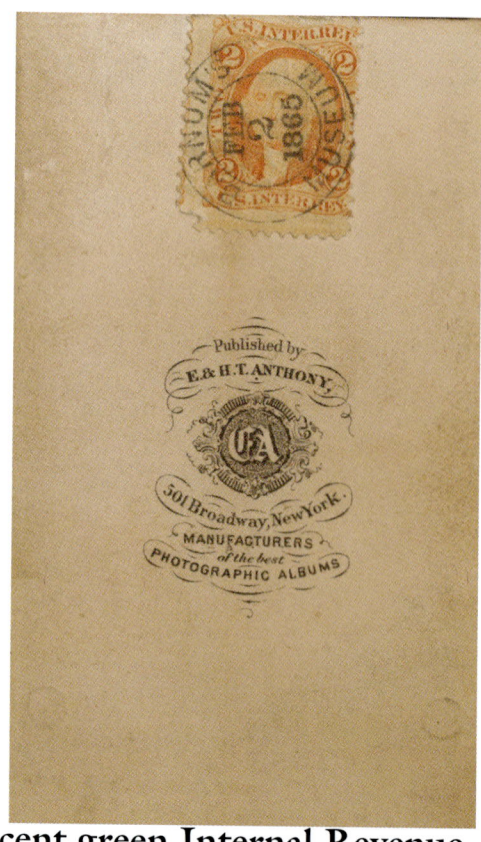

Three cent green Internal Revenue stamp was cancelled with the Barnum killer including the date.

38

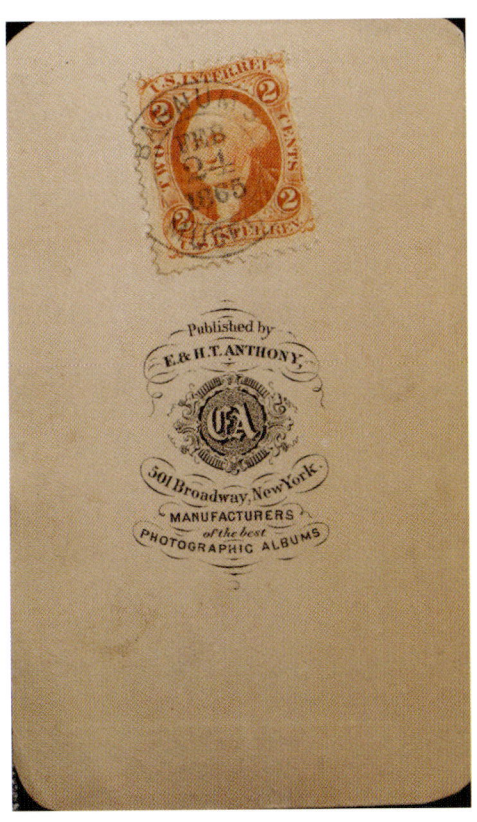

Two cent orange Internal Revenue stamp with the Barnum cancellation.

The carte of Mrs. J. J. Prior, a vocalist, sold at Barnum's Museum.

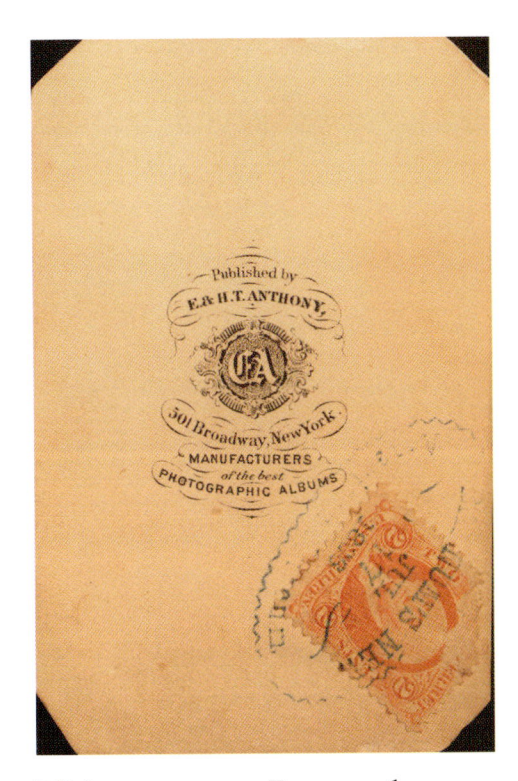

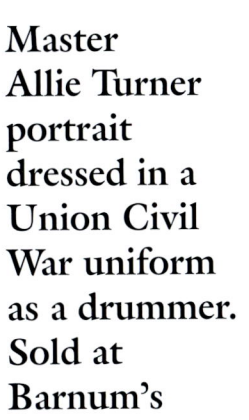

This two cent Internal Revenue stamp was cancelled just prior to the end of the stamp era.

Master Allie Turner portrait dressed in a Union Civil War uniform as a drummer. Sold at Barnum's New Museum shortly after the first museum burned. The new museum would suffer a similar fate within two years.

39

Zaruby Hannum portrait, a Circassian at Barnum's Museum.

Two cent orange Internal Revenue stamp on the reverse of Zaruby Hannum portrait.

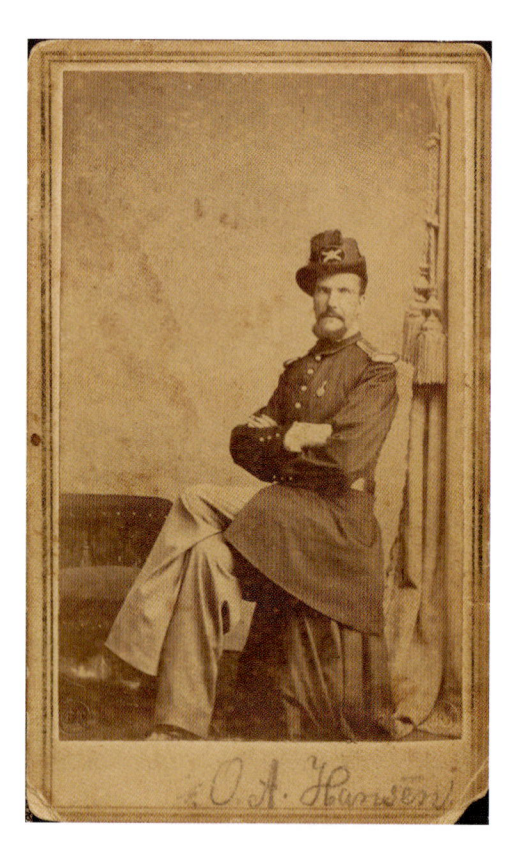

O. A. Hansen, another of Barnum's giants, at 8' 1 1/2" tall. CDV sold at Barnum's Museum.

This two cent orange Internal Revenue stamp was cancelled by the Barnum Museum.

The Disabled

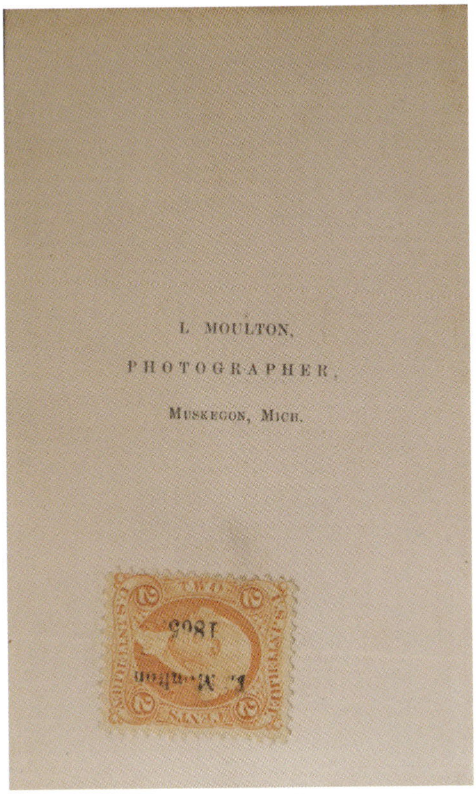

Two cent orange Internal Revenue stamp cancelled with the killer of the photographer's name and date.

Bearded man with arm, hand and leg deformities riding in a specially built cart drawn by two dogs.

Two cent orange stamp, unknown title.

Anne E Leak, born without arms near Valdosta Georgia, learned to write with her feet and signed cards (this one front and back) to earn a living.

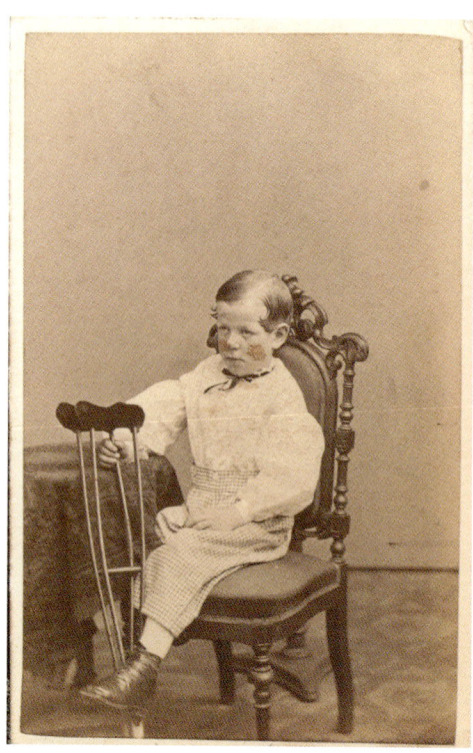

Portrait of a young boy missing his right leg and holding a crutch. It is hard to imagine, but he may have lost his leg in battle.

Three cent green Proprietary stamp paid the tax on this photo.

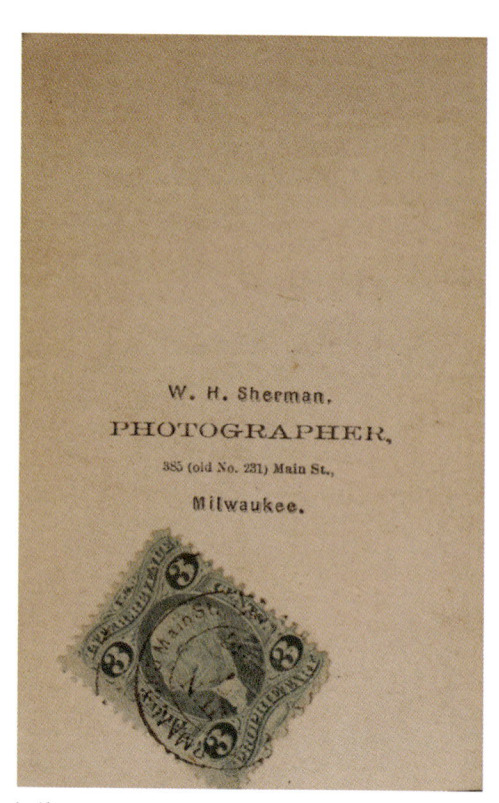

Second from left is an albino. This is probably a family photo. Note the enlarged image above the CDV.

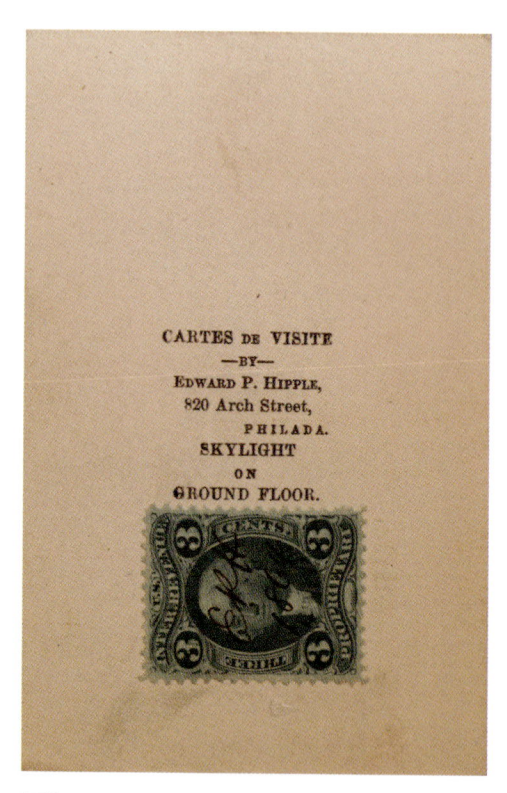

Three cent green Proprietary stamp.

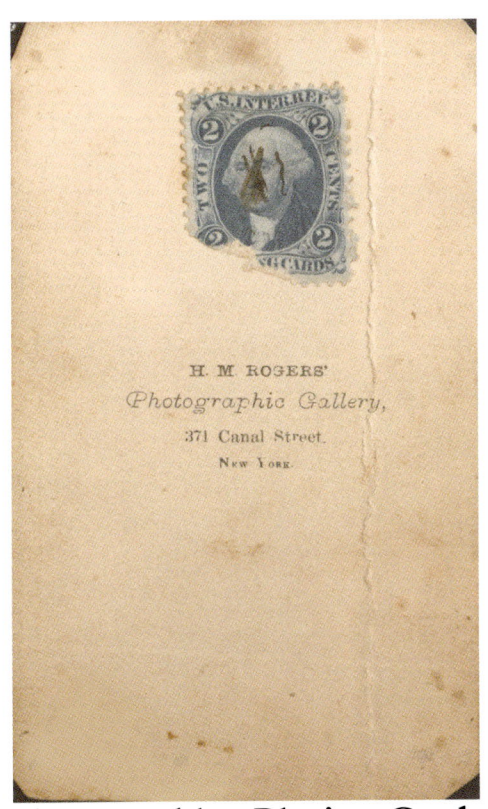

Two cent blue Playing Cards stamp.

Civil War officer with a hook, his hand probably lost in battle.

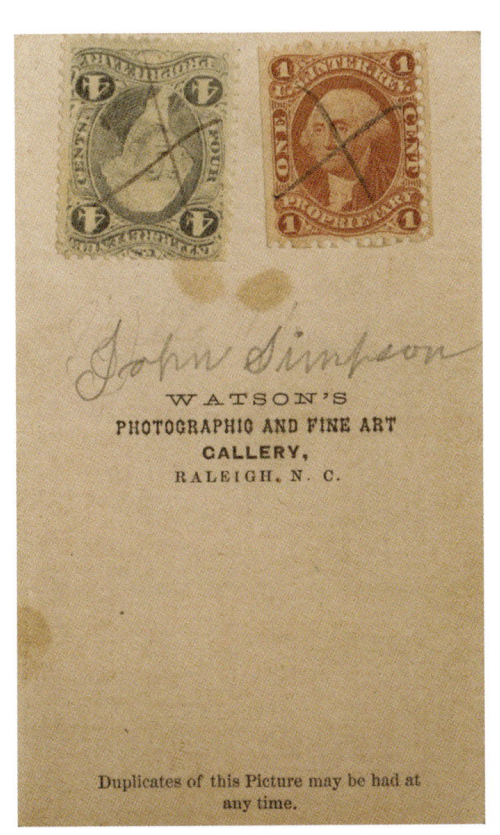

One cent and four cent Proprietary stamps used to pay tax. Dual frank.

Portrait of John Simpson, instructor at the Blind School in Raleigh, N.C. He appears to be visually impaired.

Ethnic

Alfred Wade, Governor of the Indian Territory. Typically, American Indians would dress in white man's clothes.

This image was made in Washington, DC, probably while he was there negotiating with the government.

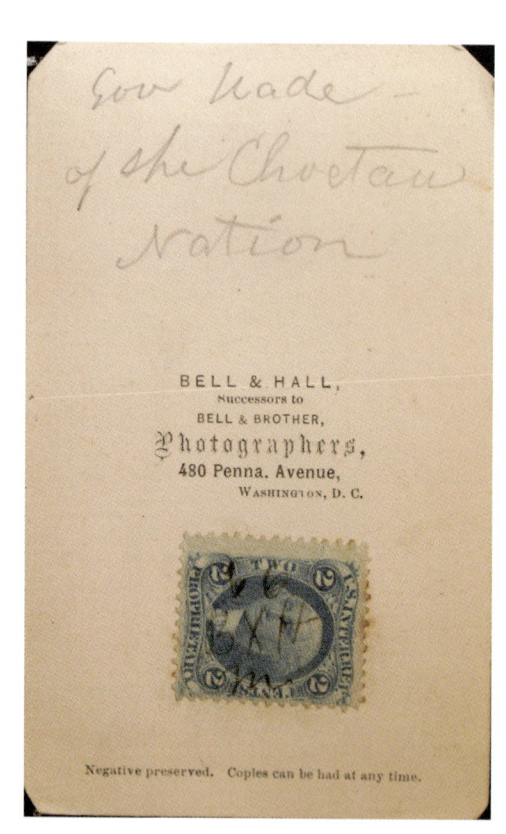

Two cent blue Proprietary stamp.

Chinese man in San Francisco, CA.

Two cent blue Proprietary stamp.

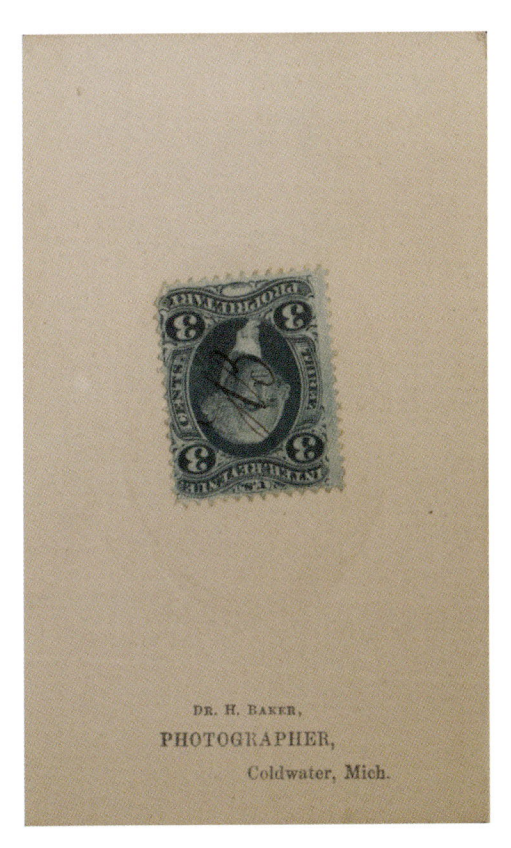

Three cent green Proprietary stamp pays the tax.

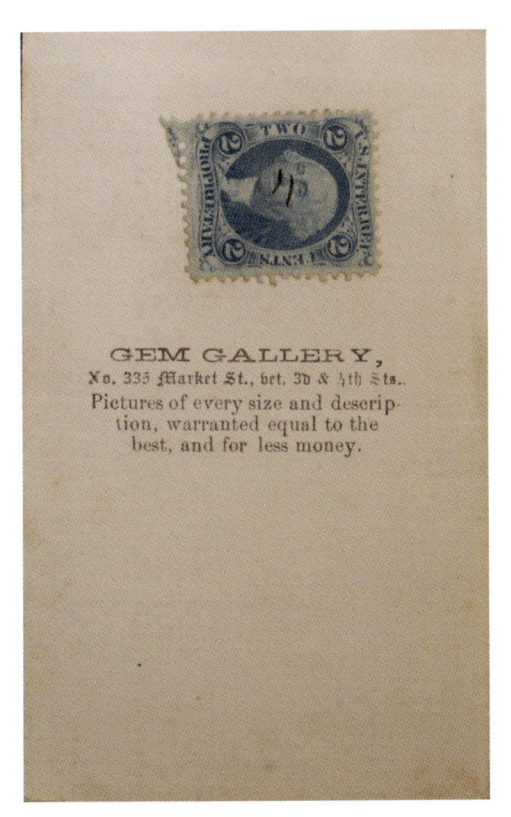

Two cent blue Proprietary stamp cancelled with two ink strokes pays the tax.

Native American dressed in white man's clothes.

The same Native American in his military uniform. He probably was a scout.

Gray Eyes was an American Indian who served as a military scout.

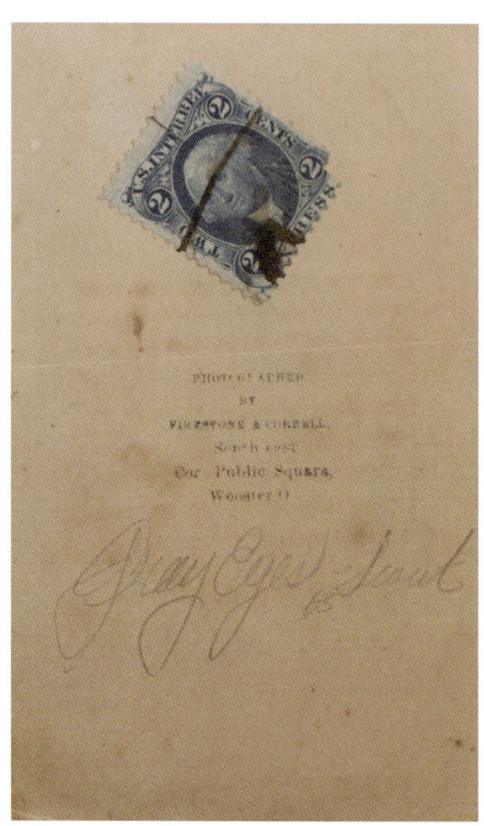

Two cent blue Express with a simple line cancellation.

Well-dressed Negro from Vermont, probably a freedman.

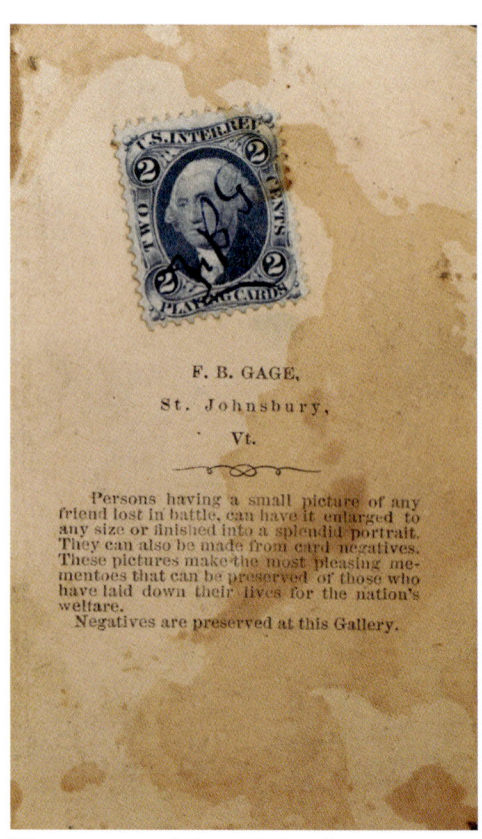

Two cent blue Playing Cards stamp.

"Freaks" and Other Circus Performers

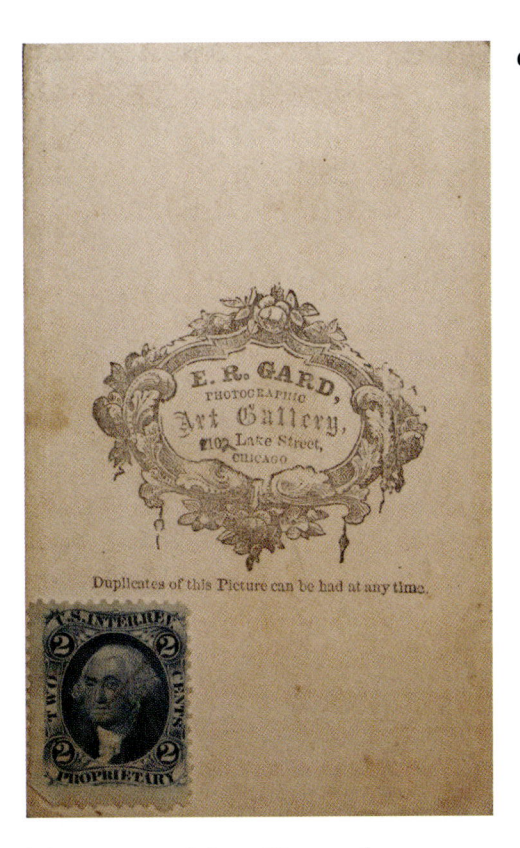

Two cent blue Proprietary stamp.

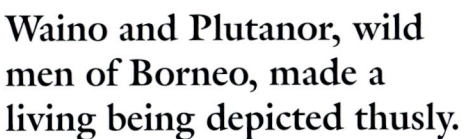

Waino and Plutanor, wild men of Borneo, made a living being depicted thusly.

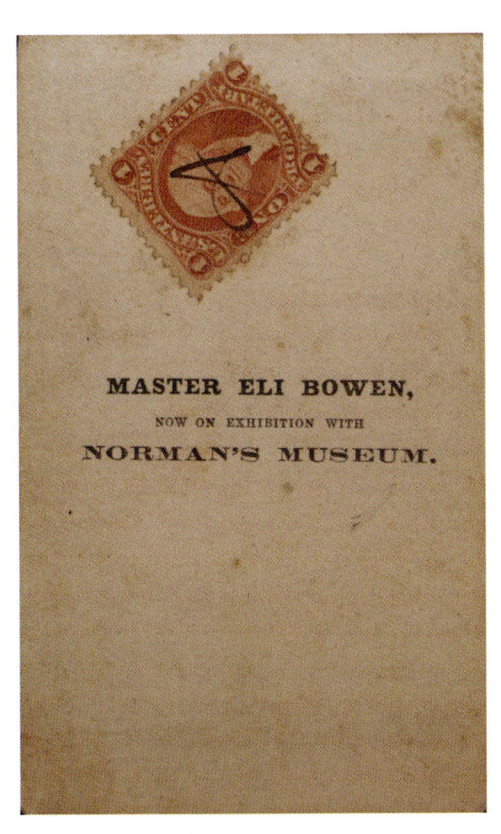

One cent red Proprietary stamp with the name of the museum and name of subject.

Eli Bowen, born without legs. He made a living working for a competitor to Barnum's Museum, the Norman Museum.

47

Madame Sherwood's statistics are listed on the card. Obesity was not very common and people would pay to see her.

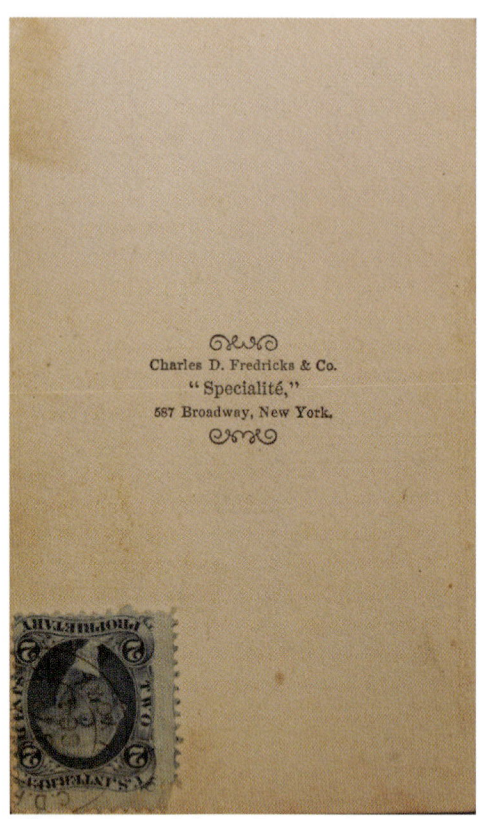

Two cent blue Proprietary stamp.

Lizzie A. Reed, midget, who made a living on exhibit. She was twenty-two years old, thirty-three inches high and weighed 35 pounds when this image was made.

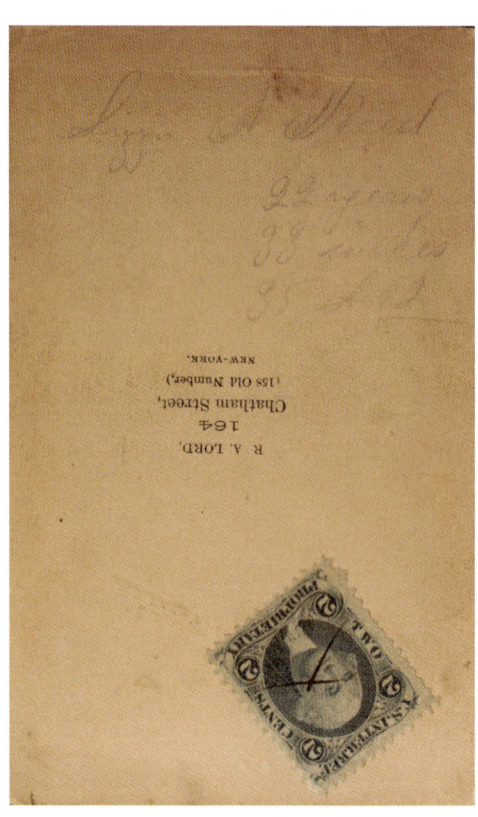

Two cent blue Proprietary stamp.

48

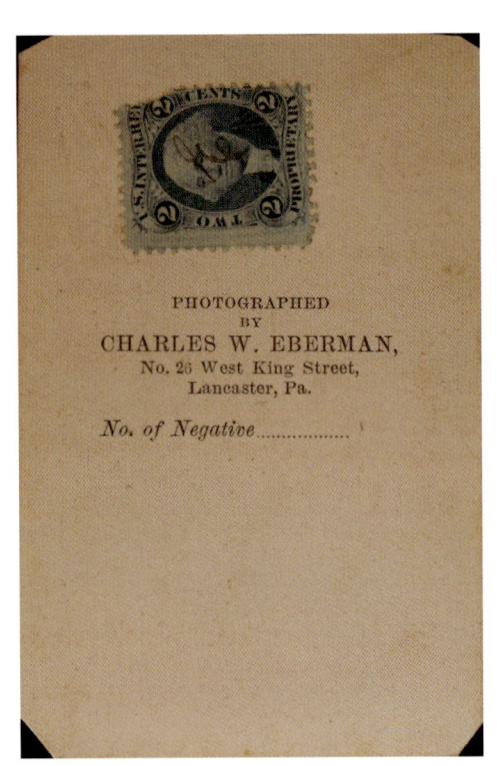

Interiors

Two cent blue Proprietary stamp.

Two cent blue Proprietary stamp.

Interior of Evangelical Lutheran Church of the Holy Trinity celebrating 100 years as indicated on the overprint on the image.

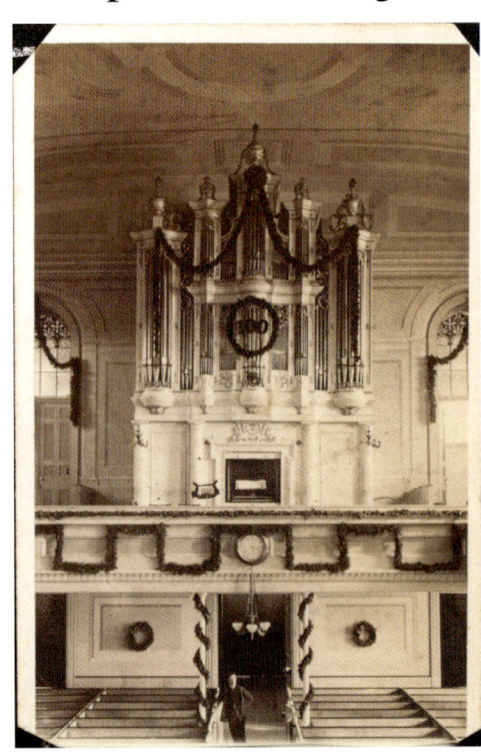

Second image of Holy Trinity, Lancaster PA.

49

Machines

The advent of the machine age was not lost to this era of photography. Machines were being perfected to perform many tedious and arduous chores. The steam engine, although in use for decades to drive trains, was being adapted to perform other mechanical feats. Most new processes or mechanisms were photographed in the model form and submitted for a patent together with drawings and descriptions. Photography of the model was probably used to market the idea for sale of the product. The photograph could also be displayed to wary investors. Although these images are scarce, they represent a glimpse of the marketing potential of photography.

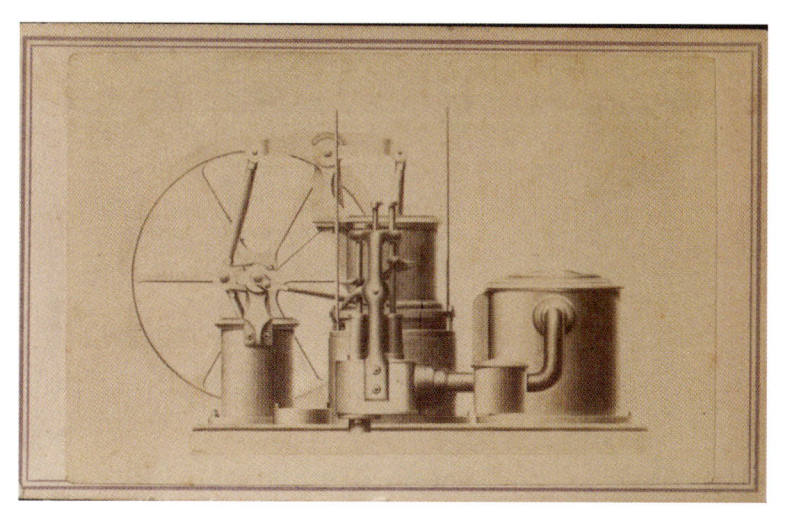

Artistic rendering of a model steam-operated apparatus.

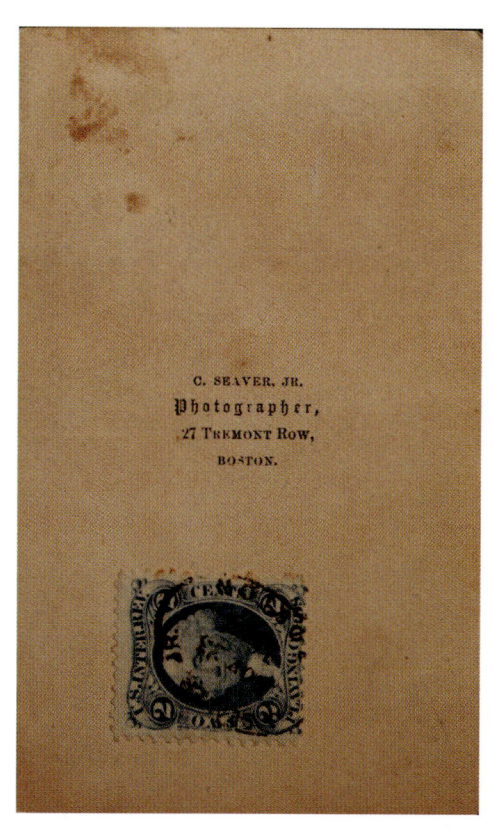

Two cent blue Playing Cards stamp.

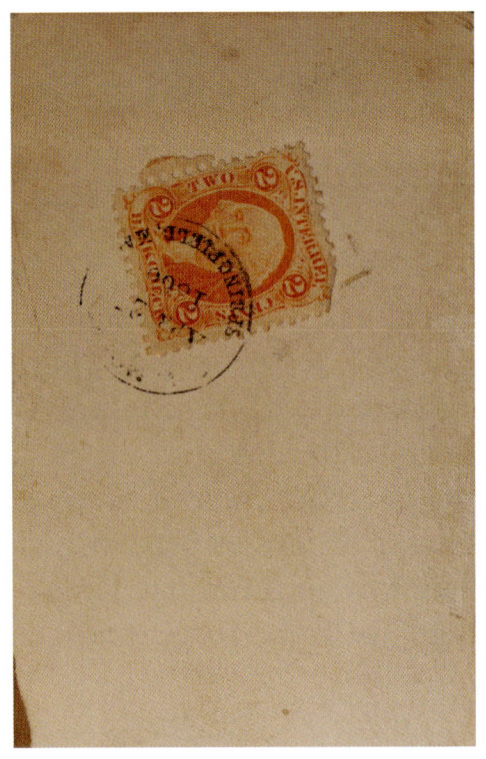

Two cent orange Bank Check stamp.

Photo of a sewing device.

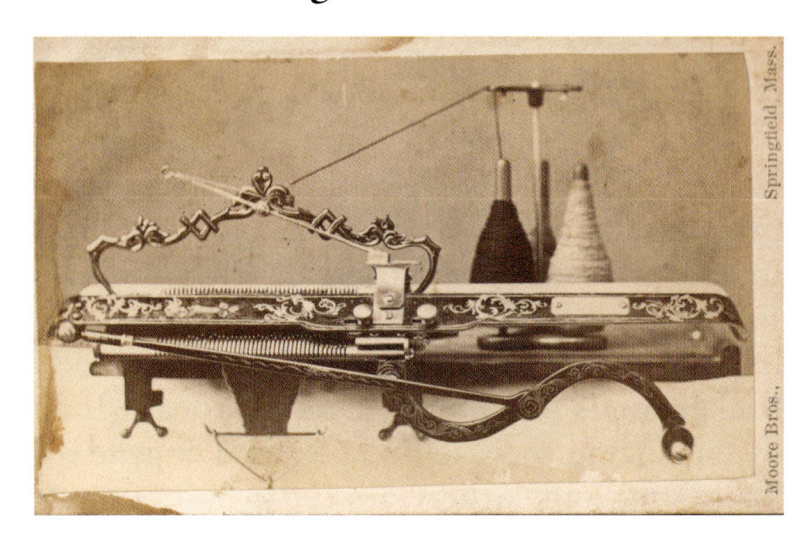

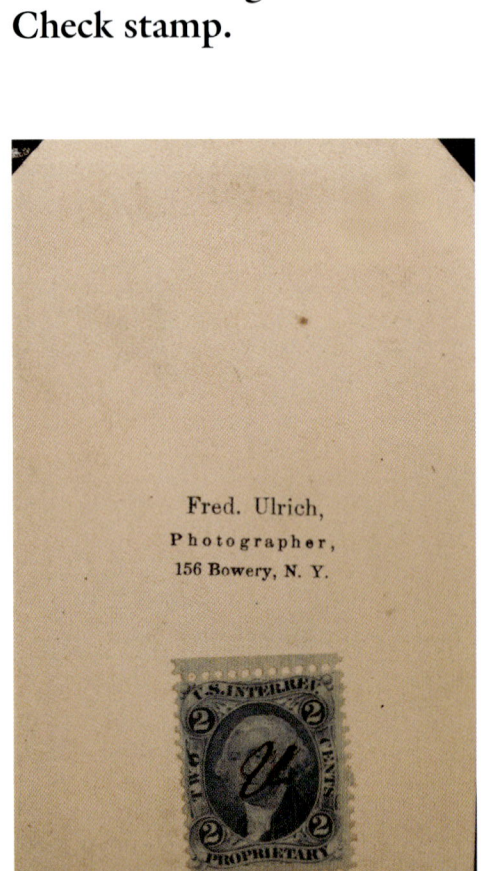

Two cent blue Proprietary stamp.

Another steam operated mechanism, possibly an early lathe.

51

Masonic Orders

Images of people in Masonic regalia are uncommon during the tax period. This is probably the result of the inherent value of keeping secret organizations secret. These images are sometimes confused with military images and regarded with that import. From the membership of George Washington to today, Masonic Orders play an important role in the fabric of American society by bringing together men of diverse backgrounds to embrace Utopian ideals. Individual members' lives are improved by enhancing their self-respect and engendering a strong sense of community. The images we look at here are the proud reminders of a heritage not to be forgotten.

Appears to be an "Odd Fellow" in full regalia.

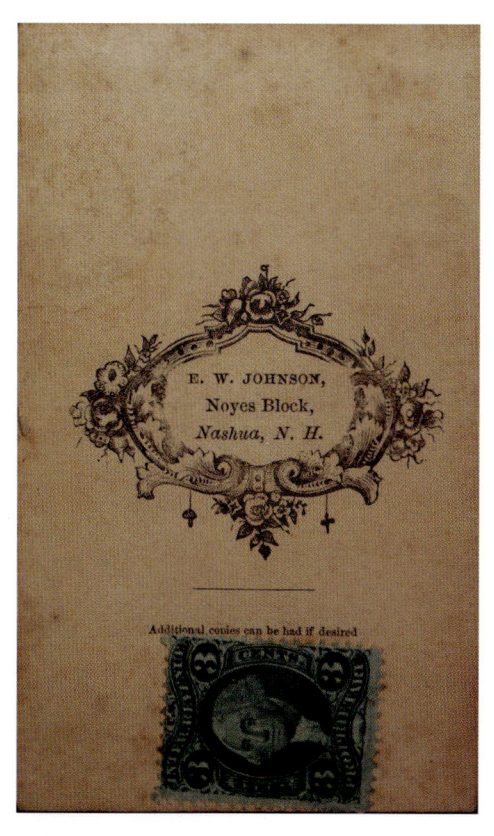

Three cent green Proprietary stamp.

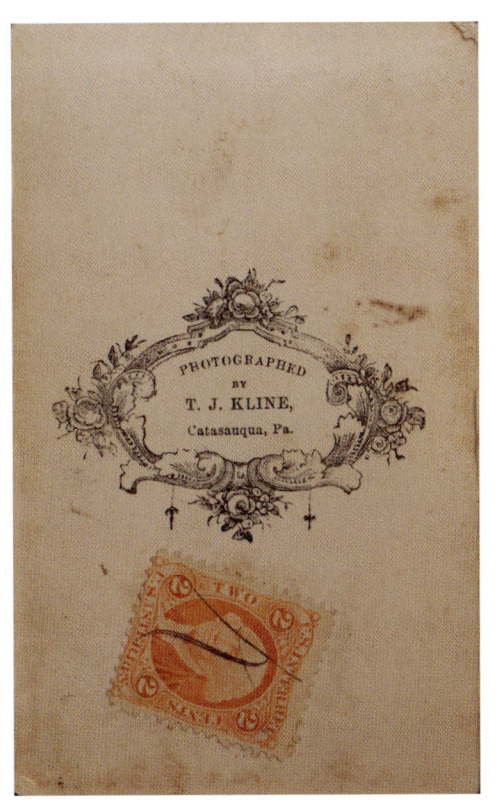

Two cent orange Internal Revenue stamp.

Masonic style sash.

One cent red Proprietary stamp.

One of the Masonic group dressed in a traditional apron.

Military

Portrait of General James Garfield. He served as president from 1881 until he was assassinated and died on September 19. 1881.

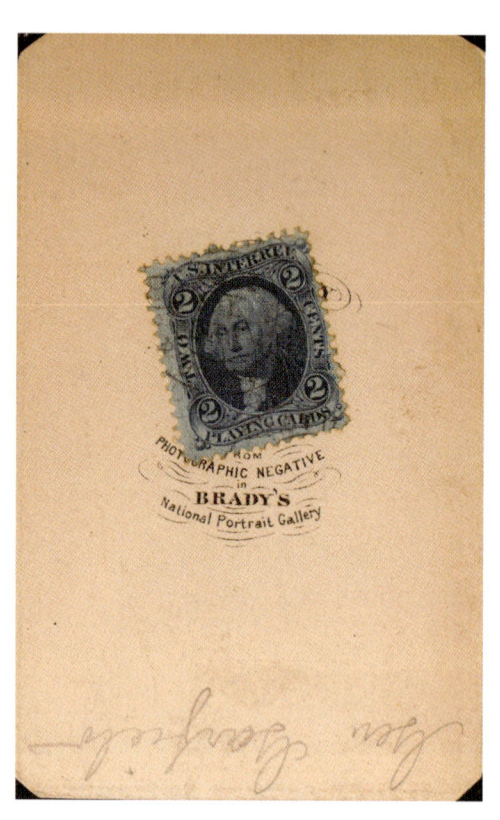

Two cent blue Playing Cards stamp.

Autographed card of J. M. Thompson, Captain Company I 12th Maine Volunteers. Photo made in Savannah, Georgia.

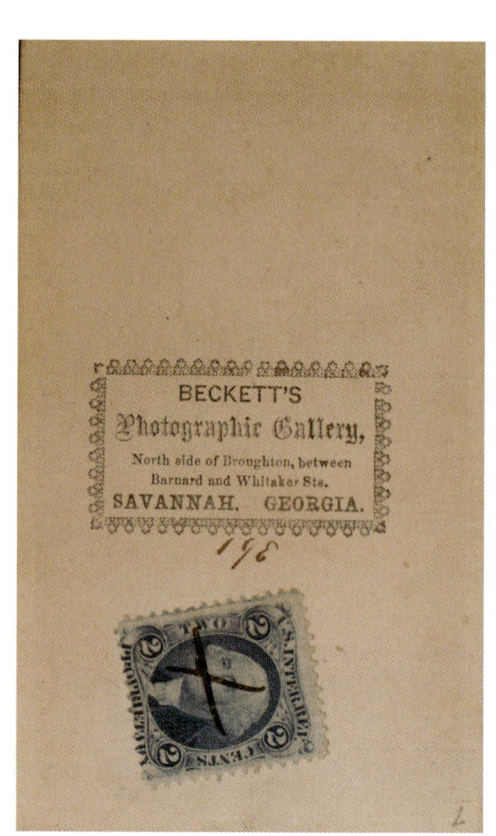

Two cent blue Proprietary stamp.

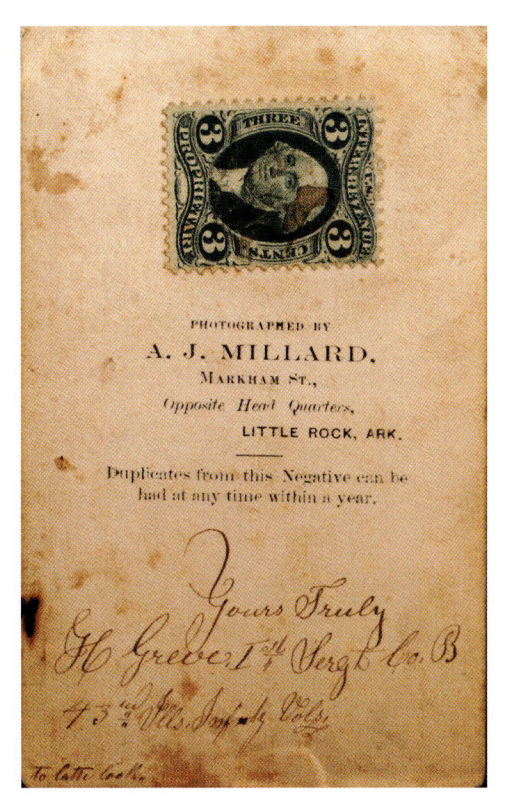

Three cent Proprietary stamp.

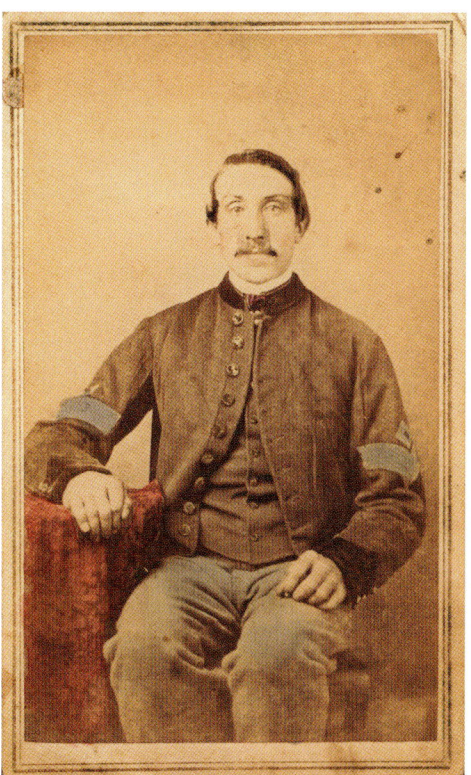

Union Soldier in Little Rock, Arkansas. Images from Arkansas during this period are very scarce.

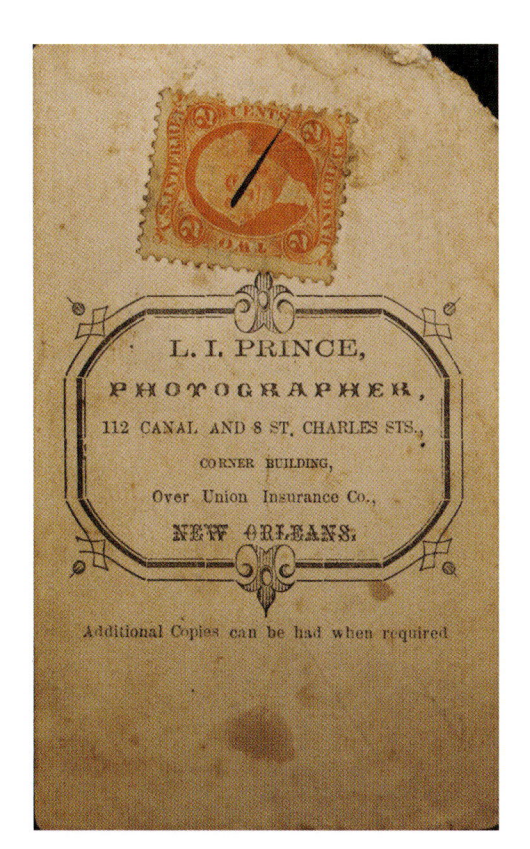

Two cent orange Bank Check stamp.

Appears to be a Confederate in uniform after the surrender of New Orleans, LA. Note the worn state of apparel.

55

Union General Hurlburt in New Orleans taken at Lillenthal's Studio. The imprint shows a depiction of the studio. Also note copyright on front of card.

Two two cent orange Bank Check stamps.

J. H. King, Roswell, GA. Mr. King owned a button and uniform manufacturing facility in Roswell, GA which was burned by Sherman's Troops.

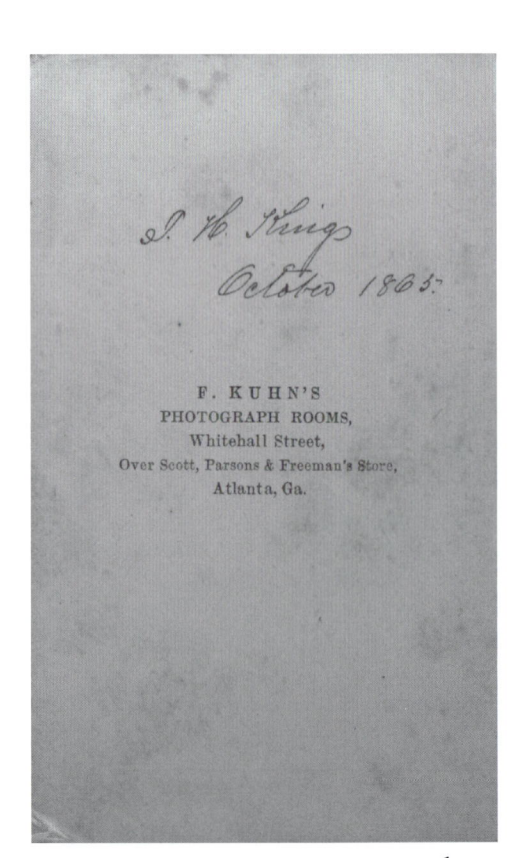

Note: No tax stamp on the photo, yet it is dated well within the tax period.

56

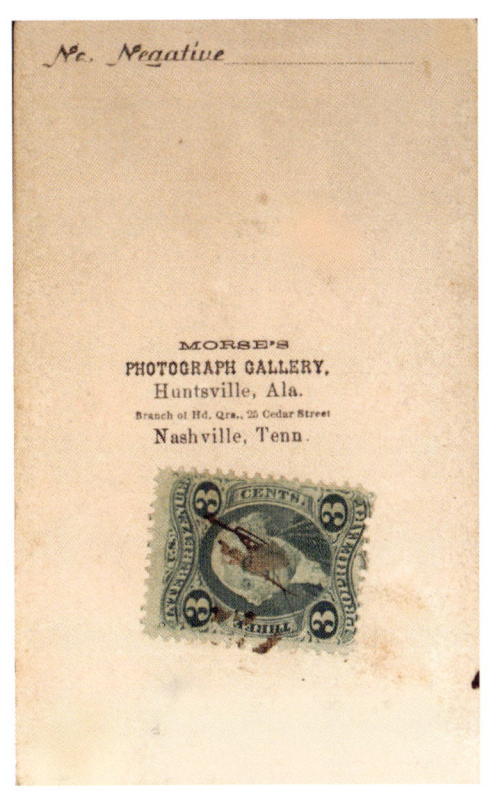

Three cent green Proprietary stamp.

Union General Morgan Lewis Smith, commander of a brigade under Lew Wallace at Shiloh. Promoted to Brigadier General July 16, 1862. In charge of the XV Corps during the Battle of Atlanta. Appointed by President Johnson as U. S. Consul to Honolulu and also served under President Grant. Image taken at Morse's Branch office in Huntsville, AL. Alabama images are scarce.

Dual frank. One cent red Proprietary and two cent orange Bank Check.

Union Civil War officer. Image taken at New Bern, NC. North Carolina CDVs with tax stamps are scarce.

57

U. S. Naval seaman of Oriental origin taken by J. M. Van Orsdell, Wilmington, NC.

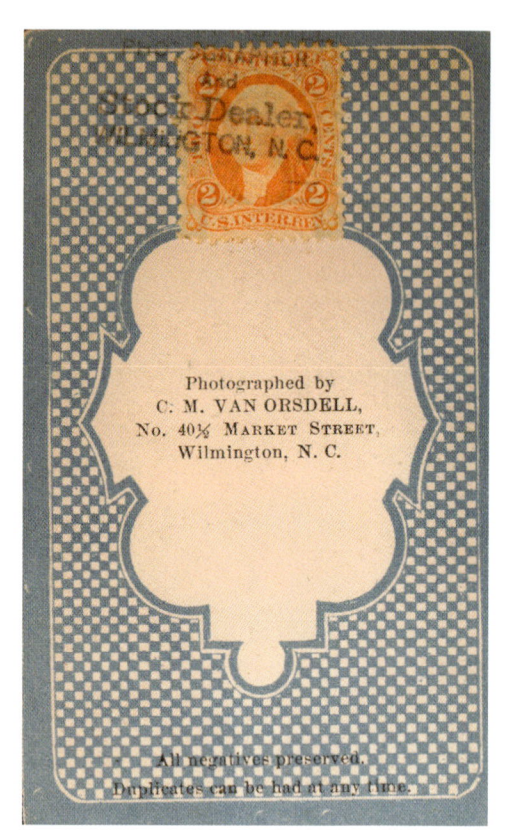

Note the killer ties the stamp to the card. Two cent orange Internal Revenue stamp.

Union General Hugh Judson Kilpatrick at Brady's NY studio.

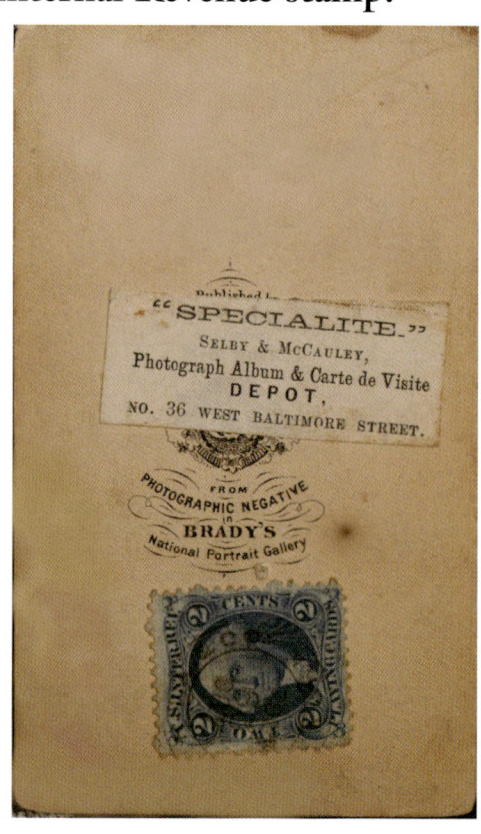

Strip label over Anthony's logo to indicate sales location. Two cent blue Playing Cards.

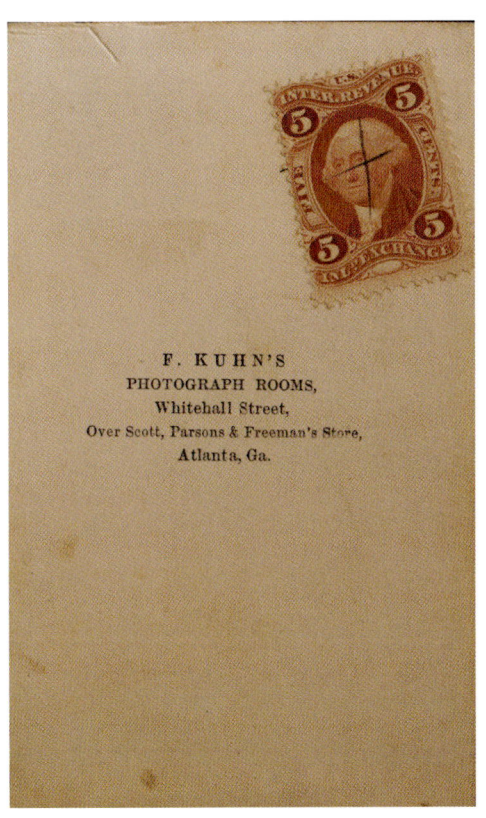

Five cent red Inland Exchange stamp.

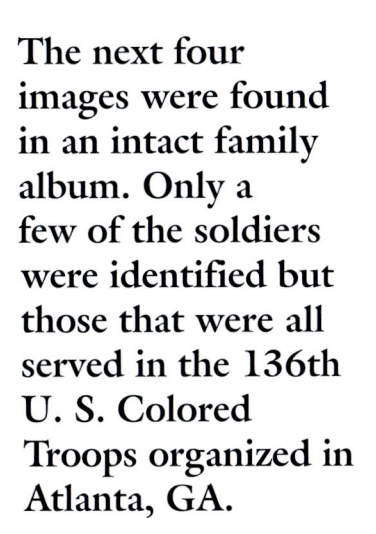

The next four images were found in an intact family album. Only a few of the soldiers were identified but those that were all served in the 136th U. S. Colored Troops organized in Atlanta, GA.

A. J. Jones, Lieutenant Colonel, USCT.

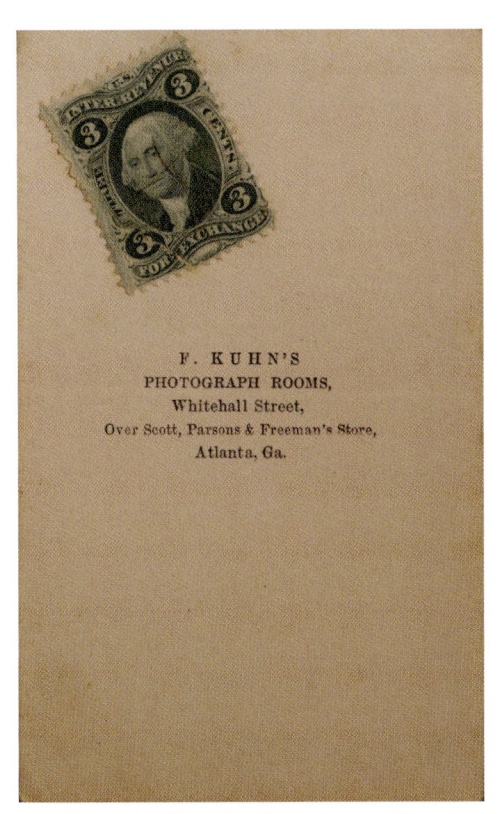

Three cent green Foreign Exchange stamp.

Unidentified Union soldier found in 136th USCT Album.

59

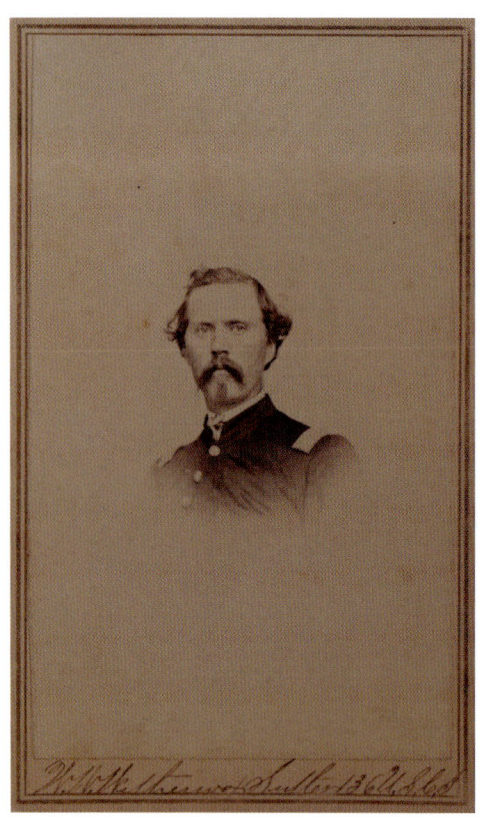

W. W. Weatherwax, Sutler, 136th USCT. This and the photo below are of brothers.

Two cent blue Playing Cards stamp on the W. W. Weatherwax CDV.

Jacob Weatherwax served in the 10th Michigan Cavalry and later in the 136th USCT.

Two cent orange Bank Check stamp.

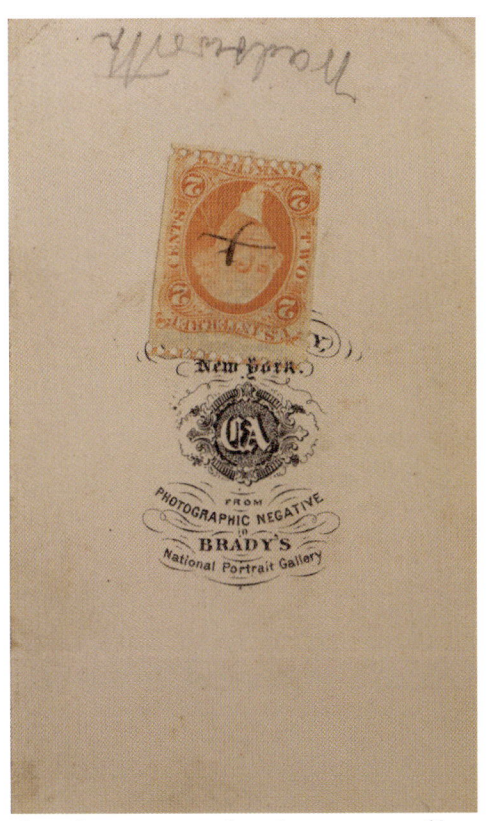

Anthony card, photo credit given to Brady. Two cent orange Bank Check stamp.

General James Samuel Wadsworth is regarded as being the wealthiest casualty of the Civil War. His father was one of the largest owners of cultivated land in New York state.

The United States Revenue Service was the predecessor of the Coast Guard.

Two cent orange Internal Revenue stamp tied by Wilmington, NC cancel.

G. Polhamus served on a USRS ship. Note wheel device on epaulet.

61

Union Infantry officer in Portland, OR.

Three cent green Proprietary stamp.

A family resemblance, possibly brothers, one of whom is a Union soldier.

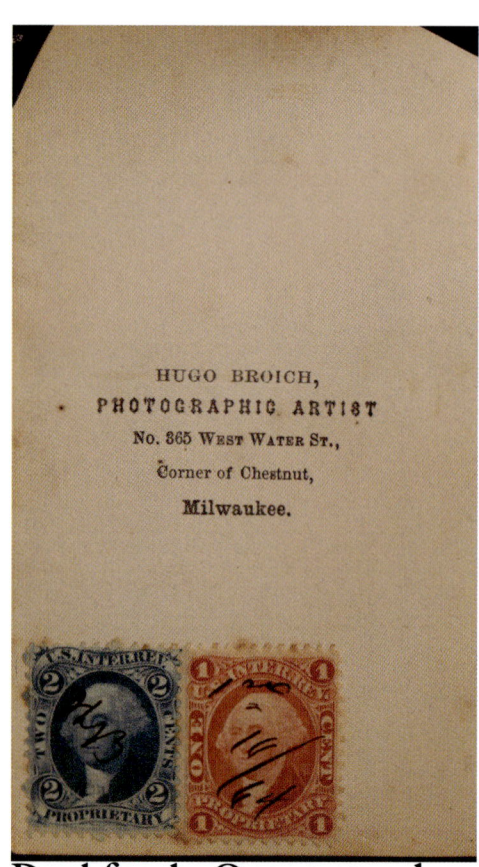

Dual frank. One cent red Proprietary and two cent blue Proprietary stamps.

Tax stamp signed Pierce to cancel two cent orange Bank Check stamp.

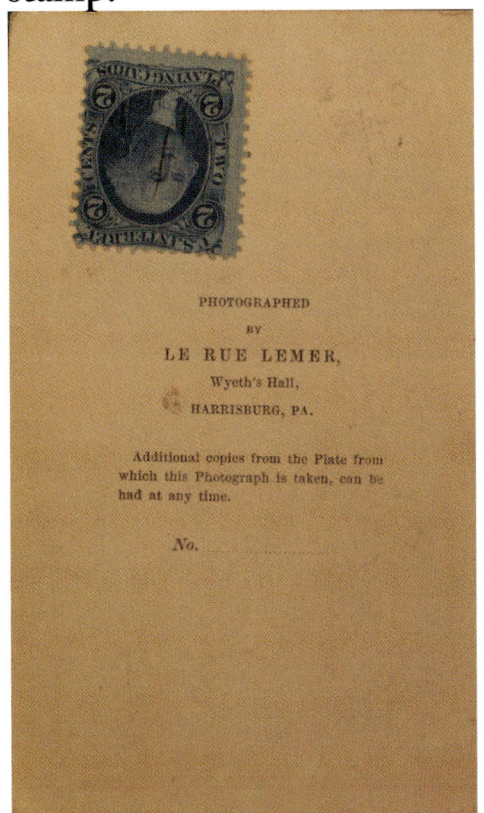

Two cent blue Playing Cards stamp.

Vignette portrait of E. J. Ford, surgeon, 101st Regiment of the USCT.

U. S. Naval officer atop this pyramid of couples.

63

Copy-print of Ulysses S. Grant sold by Partridge's Gallery, Wheeling, WV. He graduated 21st in his class at West Point in 1843. General Robert E. Lee surrendered to General Grant at Appomattox on April 9, 1865. Grant's simple honesty after the war aided him in being elected President of the United States in 1868 and re-elected in 1872.

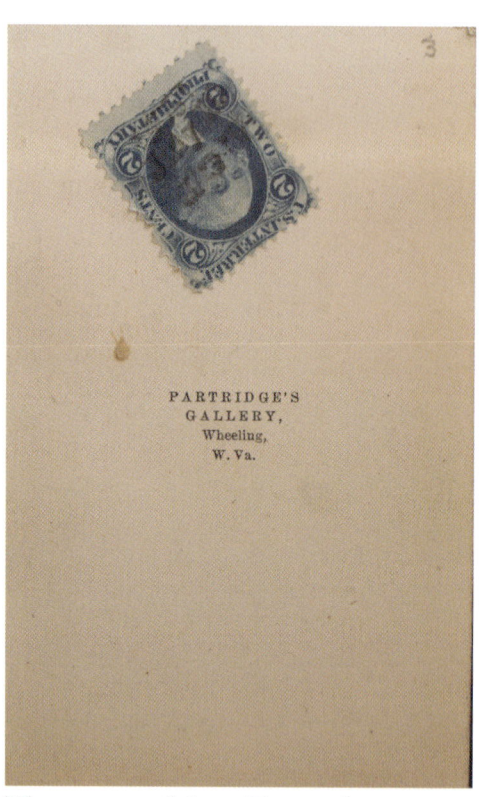

Two cent blue Proprietary stamp used to pay tax.

From life portrait of General William Tecumseh Sherman taken at Fassett's Gallery, Chicago, IL. He is well-remembered for the theory of modern warfare. This is the total destruction of anything in the path of the advancing army. He sacrificed 3000 men in a frontal assault at Kennesaw Mountain, GA. His famed "March to the Sea" included the capture and burning of the city of Atlanta, GA.

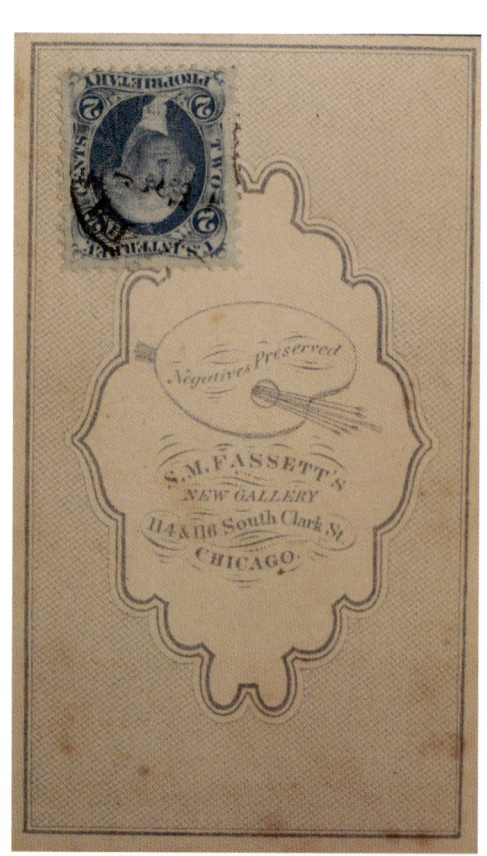

Two cent blue Proprietary stamp with Fassett's circular date cancel used to pay the tax.

64

Musical

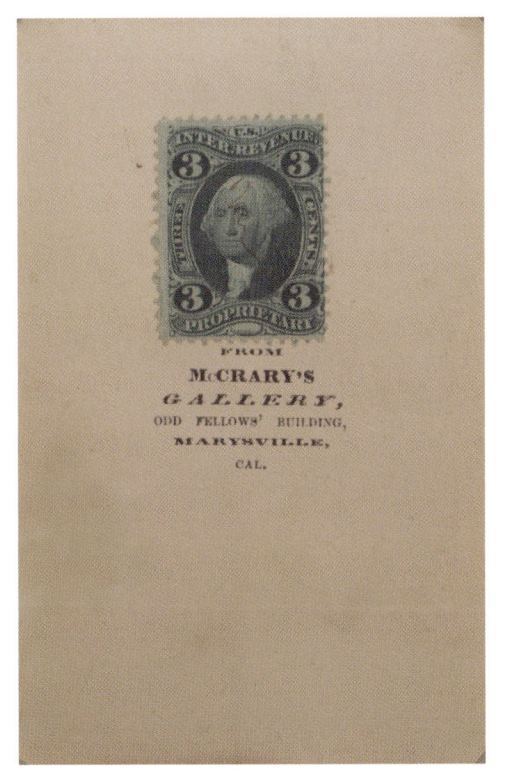

Three cent green Proprietary stamp.

California military band member.

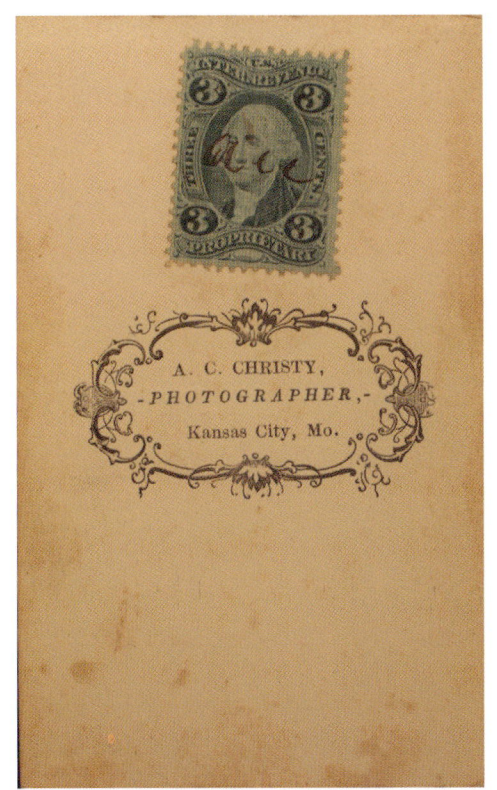

Three cent green Proprietary stamp cancelled by a Kansas City, MO photographer.

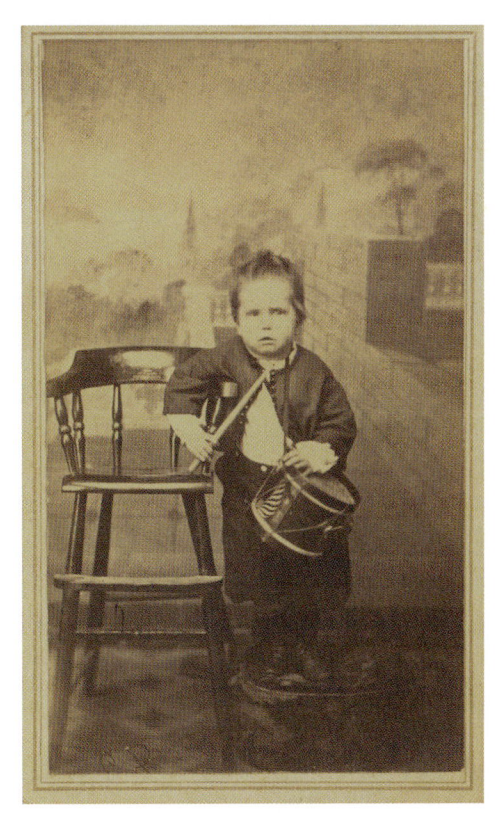

Patriotic youth with drum.

65

Street scene in New Orleans, LA depicting a broken wagon and a traveling troubadour with his guitar on his shoulder. This enlargement shows the bearded minstrel in more detail.

Two cent blue Proprietary stamp.

A Newburgh, NY band with all members including the dog.

Two cent blue Playing Cards stamp.

66

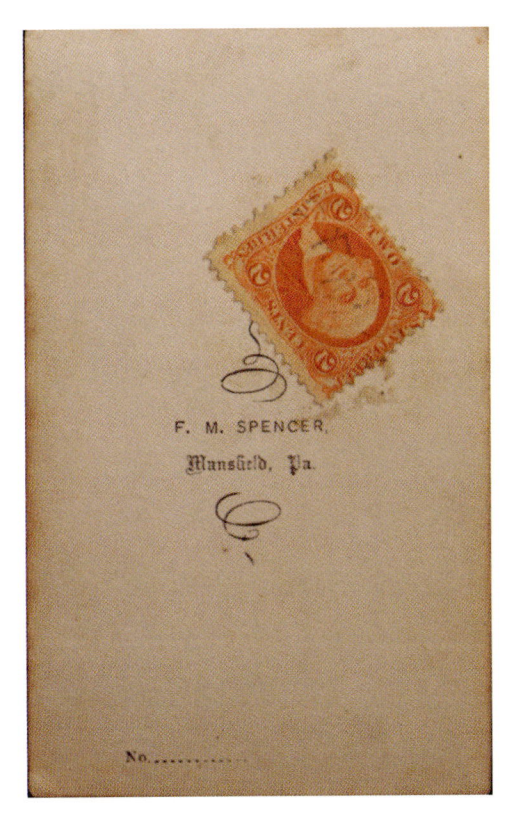

Two cent orange Internal Revenue stamp.

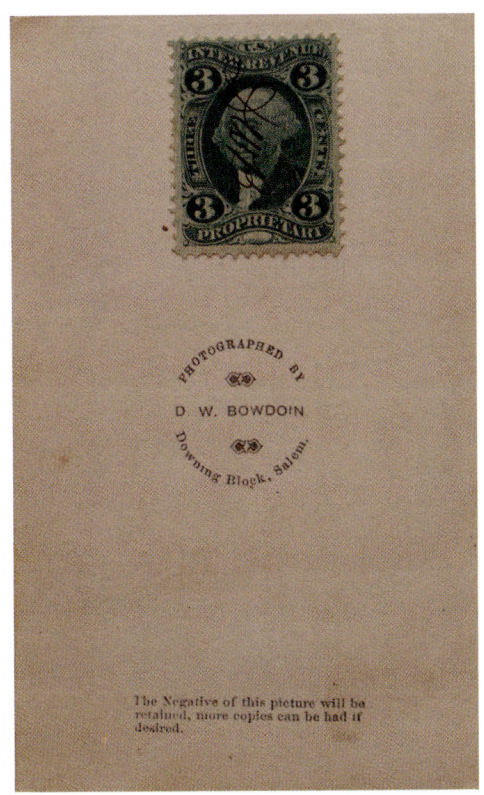

Three cent green Proprietary stamp.

One of the bagpipers of a Scottish unit during the Civil War.

Two men with musical instruments, a guitar and a fiddle.

Modern acoustic guitars are wider and the waist is less feminine in appearance. This enhances the volume and tone, providing a more robust and warmer sound.

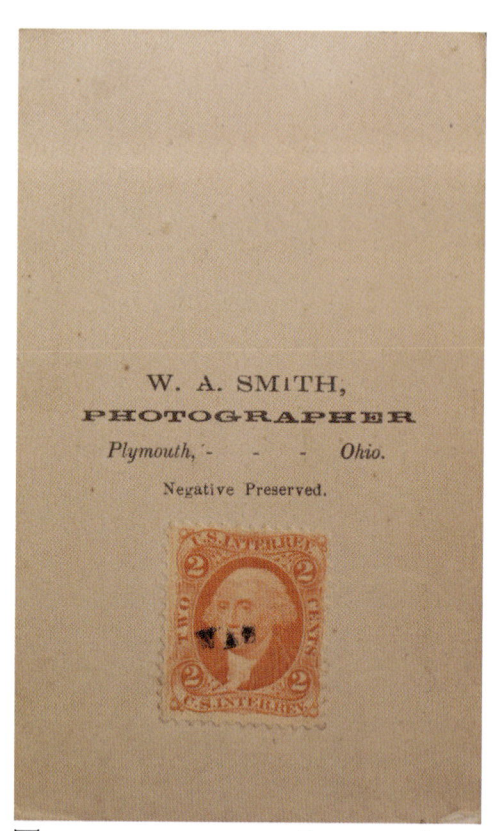

Man with his guitar. Note the elongated shape, not commonly seen in today's guitars.

Two cent orange Internal Revenue stamp.

Two women at a piano. One is probably the vocalist.

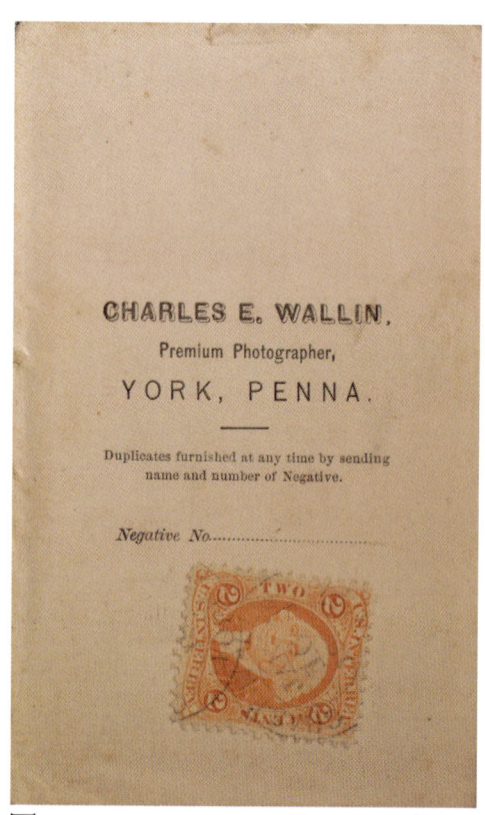

Two cent orange Internal Revenue stamp.

Occupational

Two cent orange Bank Check stamp.

Fireman dressed in uniform with his head gear on the table.

Two cent blue Proprietary stamp.

Fireman in street clothes and helmet on the table.

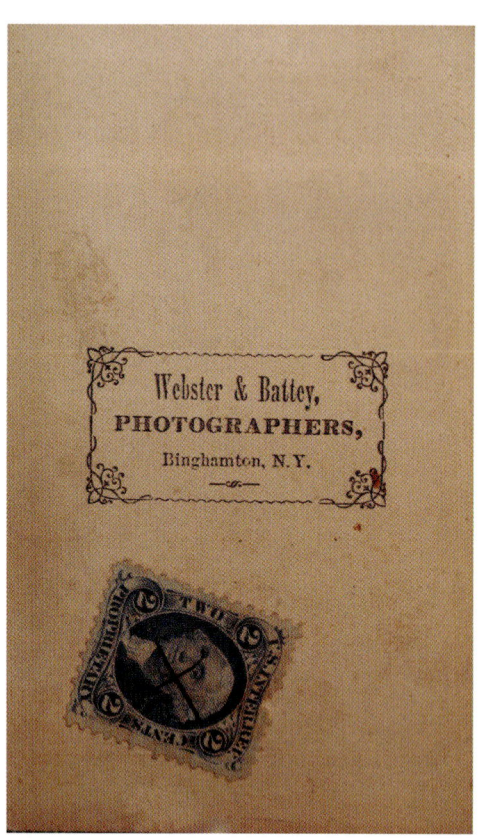

Fireman wearing fire gear and holding the hose nozzle.

Two cent blue Proprietary stamp.

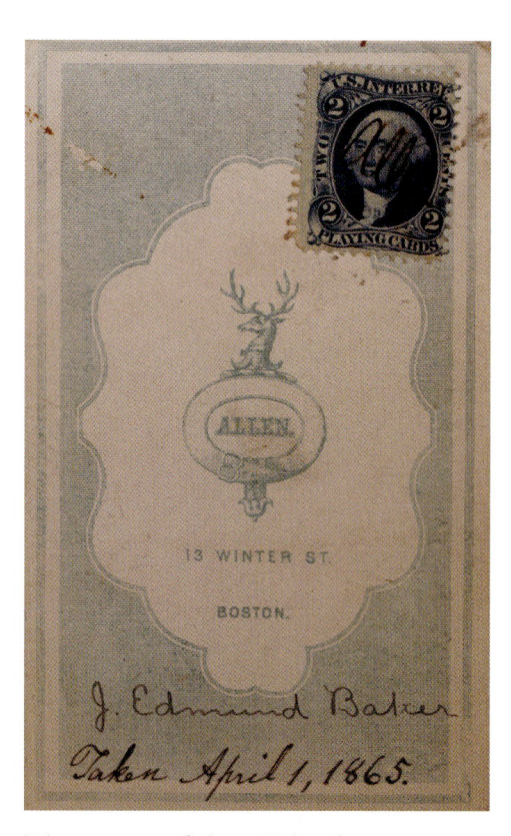

J. Edmond Baker as his name implies with a rolling pin, apron and hat.

Two cent blue Playing Cards stamp.

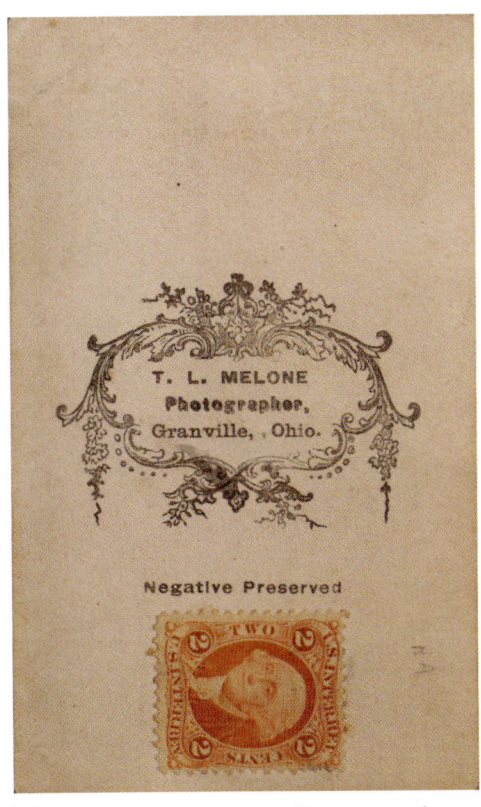

Two cent orange Internal Revenue stamp.

Two happy gamblers who seem intent on the game.

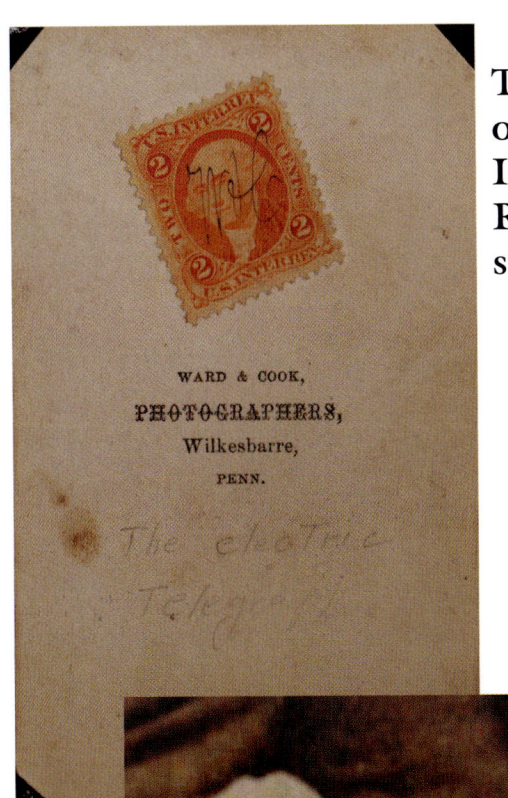

Two cent orange Internal Revenue stamp.

A telegrapher and his assistant, probably his son, at his key. See enlargement below for details of the telegrapher's key.

Caly Curtiss, ice skating Union soldier.

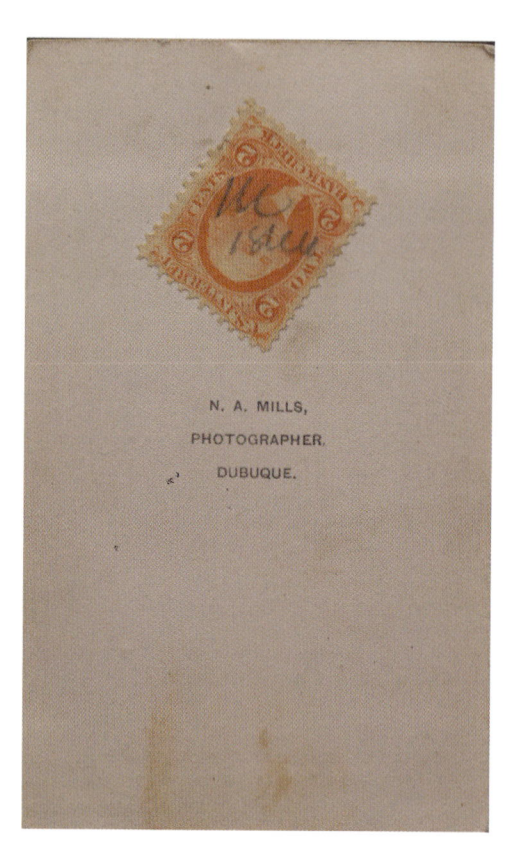

Two cent orange Bank Check stamp.

Carpenter with tools of his trade, hammer, saw and square.

Two cent orange Internal Revenue stamp.

72

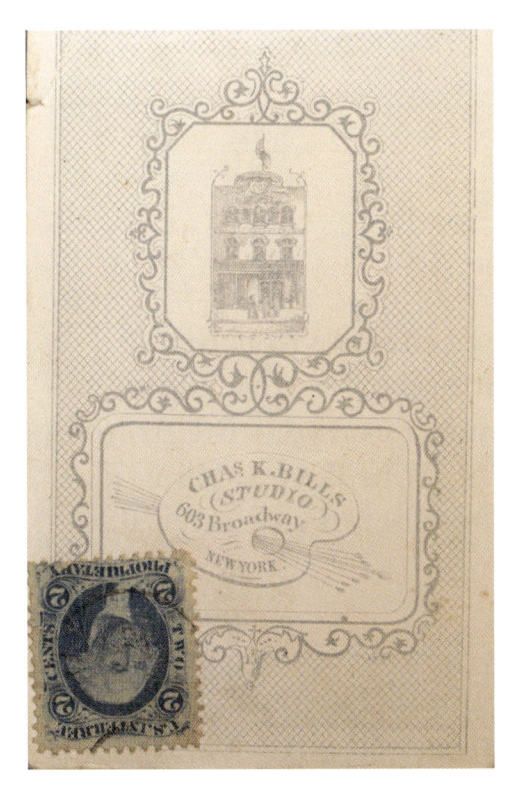

Note this back has a stamp block designed for placement. The block is unused because it contains a graphic of the photographer's studio.

Man with knife peeling apple. Most likely a fruit vendor, fruit wholesaler or apple farmer.

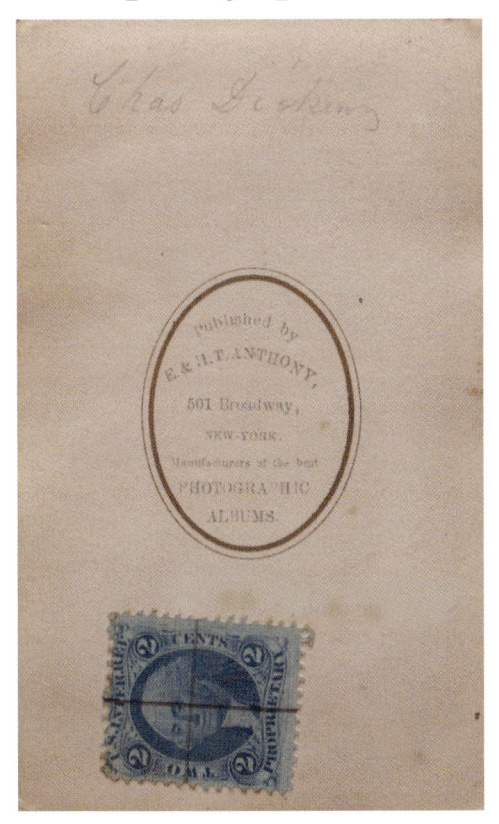

Two cent blue Proprietary stamp.

Charles Dickens, popular English novelist, author of *Oliver Twist*, *A Christmas Carol*, and *David Copperfield*.

73

Outdoor Scenes

The following images offer a little insight into the beautiful vistas that attracted the attention of photographers. In addition, we get a peek into the lives of some of the people of that era with views of everyday life from a child on horseback to men being transported to or from Fort Snelling via ferry. We even see what today would probably be considered a disaster area in the photograph of a flooded town.

The portraits throughout the book provide some evidence of how people lived in the two year span of concentration of this book. The outdoor scenes show the structures they erected, their lifestyles and what interested them.

Western waterfall "Silver Cascade," MN. Note the soldiers at the top of the waterfalls.

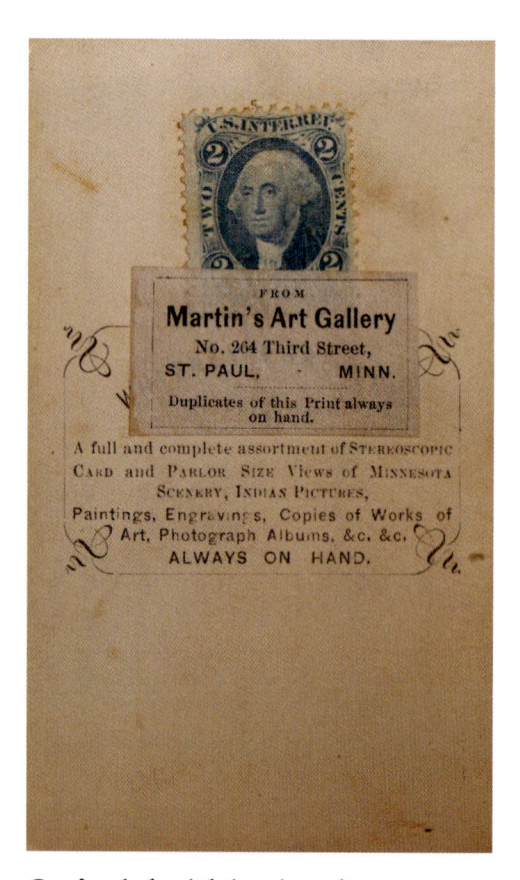

Strip label blocks the original photographer's name and partially covers the two cent blue stamp.

Two cent blue Proprietary stamp.

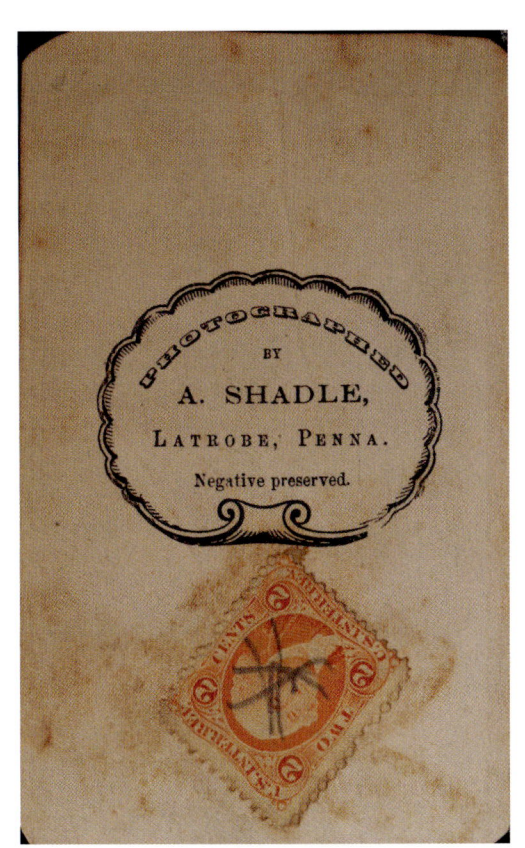

View of an attempt to harness the water energy for a lumber mill at the Falls of St. Anthony, MN.

Two cent orange Internal Revenue stamp.

Outdoor CDV of a youth on horseback.

75

Photo of a two horse carriage. Note the track of the wagon pulled up to the photographer's assistant, a young black boy.

Three cent green Proprietary stamp.

The *U.S.S. Constitution*, Boston, MA

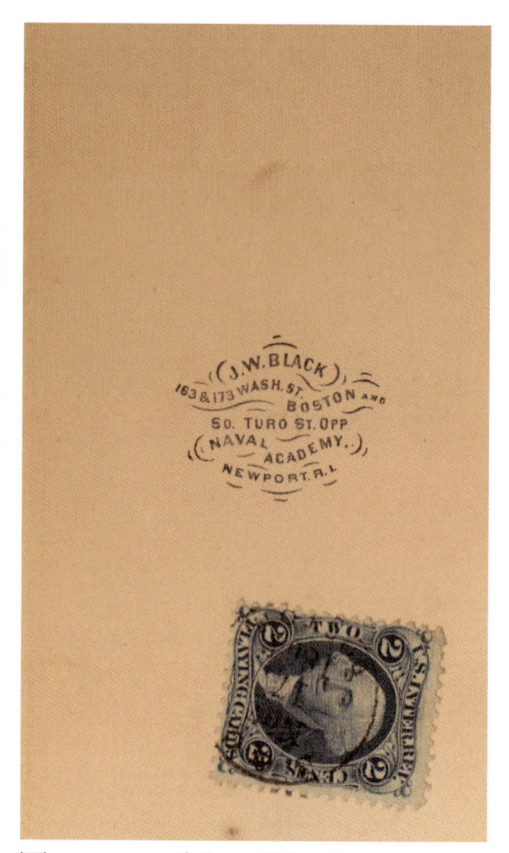

Two cent blue Playing Cards stamp.

76

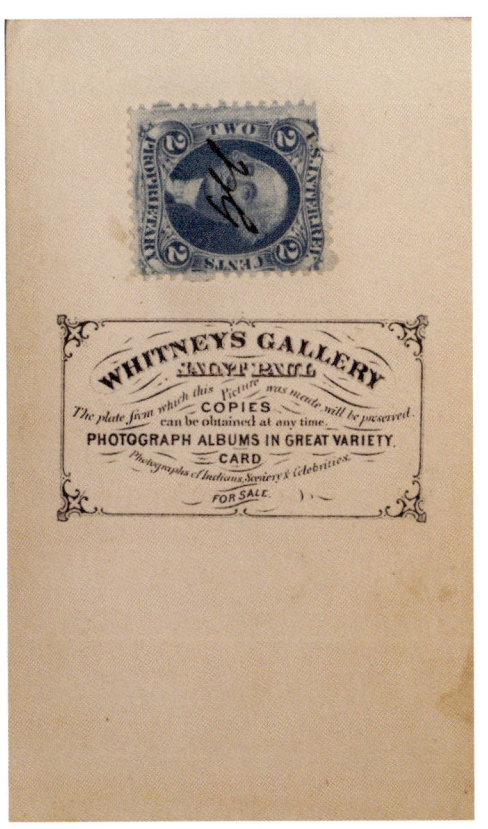

Two cent blue Proprietary stamp.

Outdoor CDV of a bridge over the Mississippi River at St. Paul, MN.

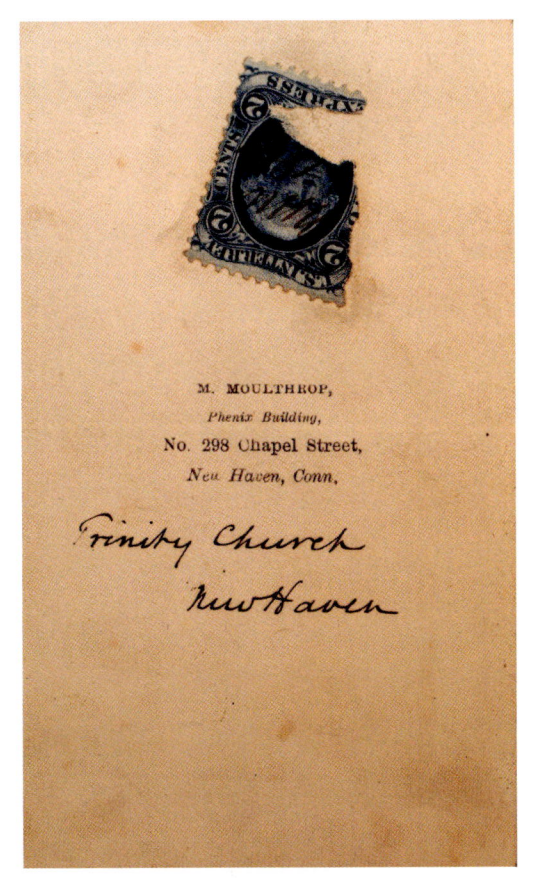

Two cent blue Express stamp.

View of Trinity Church, New Haven, CT. Note the contrast in the clouds.

77

Bridge in Nashville, TN, removed in 1999. The bridge moved on a pivot to allow large boats through.

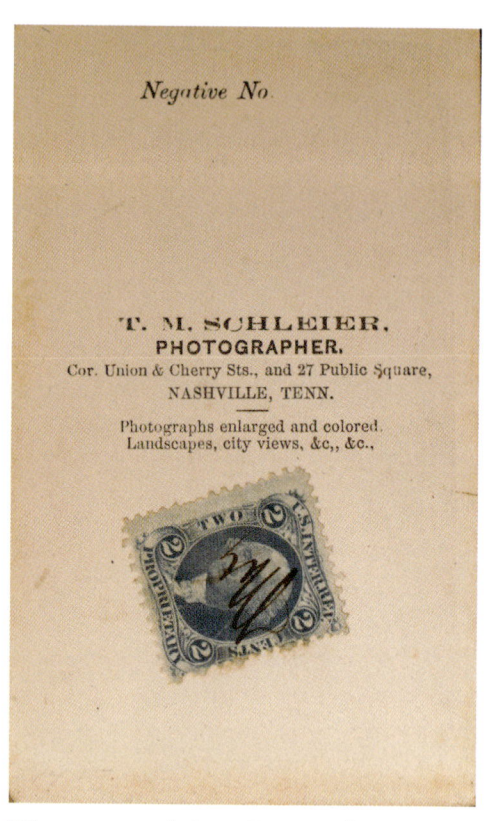

Two cent blue Proprietary stamp.

Catholic church in Brownsville, TX near the time of the last Civil War battle which was fought a few miles from here at Palmetto (Palmitto) Ranch, TX, a Southern victory.

Two cent orange Internal Revenue stamp.

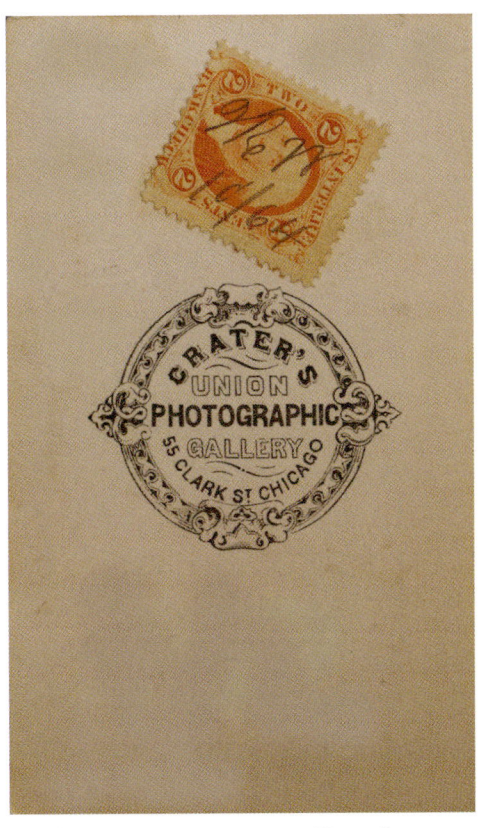

Two cent orange Bank Check stamp.

Two ships on the waterfront in Chicago, IL.

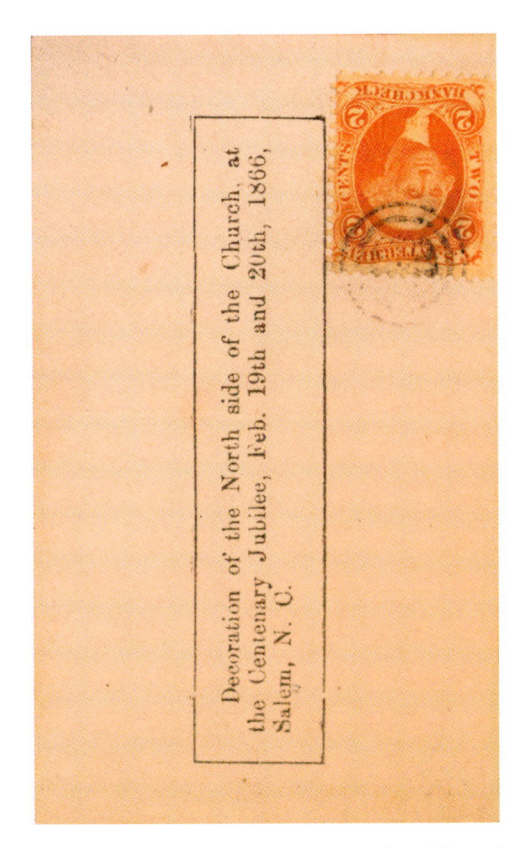

Two cent orange Bank Check stamp tied by a cork killer cancel.

Outdoor scene of decorations celebrating one hundred years of this unknown church in Salem, NC.

Ox drawn wagon hauling men at Lookout Mountain, TN. The man in the stove-pipe hat is R. M. Linn, the photographer.

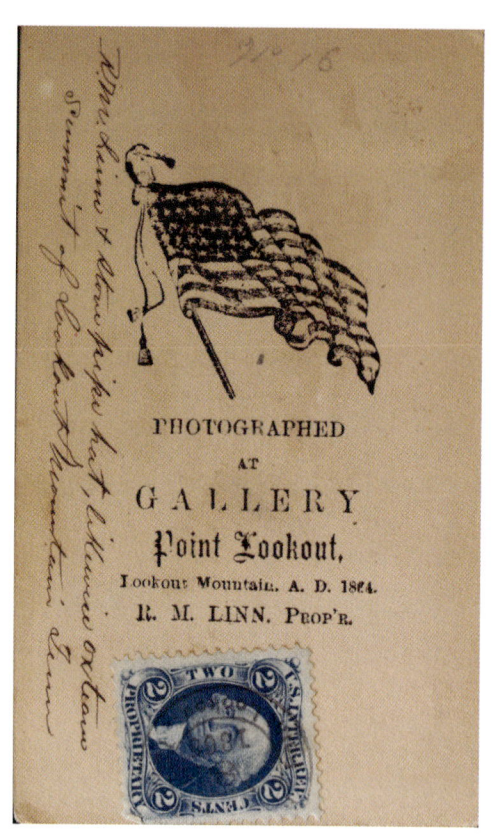

Two cent blue Proprietary stamp.

The U. S. Mint, Denver, Colorado Territory. Prior to being operated as a U. S. Mint, it had operated as a private mint issuing gold coins.

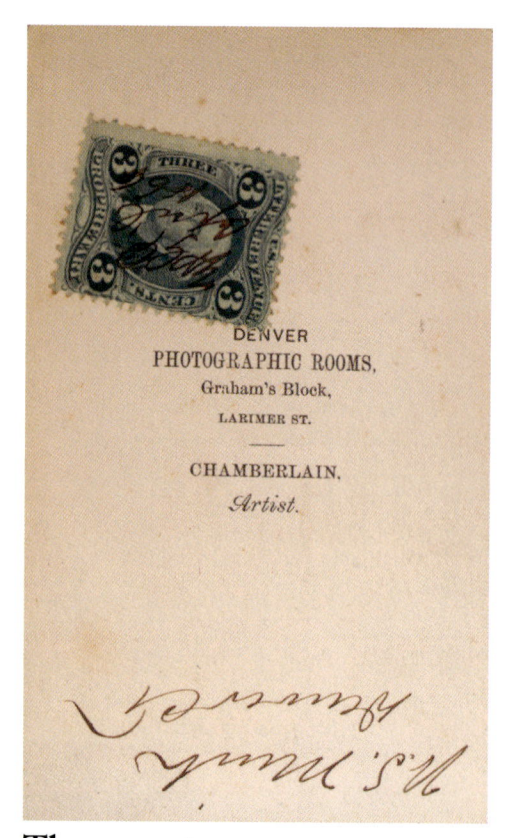

Three cent green Proprietary stamp.

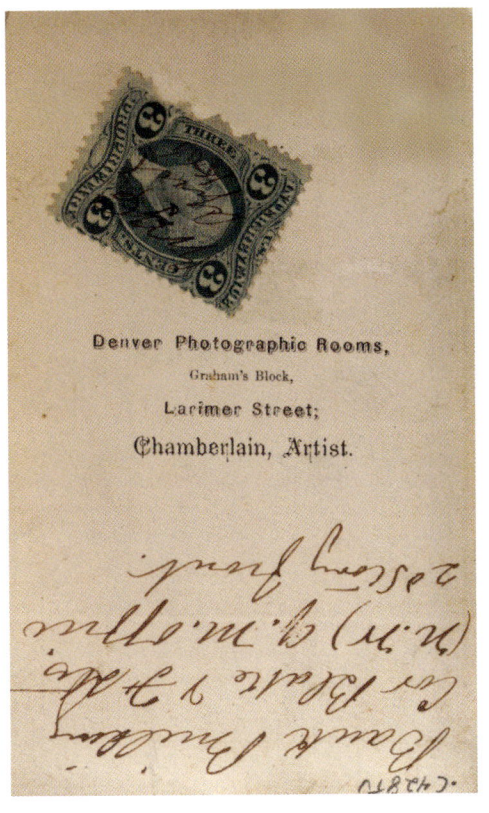

Three cent green Proprietary stamp.

The First National Bank at Denver, Colorado Territory.

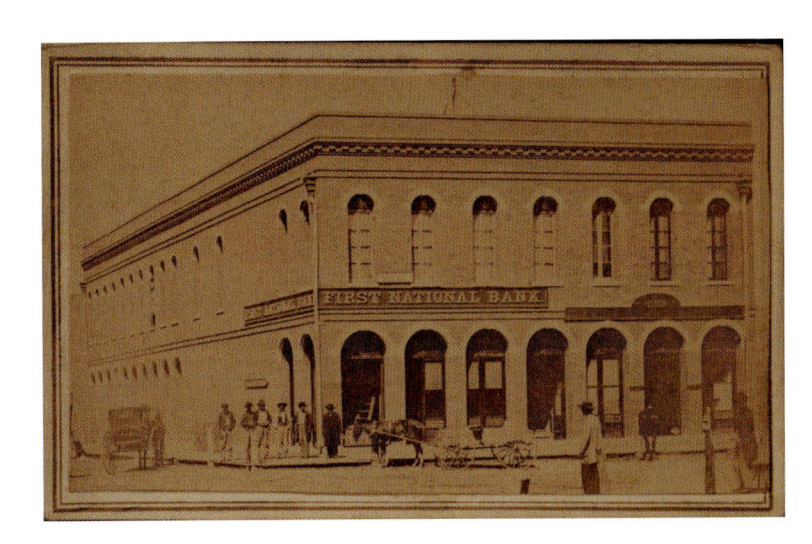

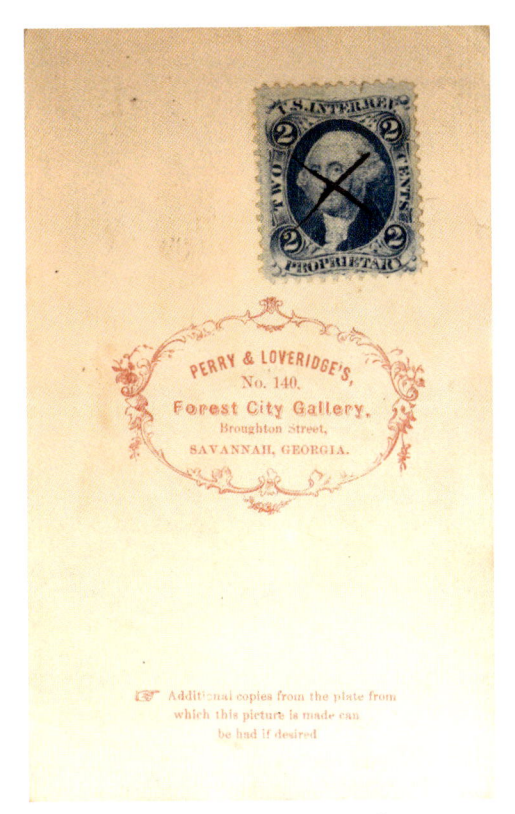

Two cent blue Proprietary stamp.

Spanish architecture influenced this unknown church in Florida. Image taken by Georgia photographers, Perry and Loveridge.

81

Fort Marion, FL. image taken by Georgia photographers, Perry and Loveridge.

Two cent blue Proprietary stamp.

Ruins of church in Charleston, SC taken by Georgia photographers, Perry and Loveridge.

Two cent blue Proprietary stamp.

Two cent orange Internal Revenue stamp.

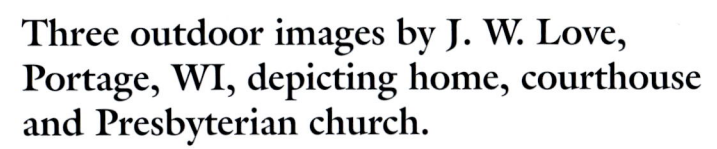

Two cent orange Internal Revenue stamp.

Three outdoor images by J. W. Love, Portage, WI, depicting home, courthouse and Presbyterian church.

Columbia County Courthouse, Portage, WI.

83

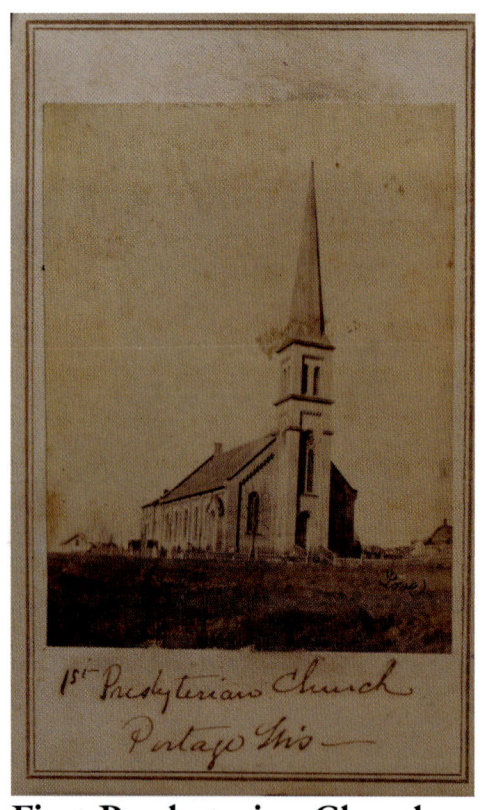

First Presbyterian Church, Portage, WI.

Enlargement of J. W. Love's signature etched into the negative of the First Presbyterian Church image.

Two cent orange Internal Revenue stamp.

The falls at St. Anthony, MN where debris has collected from previous flooding.

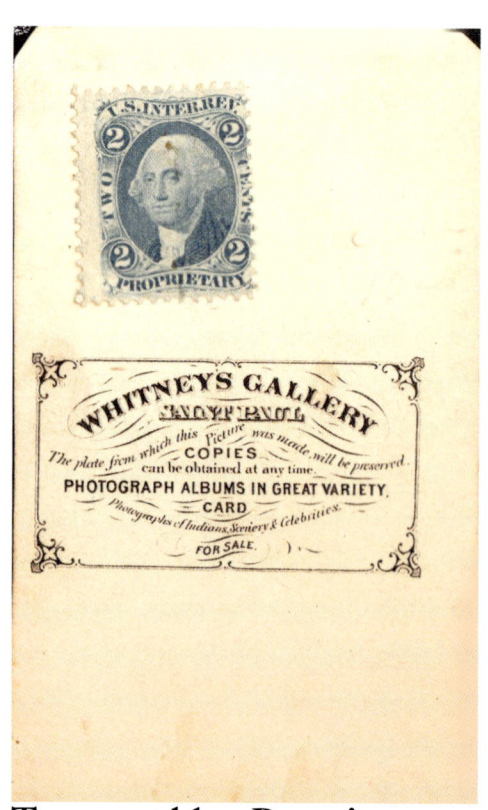

Two cent blue Proprietary stamp.

Two cent orange Bank Check stamp.

Oil City, PA during a flood. Unable to determine photographer from cancellation on the stamp.

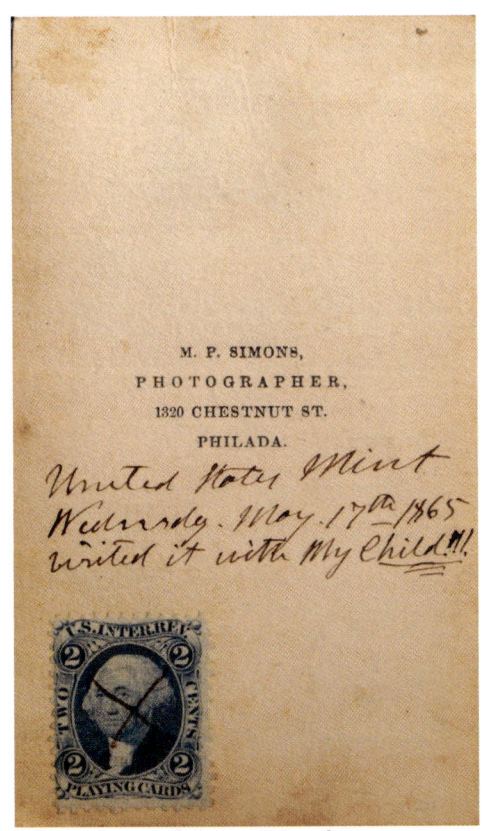

Two cent blue Playing Cards stamp.

Image of the U. S. Mint, Philadelphia, PA.

85

Docked Mississippi paddle wheel riverboat, *Magenta,* at St. Louis, MO.

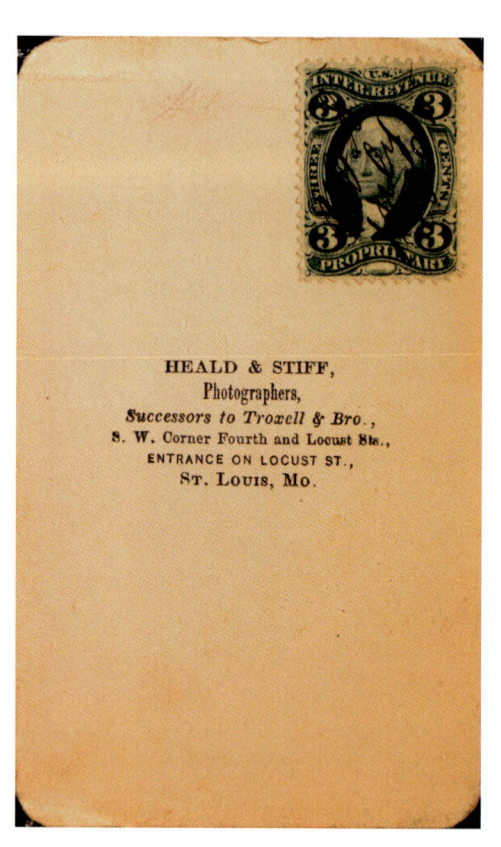

Three cent green Proprietary stamp.

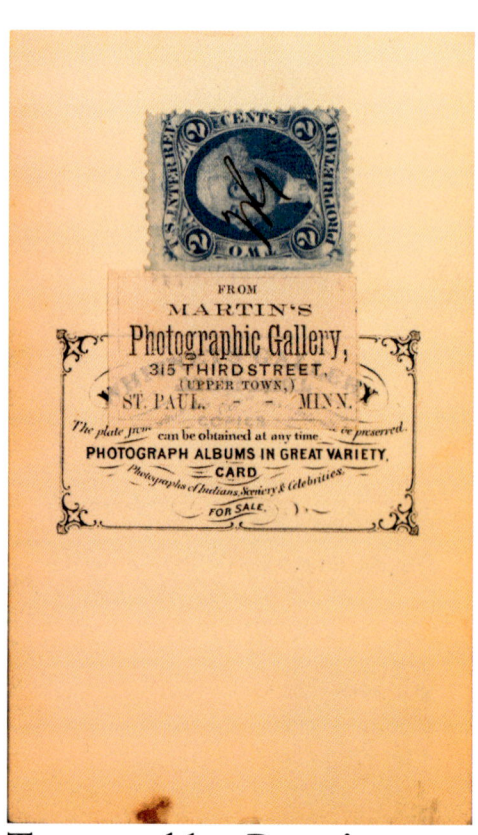

Ferry at Fort Snelling, MN. Note the clarity of the image. Even the ropes for the ferry are apparent.

Two cent blue Proprietary stamp.

86

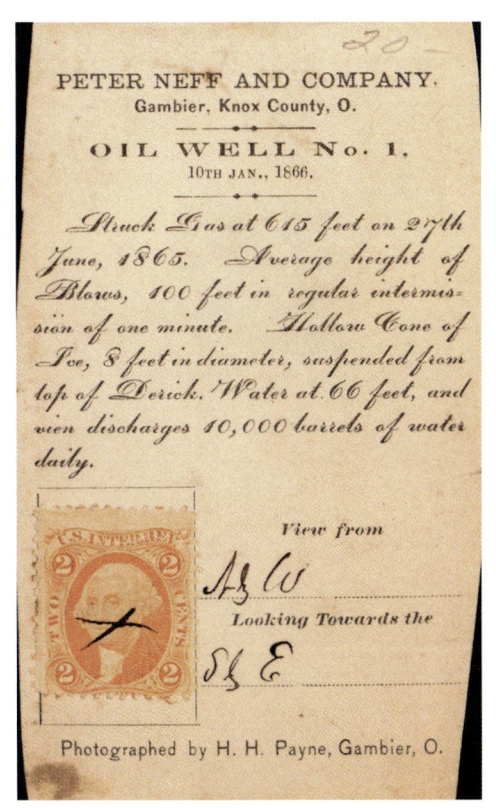

Two cent orange stamp with no bottom label.

Neff photo of oil well used for enticing investors. Neff is also known as one of the inventors of the tin-type c. 1854-1856.

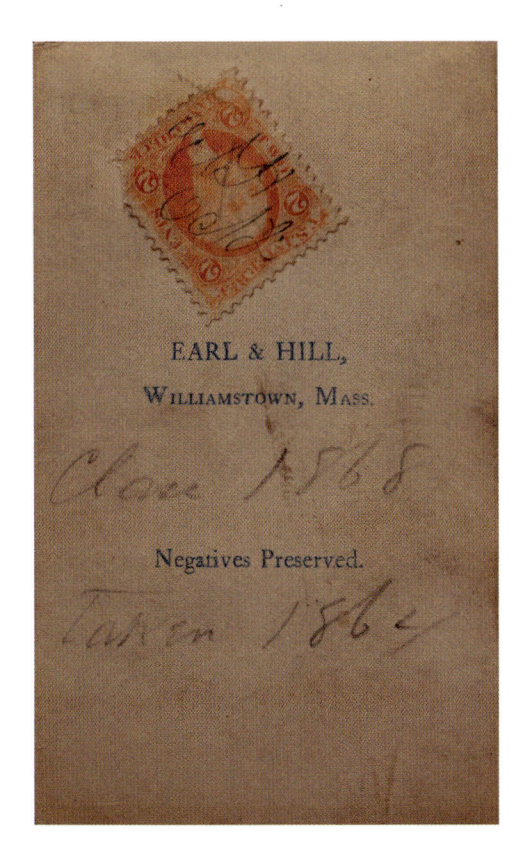

Two cent orange Internal Revenue stamp.

Landscape portrait of Williams College Class of 1868. Photograph taken in the Autumn of 1864.

87

An Indian mound was turned into a garden by the occupying Union troops in Chattanooga, TN. Today this is the site of the waterworks.

Two cent Proprietary blue stamp.

Outdoor CDV of the State House at Nashville, TN. Note the tents of the occupying troops around the capitol.

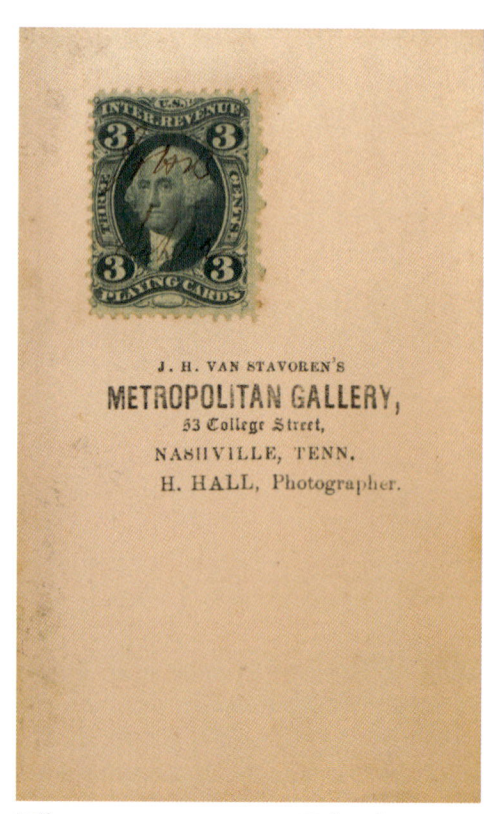

Three cent green Playing Cards stamp.

88

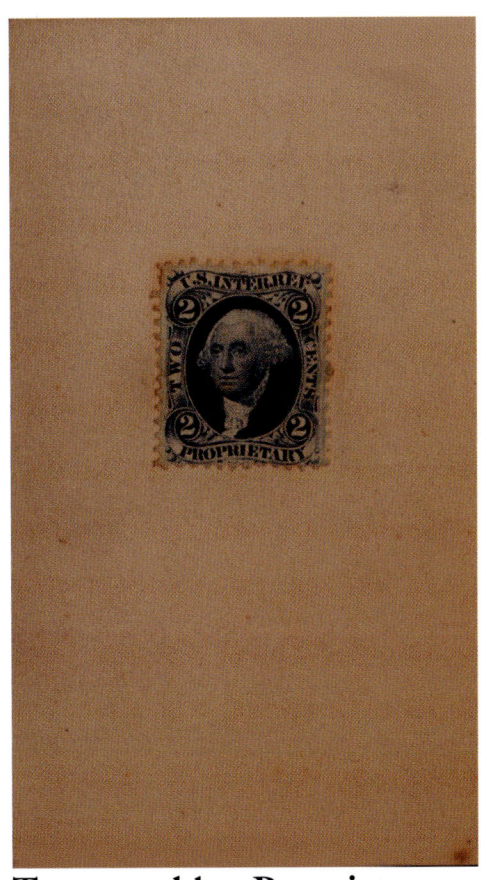

Two cent blue Proprietary stamp.

Famous sandstone formation frequently visited by people heading west from St. Paul, MN.

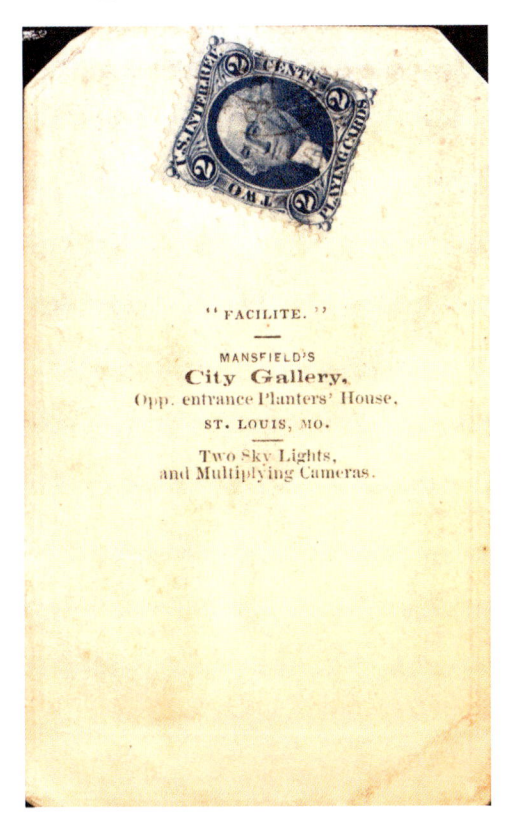

Two cent blue Playing Cards stamp.

Outdoor scene along a river near St. Louis, MO.

89

Elevated bridge in Chicago, IL.

Two cent orange Bank Check stamp.

Outdoor scene by R. M. Linn of one of the beautiful waterways on top of Lookout Mountain, TN.

Two cent orange Bank Check stamp.

Mount Vernon

All views of Mount Vernon depicted here have a similar cancel on the stamp: MVLA. The Mount Vernon Ladies Association is the oldest non-profit organization operating in the United States.

Ann Pamela Cunningham from South Carolina took possession of Mount Vernon on February 22, 1860 to preserve President George Washington's historic home. After the Civil War broke out in 1861, she gained an audience with General Winfield Scott and obtained a letter barring Union soldiers carrying arms on the property. She secured the same promise from the Governor John Letcher of Virginia.

In 1864, the MVLA sold potatoes, peaches, pears, tomatoes, cabbages, hay, photographs of Mount Vernon and handmade bricks, grossing $118.03. They also earned $230.00 from visitors admissions at no more than twenty-five cents each.

Two cent orange Internal Revenue stamp.

Washington's design of a round barn where the cattle entered on the second level and thrashed wheat depositing the grain on the lower level through cracks in the floor above.

Washington's tomb, Mount Vernon.

View of Mount Vernon from the Potomac River.

When Miss Cunningham took possession, Mount Vernon, she found nothing but the key to the Bastille, which had been given to Washington as a gift by Lafayette, a globe in Washington's study, and a bust by Jean-Antoine Houdon, a French sculptor who created the masterpiece from a mask made of Washington's face.

Two cent orange Bank Check stamp cancelled by MVLA.

Various official photographers at Mount Vernon include Alexander Gardner, N.G. Johnson, and Luke G. Dillon.

92

Patriotic Children

Patriotic albumen CDV of a youth with an American flag. Note the photograph album on the table. Two cent orange Bank Check was typical usage on CDVs.

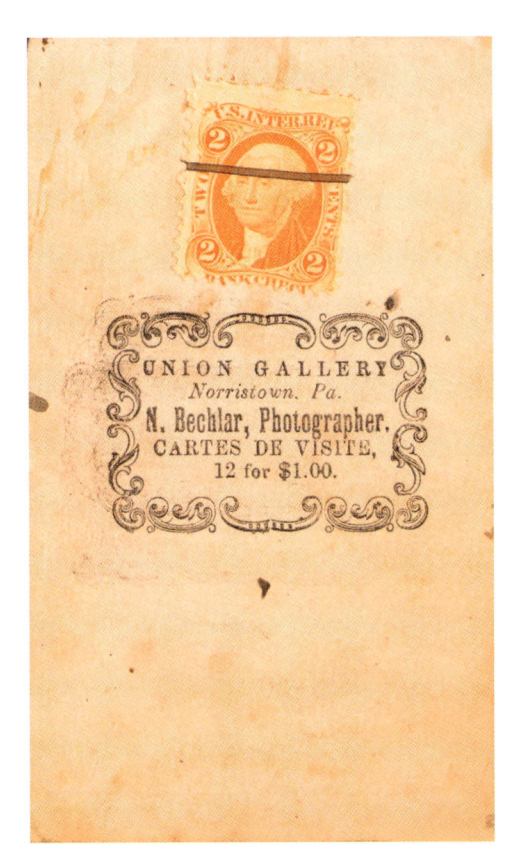

Two cent orange Bank Check stamp.

CDV of a patriotic youth holding a flag at the Union Gallery.

93

Personalities

CDV of newspaperman, Horace Greely. He is famous for the quote, "Go west, young man." He edited both *The Jeffersonian* and *The New York Tribune*.

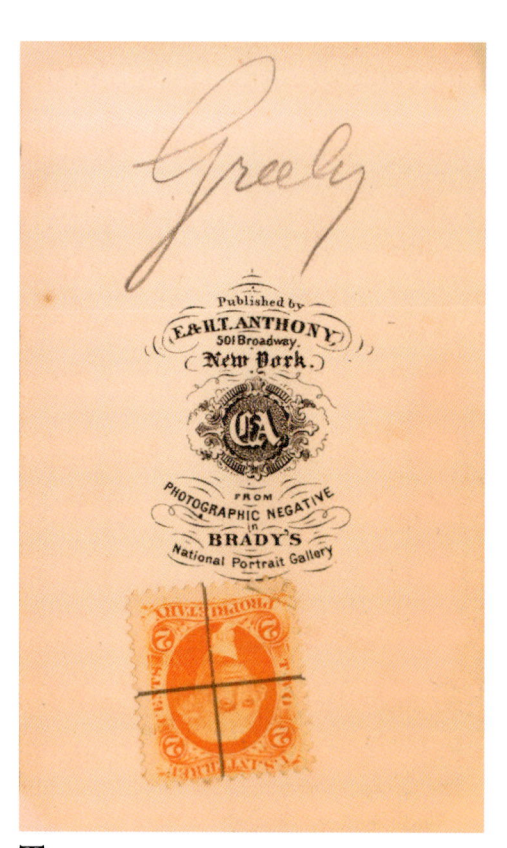

Two cent orange Proprietary stamp.

Vignette of President Andrew Johnson by Alexander Gardner, Washington, DC. He served as the military governor of Tennessee during the Civil War and was only one of two Senators from Southern states who kept his seat and adhered to the Union. Johnson served as president from 1865 to 1869.

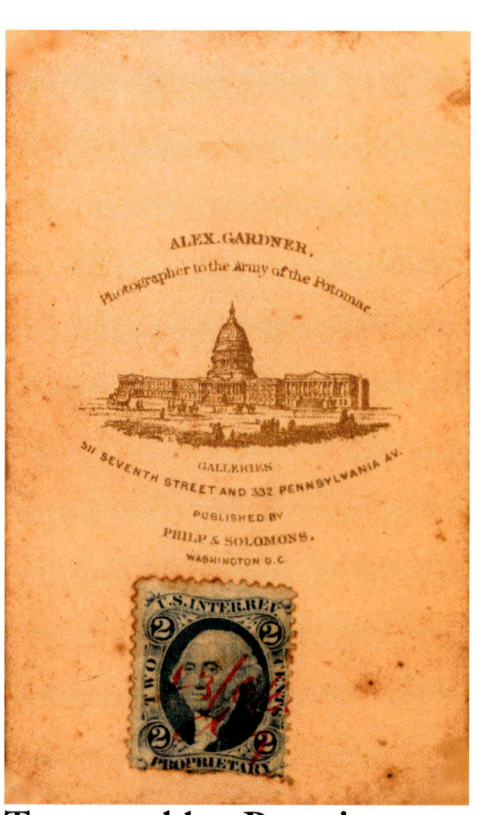

Two cent blue Proprietary Stamp.

94

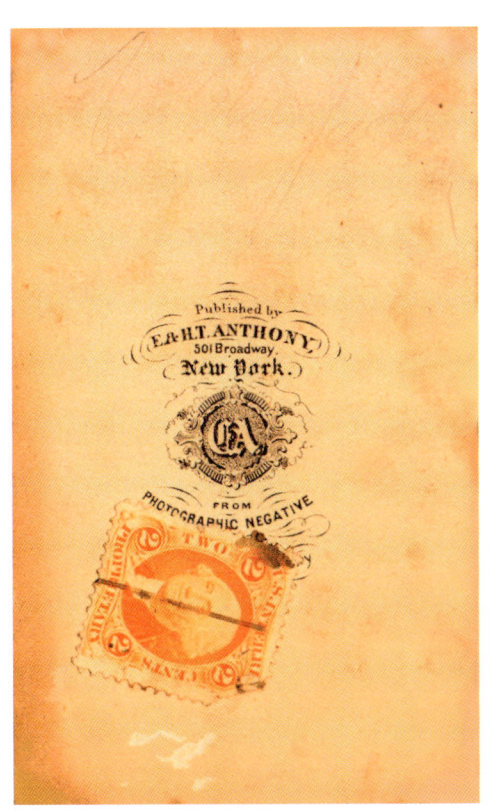

Two cent orange Proprietary stamp.

Two cent blue Proprietary stamp.

CDV of President Andrew Jackson from a Brady negative and published by E & H.T. Anthony. He served as a Major General in the War of 1812 and became a hero when he defeated the British at New Orleans. He was elected President and 1829 and again in 1833. He was the first president to endure an assassination attempt. The attempted assassin had two pistols, both of which misfired.

John Wells Foster who served as Vice-President under Andrew Johnson after the assassination of President Lincoln.

95

Postmortem

These sad remembrances may seem macabre, but they are the only visual reminder of the family member. In this era, mortality rates among children less than two years old were much higher and death was an unhappy occurrence cruelly visited on these people.

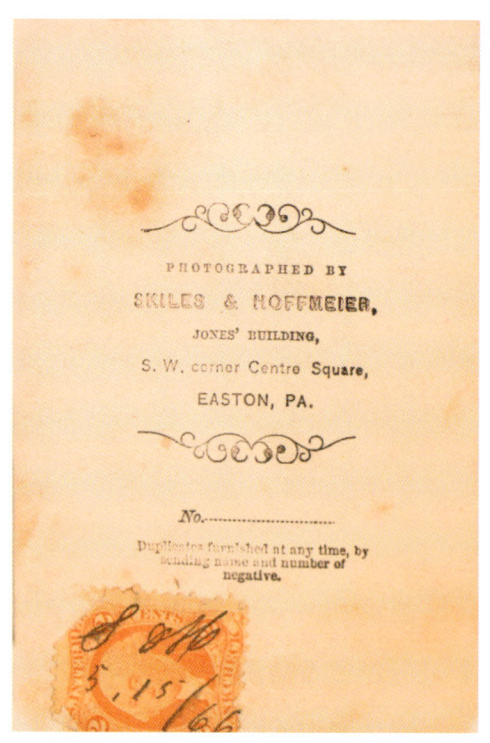

CDV of a mother holding the body of her recently deccased baby. Note the despair in her face.

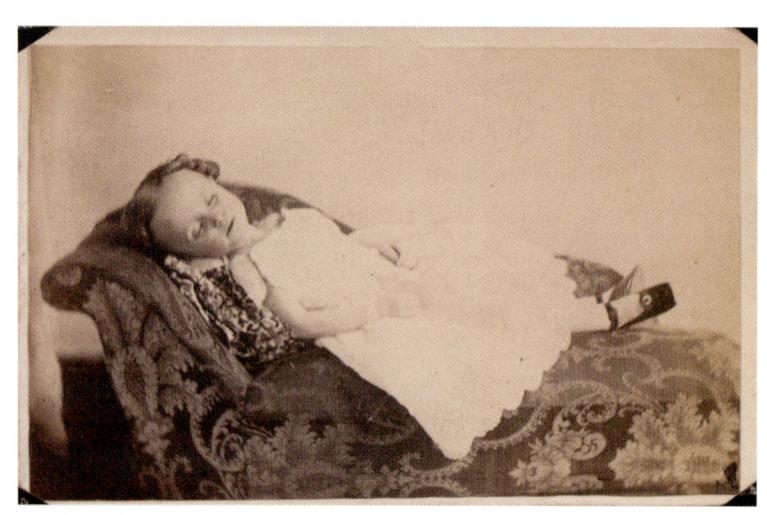

CDV of a child postmortem laid out on a chaise.

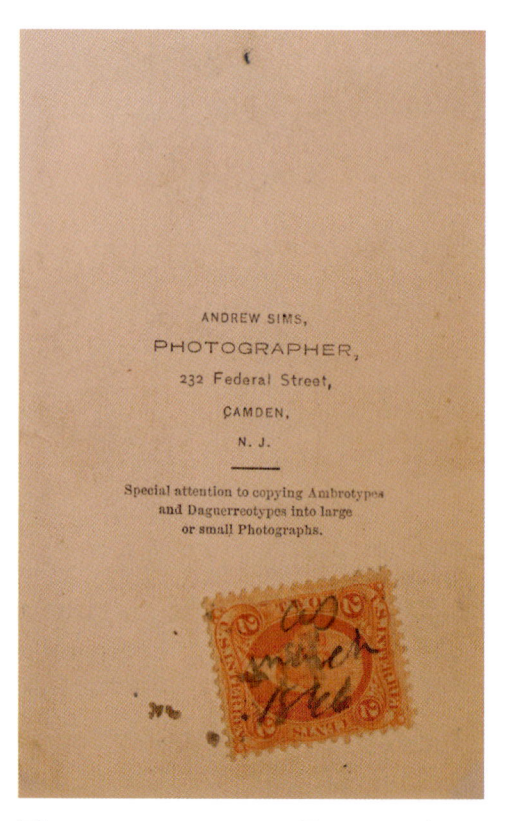

Two cent orange Bank Check stamp.

Two cent orange Internal Revenue stamp.

96

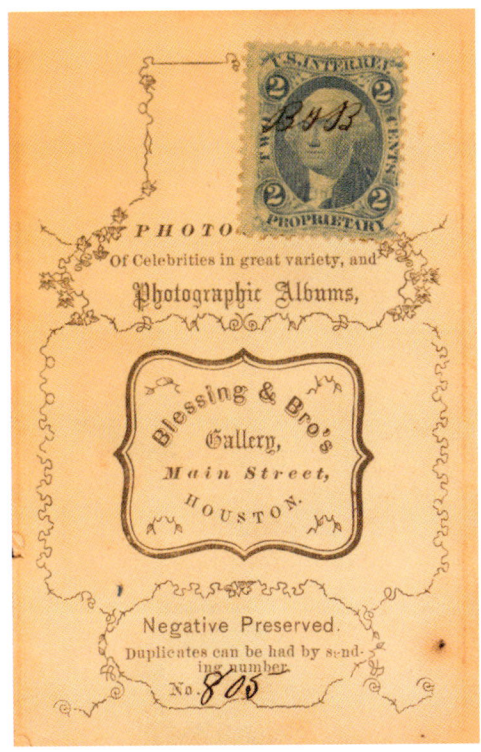

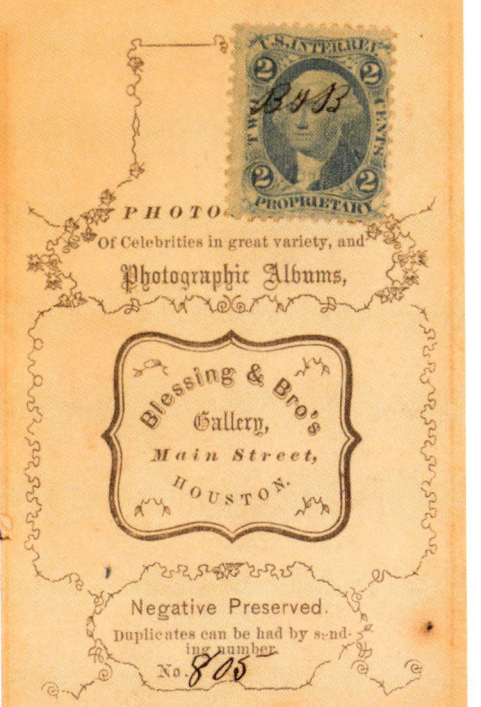

Two cent blue Proprietary stamp.

CDV of a child postmortem taken in Houston, TX.

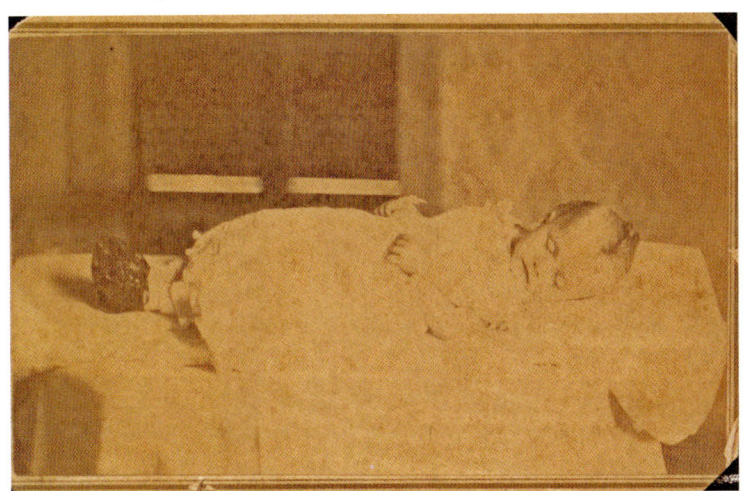

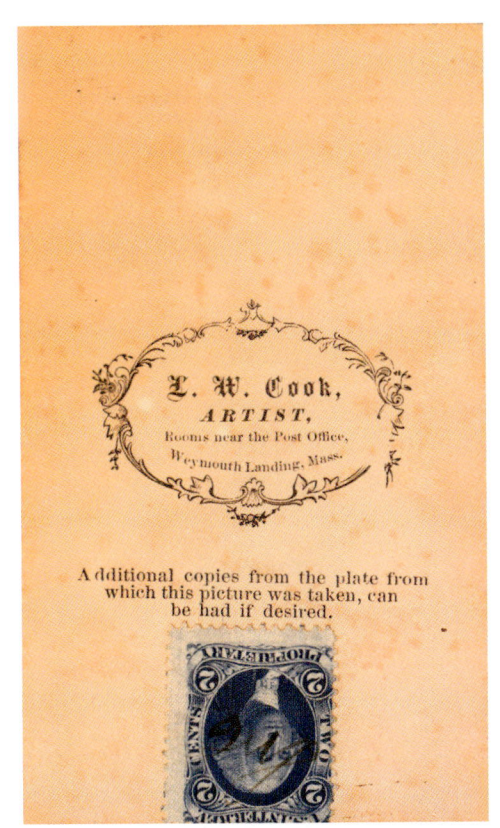

Two cent blue Proprietary stamp.

Vignette of a man postmortem.

97

Statuary and Works of Art

CDV of a copy of art entitled, "Life on the James, 1864-5 before Richmond."

Two cent blue Playing Cards Stamp.

CDV of a copy of art showing a military parade in San Francisco, CA.

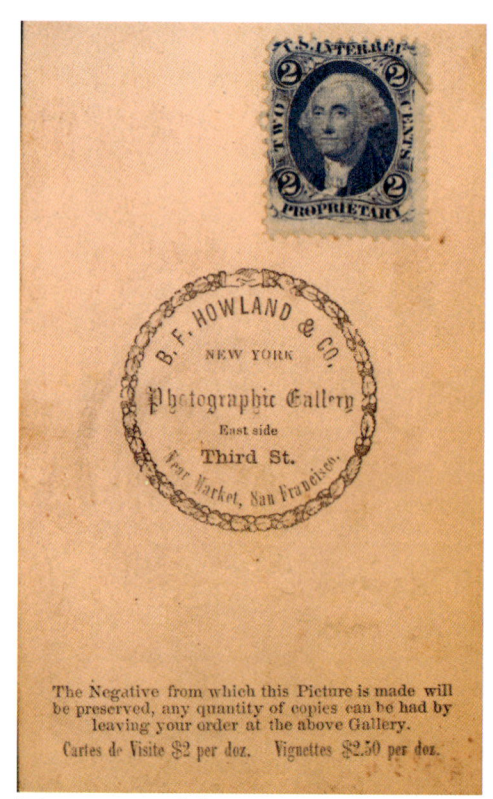

Two cent blue Proprietary stamp.

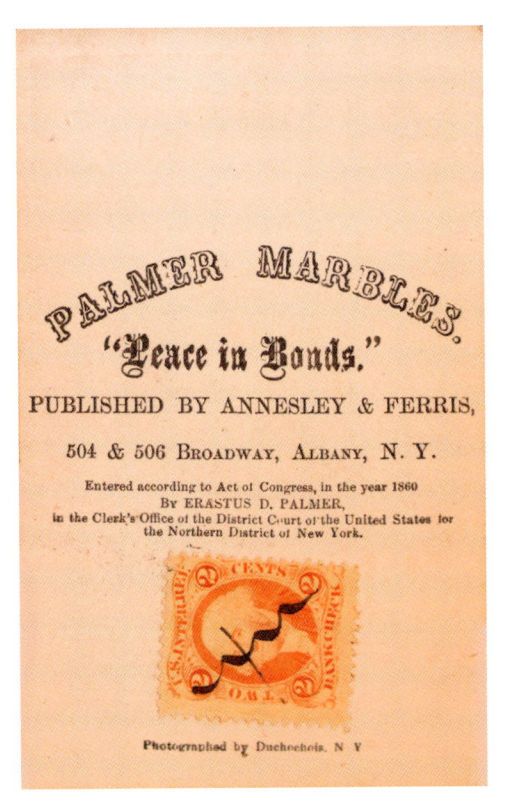

Two cent orange Bank Check stamp.

Peace in Bonds

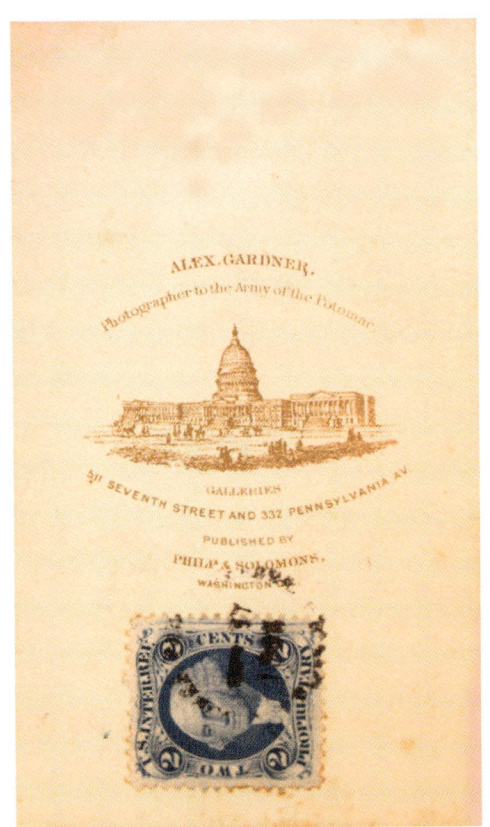

Two cent blue Proprietary stamp.

Copy of art depicting a young woman in a theatrical pose.

Copy of art of an American ocean-going side wheeler by an unknown artist.

Two cent blue Proprietary stamp with a blue circular date cancel.

Humor, depiction of an ancestral congregation sleeping through a sermon.

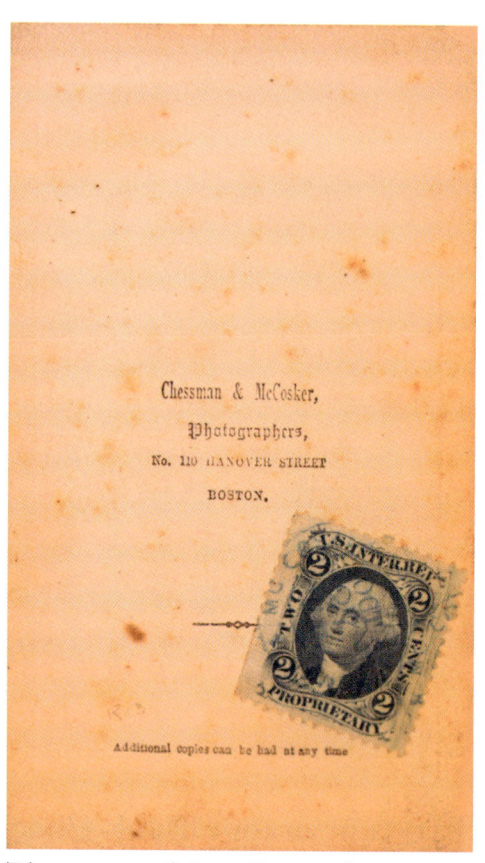

Two cent blue Proprietary stamp.

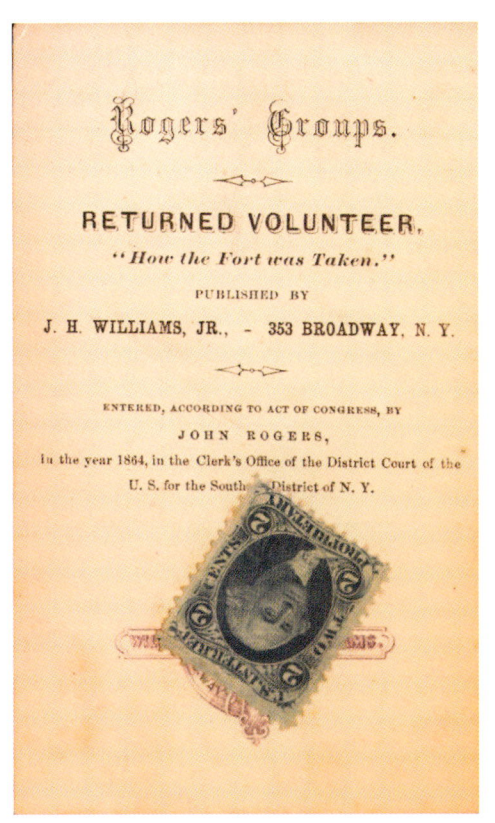

The following eight CDVs are images of Rogers' Groups. John Rogers was a famous sculptor of the period who did a series of Civil War related topics.

Two cent blue Proprietary stamp.

Returned Volunteer

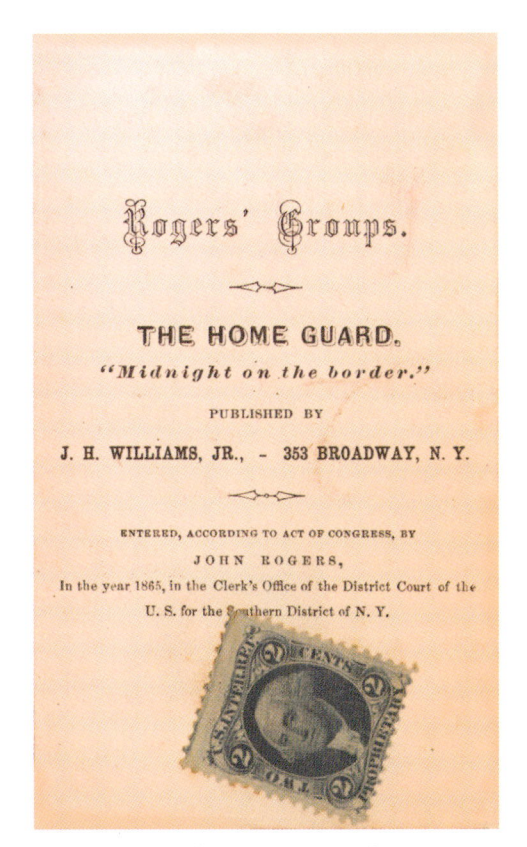

Two cent blue Proprietary stamp.

The Home Guard

101

One More Shot

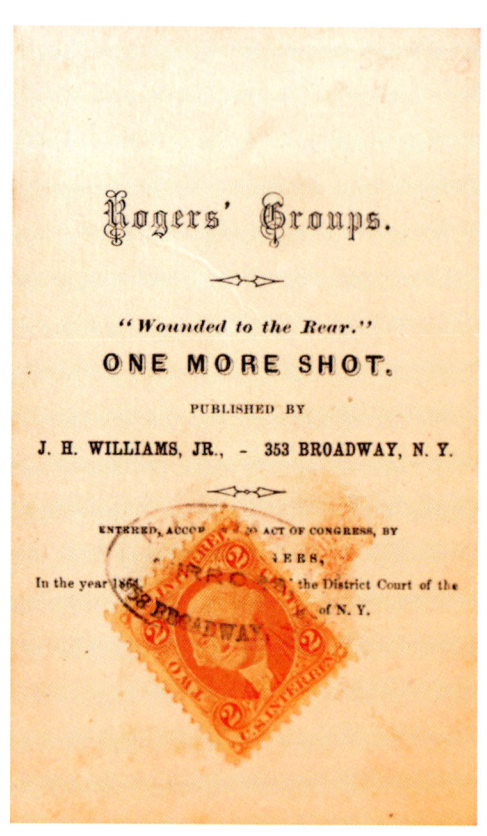

Two cent orange Internal Revenue stamp.

Mail Day

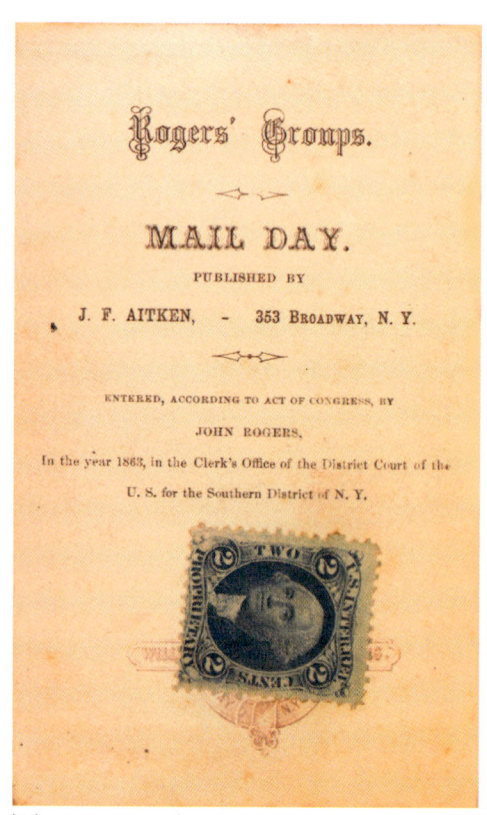

Two cent blue Proprietary stamp.

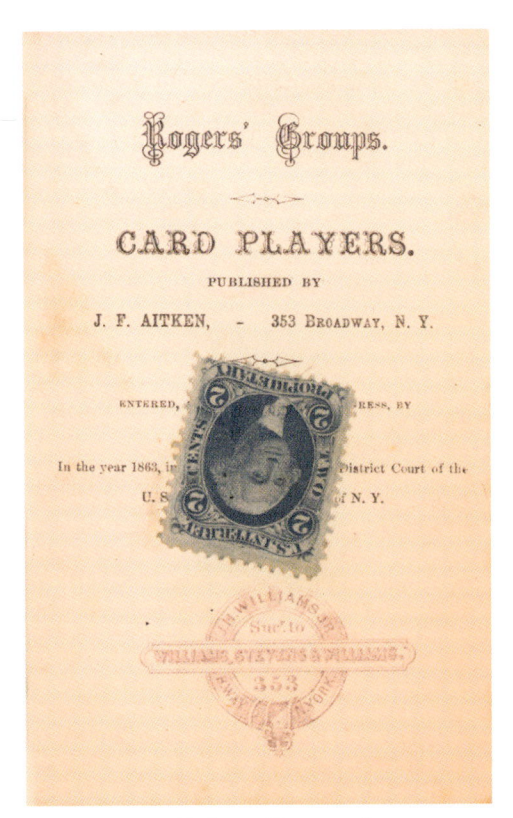

Two cent blue Proprietary stamp.

Card Players

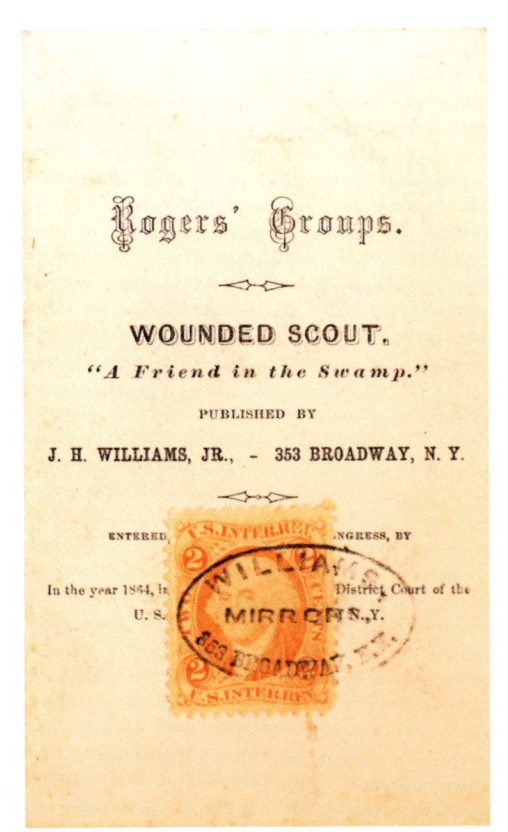

Two cent orange Internal Revenue stamp.

Wounded Scout

103

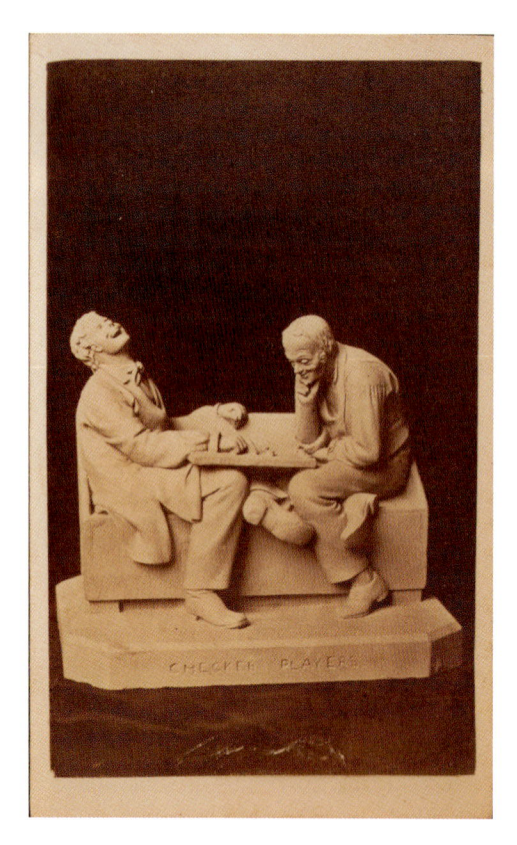

Checker Players

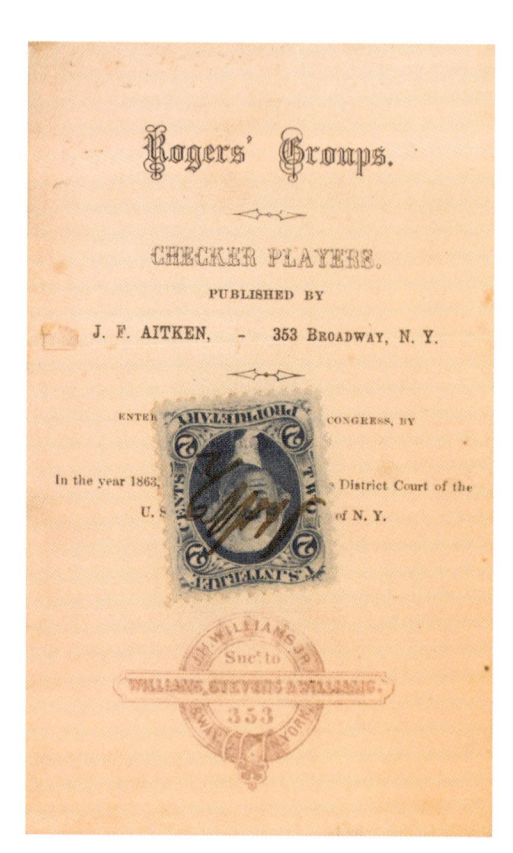

Two cent blue Proprietary stamp.

Camp Fire

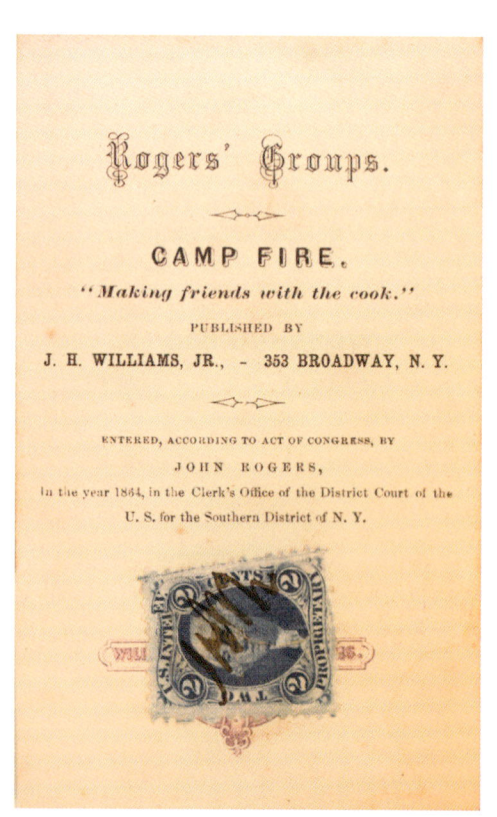

Two cent blue Proprietary stamp.

Stereo Viewers

Stereo views became a primary source of entertainment in the 19th century. It is no surprise to find images of people in studios with viewers. The stereo view, when placed in a viewer, makes the two adjacent views appear as one. The merged view has a third dimension, depth. This is accomplished by placing the view in the mobile carrier and looking through the lenses. The view is then adjusted to bring the two views into focus. Once this is complete the person doing the viewing is magically transported through time and space to the subject titled on the card. A person could then study the images in detail and pass the viewer to the next person for a similar experience.

Any home with views had at least one viewer. Viewers were an item available at the photographer's studio and may have been used as props. The images of people with viewers is a sought subject because it brings the subjects of people and photography together.

Two cent blue Proprietary stamp.

CDV of a young girl with a stereo viewer and views in her lap.

The enlargement of this viewer revealed a stereo view of the U. S. Capitol.

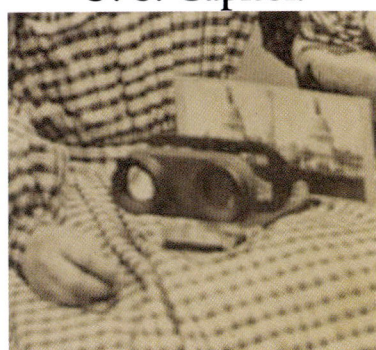

A couple with a Brewster stereo viewer between them.

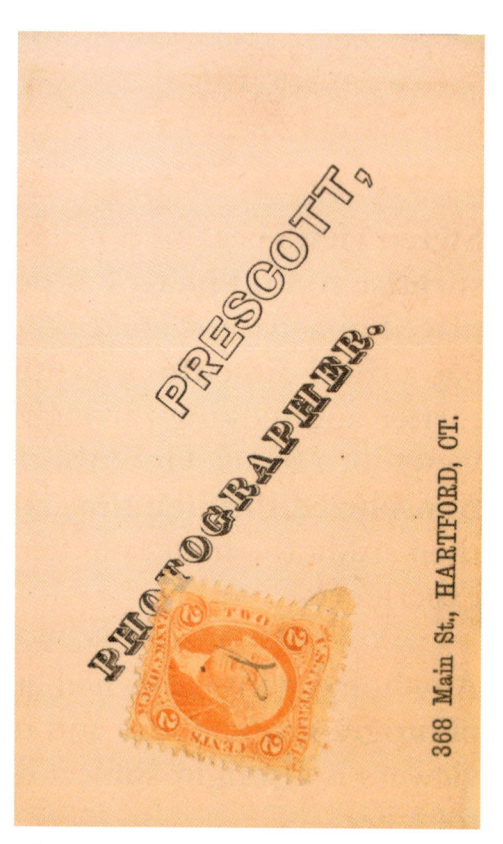

Two cent orange Bank Check stamp.

A teenager with a stereo viewer and card on the table next to him.

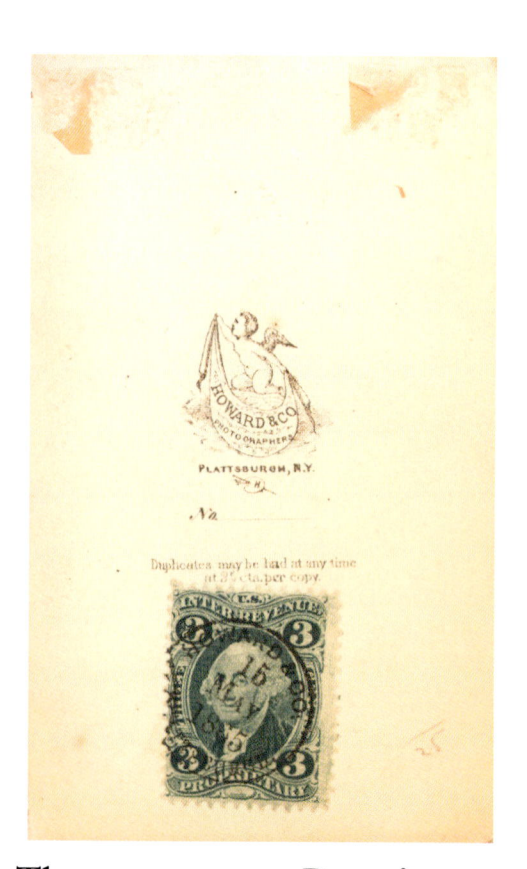

Three cent green Proprietary stamp.

Toys

The toys of an era provide evidence about how advanced the society may have been. In the images following, we see the typical toys that were available to children of this time period. These children were perfectly content to play with dolls, hoops, rocking horses and other simple toys. However, even though we may describe these toys as simple, they were not. These items were all handmade by craftsmen using crude tools. The fit and finish of the toys personify some important aspects of the era, such as fine craftsmanship, attention to detail and ingenuity.

On the back is a Matches tax stamp properly initialed by the photographer. The Matches stamp applied was the only Match stamp that did not have a private vendor's name. It was to be used by special permission, by four small match manufacturers in the Philadelphia area.

CDV of a boy with a hoop.

107

Young girl astride a rocking horse. She is holding a riding crop.

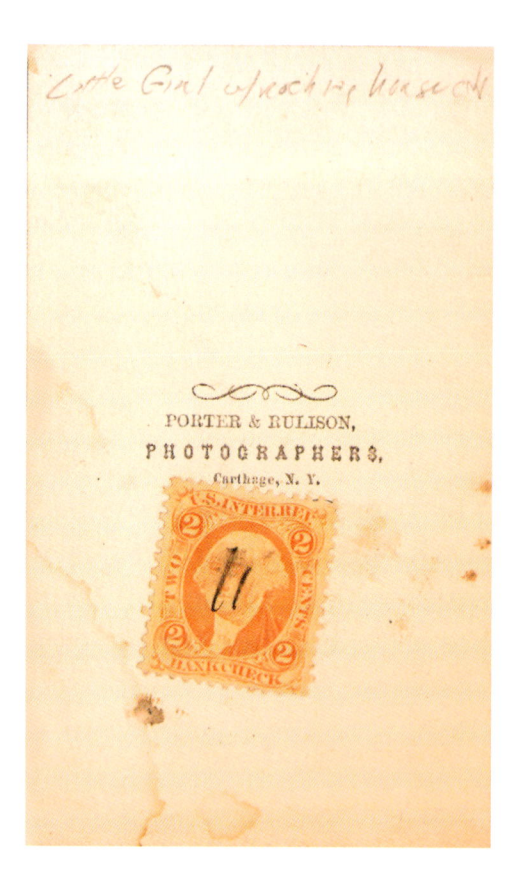

Two cent orange Bank Check stamp.

This young girl is holding a doll almost half her size.

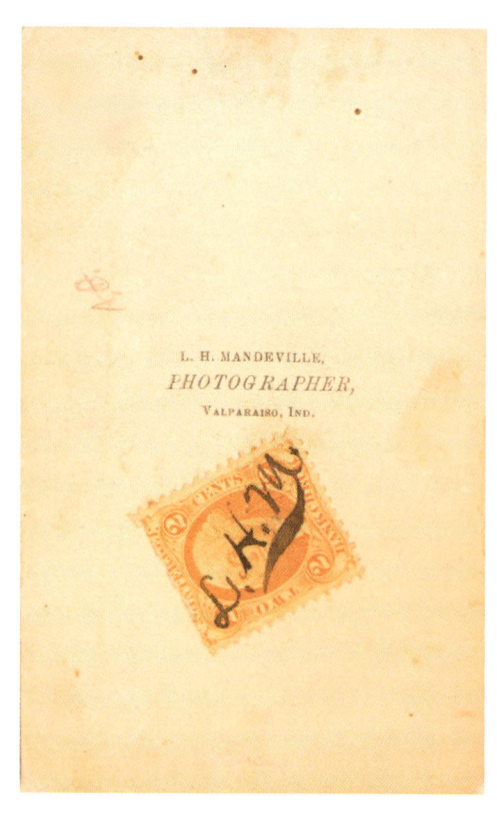

Two cent orange Bank Check stamp.

Two cent orange Bank Check stamp.

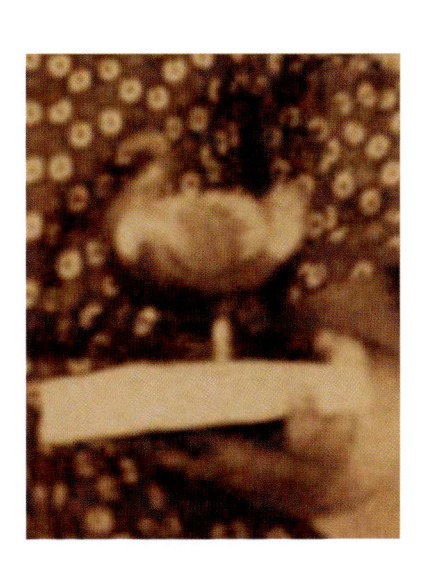

This girl is holding a model of a bird on a platform. The CDV was trimmed at the bottom by an overzealous person to fit his or her album.

Two cent orange Bank Check stamp.

A boy standing next to a rocking horse.

109

Weddings

During this era, it was customary to be married in a special, well-made dress. Wedding gowns as fancy as those depicted here were atypical for the period. Gowns were generally passed down to the daughters in a family, sometimes for generations. Although there are portraits of brides in fancy gowns, they are nothing like today's bride's product-driven quest for a fairy-tale wedding. Also evident is the photographer's role in this event. Today, wedding photography is an industry. In earlier times, the wedding portrait may have been little more than an afterthought.

A beautiful bride. Images of brides during this period are extremely scarce.

Two cent blue Proprietary stamp.

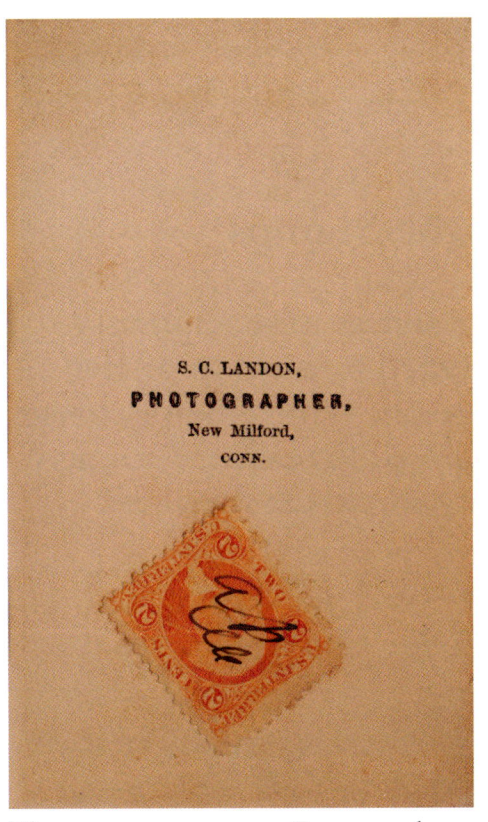

Two cent orange Internal Revenue stamp.

CDV of a bride holding a feather fan and a bouquet.

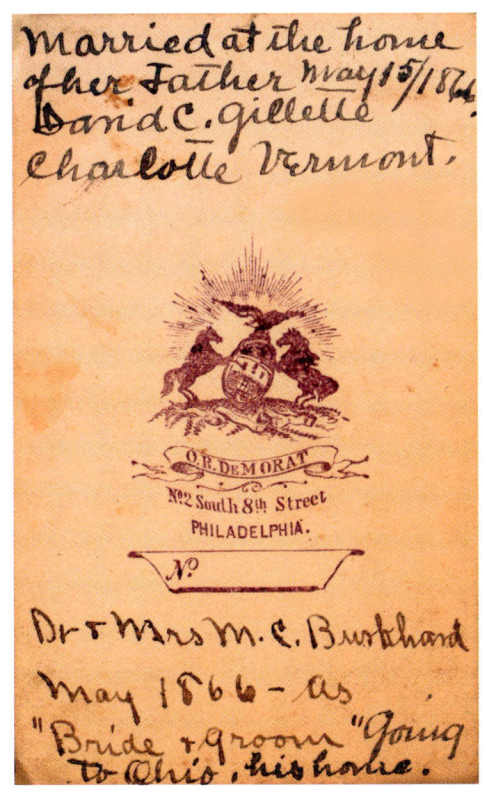

Notice that the image is dated May 15, 1866, well within the tax period and no stamp present.

A couple on their wedding day.

111

Chapter Three

Photography, the Stamp Law and the Stamps

From August 1, 1864 to July 31, 1866, American photographers were required to collect a tax and pay with proof that the tax had been collected by purchasing the appropriate stamp, canceling it and affixing it to a photograph. With a minor change in the law enacted on, March 3, 1865, all photographs exposed for sale had to carry a tax stamp. The law concerning rate and collection of ad valorem tax remained constant.

The penalties for violating the newly established tax law were as follows:
Counterfeiting the stamp $1000.00 fine
Failure to cancel stamp   50.00 fine
Failure to affix a stamp   10.00 fine.

Under Schedule C of the Act of 30th June 1864, House Bill No. 513 the rates established for photographs were:

    Photographs, ambrotypes, Daguerreotypes, or any sun picture, except as hereinbefore provided, upon each and every picture of which the retail price shall not exceed twenty-five cents, two cents   .02
    Exceeding the retail price of twenty-five cents, and not exceeding the sum of fifty cents, three cents   .03
    Exceeding the retail price of fifty cents, and not exceeding one dollar, five cents   .05
    Exceeding the retail price of one dollar, for every additional dollar or fractional part thereof, five cents   .05

The law also dictated that each cancel must carry the date of sale and the photographer's name.

This law was not popular with photographers, even though their patriotism and willingness to abide by the law was not in question. Photographers' complaints included:
    a) stamps ruined their images when stacked

     b) stamps were unavailable in quantities needed
     c) unfair taxation because frames were considered part of the photograph and taxes could not be collected through normal accounting methods such as was provided for in Section 94. Photographs that were " copies of engravings, works of art and photographs so small that stamps cannot be affixed" were to be taxed at 5% ad valorem. Another minor change of March 3, 1865 was the ad valorem change to 6% for wholesale sale of less than 10 cents. This was further amended by the tax law of July 13, 1866 and effective August 1, 1866: no tax on sale of wholesale for no more than 15 cents and 5% non-stamp duty if sold wholesale for more than 15 cents or retail at any price. This statute did away with stamps on photographs.

Through a series of decisions enacted by the Commissioner of the Internal Revenue, confusion arose concerning the payment of the taxes due. Photographers lobbied to pay the tax due by affixing the stamps to their monthly sales report. In 1865 a 50 cent Proprietary die was commissioned and never used. It was created to fill the need to pay the tax in this manner.

A New York photographer shared the following correspondence with Honorable E.A. Rollins, Commissioner of Internal Revenue, in *Humphreys Journal,* 15 October, 1864, "The law requires each picture should be stamped, and not each pack of pictures as in the case of playing cards."

In the same issue, an agent of the Central Government reported "that the intention of the government was to cause as little trouble as possible to the photographer without diminishing the taxation. Card-pictures may be regarded as copies sold in quantity, to stamp would be irksome; the photographer, therefore, is requested simply to transcribe into his daily report the number of card-pictures sold and their value, for which he has to pay a tax of 5% each month. Upon this interpretation of the clause the government officer acts in making out his monthly account for all taxes thus received; and, as he states, the 'Powers that be' are satisfied."

Confusion about rates, images to be taxed and the method of payment are evident from the many examples showing "ghost rates" of none, one cent and four cent rate uncommonly found. The method of cancellation was widely divergent also, from total obedience to a single pencil mark.

This diversity is appealing to collectors who find the editorial in *The American Journal of Photography*, January 1866 true. " The stamp is an enduring memento of the times we live in. When our carte de visites turn up amongst the rubbish which shall have accumulated in a thousand years, the stamps may be more prized than our now beautiful photographs."

The Revenue Stamps

Revenues used on photographs are commonly limited to the one cent through five cent values. This limitation is due to the cost of the photograph. The tax law indicated that all types of stamps could be used for any purpose with the exception of proprietary items. Examples of proprietary items are matches, perfume, playing cards and photographs. The only first issue revenue stamps which could be used according to the prescribed tax law were the Playing Cards and the Proprietary titles. Due to the diligence of the photographer to adhere to the law, the two titles mentioned are used with greater frequency than the other titles. The other titles were to be used to pay the appropriate tax on monetary or legal papers. An example is the three cent green Playing Cards. While scarce, it can be found in greater numbers on photographs than its scarcity indicates.

One problem of the newly founded Internal Revenue was the ability to distribute the stamps in the appropriate quantities to the necessary distribution points. One decision made was to allow any unfinished stamp to be shipped. Unfinished meant perforated or not. The process of perforation was a two step job. After the stamp had been printed, the sheets moved on to be perforated. Perforation was done by hand. The sheets were shipped perforated, part-perforated, some horizontal, some vertical and imperforate. Thus for many titles there are several perforation varieties. This decision was made in 1862, and production was stepped up to produce a finished product. Afterwards if an unfinished sheet made its way to be sold, it was an error.

Some titles only made it through the initial printing. In typical Washington fashion, the titles were initially intended to provide statistical information. After the decision to use any stamp for any purpose, this information could not be gathered, but the stamps continued to be issued with various titles until 1871. The stamp laws, initiated in late 1862, were not applied to photographs until August 1, 1864. All the stamps, one cent through five cent including many perforation varieties have been found on photographs. Two cent stamps issued for the initial 1862 production were printed in two colors, orange and blue. The production of orange stamps was limited in favor of the blue. One photographic distributor, E & H.T. Anthony acquired over a half million of the remaining orange stamps to be used on their images to pay the tax. The overwhelming majority of these stamps are the scarce orange two cent Proprietary. Other photographers in the New York City area also exhibit a high occurrence of this stamp usage indicating the ties between the Anthony firm and theirs. In 1865 a new two cent stamp was designed. The color was orange, and it is known by the lower scroll which matches the upper scroll, U.S. Inter. Rev., or U. S. Internal Revenue. Orange was back in favor, and Bank Check and Express stamps were issued in greater quantities while Certificate, Playing Cards and Proprietary orange were left idle.

The Stamps

The First Issue Revenue Stamps were authorized by Act of Congress, July 1, 1862. Their purpose was to add revenue to prosecute the war, and the stamps are thus called "Civil War Revenue Stamps". The Office of Commissioner of the Internal Revenue was authorized by this same act.

These first issue revenue stamps, 102 in number, were the first gummed and perforated stamps issued by the U.S. Government. The first 29 are all that shall be considered. With few exceptions, these are the stamps used on photographs.

The exceptions are the U. S. Postage Issues:
    One Cent, blue, Benjamin Franklin, issued Aug. 17, 1861, perf. 12
    Two Cent, black, Andrew Jackson, issued July 1, 1863, perf. 12, Black Jack
    Three Cent, Pink, George Washington, issued Aug. 18, 1861 perf. 12

The Revenue Issues:
    Six Cent, orange, George Washington, Inland Exchange, perf. 12
    Ten Cent, blue, George Washington, Bill of Lading, perf. 12
    Ten Cent, blue, George Washington, Certificate, perf. 12
    Ten Cent, blue, George Washington, Inland Exchange, perf. 12
    Ten Cent, blue, George Washington, Power of Attorney, perf. 12
    Fifteen Cent, brown, George Washington, Inland Exchange, perf. 12
    Twenty-five Cent, red, George Washington, Power of Attorney, perf. 12
    One Dollar, red, George Washington, Probate of Will, perf. 12

Revenue Essay
    Fifty Cent, black, George Washington, Proprietary, on card
Prepared for use by photographers to attach to taxes due form. This method of payment rescinded by Internal Revenue Commissioner after dies were prepared.

Private Die Proprietary
    One Cent, blue, Benjamin Franklin, Matches, perf. 12
Four companies were given special permission by the Internal Revenue Commissioner to manufacture a stamp to be used by any of the four companies (later special permission rescinded). The companies were all small matches manufacturers from Philadelphia. Later two of the four issued their own private die proprietary stamp.
    One Cent, blue, George Washington, V. R. Powell, perf 12

Postage Currency
    Five Cent, brown, Thomas Jefferson, unknown perforation
Center cut from Postage Currency note to pay five cent rate.

Mexican Revenue
    ¼ Centavo, blue, lathe work
Used on a Texas photographer's work of Chihuahua and sold there, c. 1883.

One Cent Express, Red,
Imperforate

One Cent Express, Red,
Part-perforated

One Cent Express, Red,
Perforated

One Cent Playing Cards,
Red, Perforated

One Cent Proprietary,
Red, Perforated

One Cent Proprietary, Red,
Bisect

One Cent Telegraph,
Red, Perforated

116

Two Cent Bank Check, Blue, Imperforate

Two Cent Bank Check, Blue, Part-Perforated

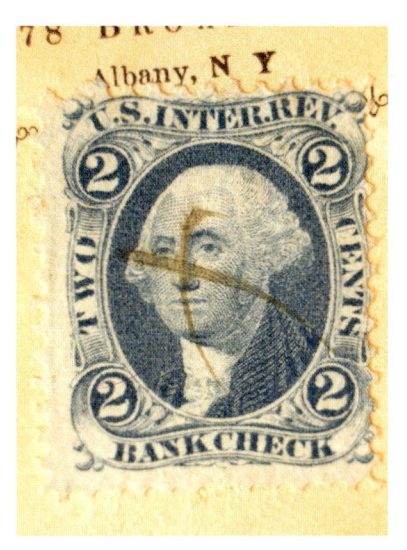

Two Cent Bank Check, Blue, Perforated

Two Cent Bank Check, Blue, Double Transfer

Two Cent Bank Check, Orange, Perforated

Two Cent Bank Check Orange, Part-perforated

Two Cent Bank Check, Orange, Double Transfer, Type I

Two Cent Bank Check, Orange, Double Transfer, Type II

Two Cent Bank Check, Orange, Bisect

117

Two Cent Certificate, Blue, Perforated

Two Cent Express, Blue, Imperforate

Two Cent Express, Blue, Part-Perforated Horizontal

Two Cent Express, Blue, Part-Perforated Vertical

Two Cent Express, Blue, Perforated

Two Cent Express, Orange, Perforated

Two Cent Playing Cards, Blue, Part-Perforated, Double Perforations, Imperforate Horizontal

Two Cent Playing Cards, Blue, Perforated

Two Cent Playing Cards, Blue, Bisect

Two Cent Playing Cards, Orange, Perforated

Two Cent Proprietary, Blue, Part-Perforated, Imperforate Vertical

Two Cent Proprietary, Blue, Part-Perforated, Imperforate Horizontal

119

Two Cent Proprietary, Blue, Perforated

Two Cent Proprietary, Blue, Double Transfer, Type I

Two Cent Proprietary, Blue, Double Transfer, Type II

Two Cent Proprietary, Blue, Bisect

Two Cent Proprietary, Orange, Perforated

Two Cent Proprietary, Orange, Double Transfer

Two Cent Proprietary, Orange, Bisect

120

Two Cent Internal Revenue, Orange, Perforated

Two Cent Internal Revenue, Orange, Bisect

Three Cent Foreign Exchange, Green, Perforated

Three Cent Playing Cards, Green, Perforated

Three Cent Proprietary Green, Perforated

Three Cent Proprietary, Green, Bisect

Three Cent Telegraph, Green, Imperforate

Three Cent Telegraph, Green, Part-Perforate

Three Cent Telegraph, Green, Perforated

Four Cent Inland Exchange, Brown, Perforated

Four Cent Proprietary, Purple, Perforated

Four Cent Proprietary, Purple Bisect

Five Cent Agreement, Red, Perforated

Five Cent Certificate, Red, Perforated

Five Cent Express, Red, Perforated

Five Cent Express, Red, Bisect

Five Cent Foreign Exchange, Red, Perforated

Five Cent Inland Exchange, Red, Perforated

Five Cent Inland Exchange, Red, Bisect

Five Cent Inland Exchange, Red, Part-Perforated

Five Cent Playing Cards, Red, Perforated

Five Cent Red Proprietary, Perforated

Six Cent Inland Exchange, Orange, Bisect

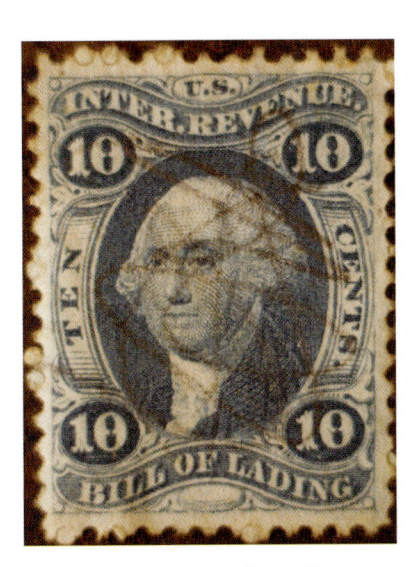

Ten Cent Bill of Lading, Blue, Perforated

Ten Cent Certificate, Blue, Perforated

Ten Cent Inland Exchange, Blue, Perforated

123

Ten Cent Power of Attorney, Blue, Perforated

Ten Cent Blue Proprietary, Blue, Perforated

Fifteen Cent Inland Exchange, Brown, Perforated

Twenty-Five Cent Power of Attorney, Red, Perforated Pair

One Dollar Probate of Will, Red, Perforated

124

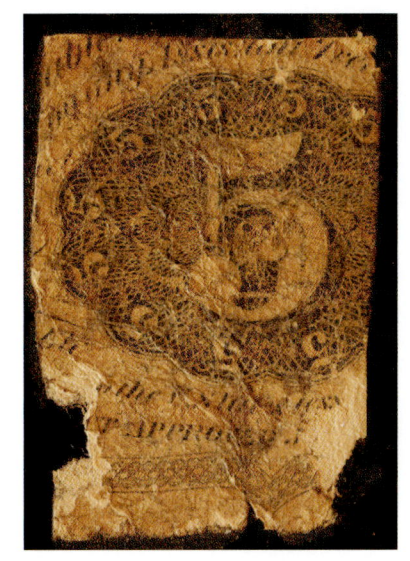

Five Cent Postal Note, Green, Reverse Side Up, Center Cut-out

One Cent Powell's Telegraph Matches, Blue, Perforated

One Cent Matches, Blue, Perforated

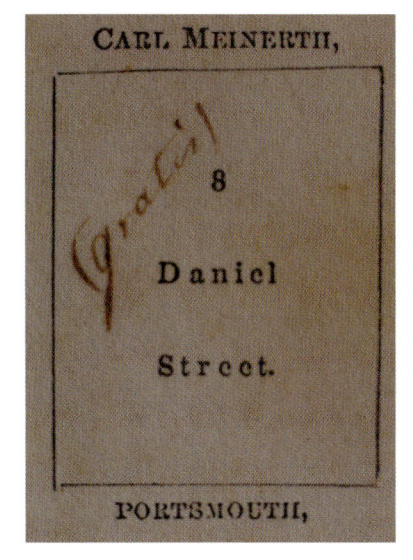

Stamp Block with Manuscript Gratis (free) therefore no tax.

One Cent US Postage, Blue, Perforated

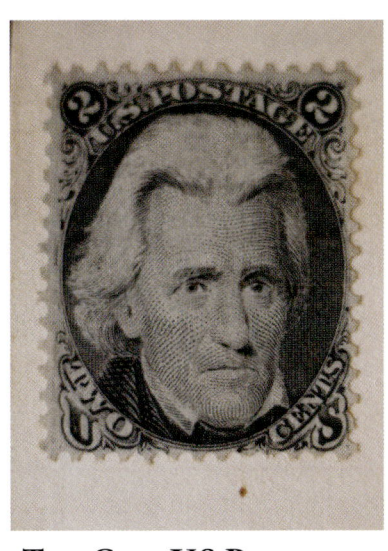

Two Cent US Postage, Black, Perforated

Three Cent US Postage, Rose, Perforated

Two Cent unknown, Orange, Double Transfer

Two Cent Proprietary, Blue, Fingerprint

Two Cent Proprietary, Blue, Double Transfer

Two Cent Internal Revenue, Orange, Double Transfer

Two Cent Bank Check, Orange, Rusted Die

One Cent Proprietary, Red, Plate Imprint

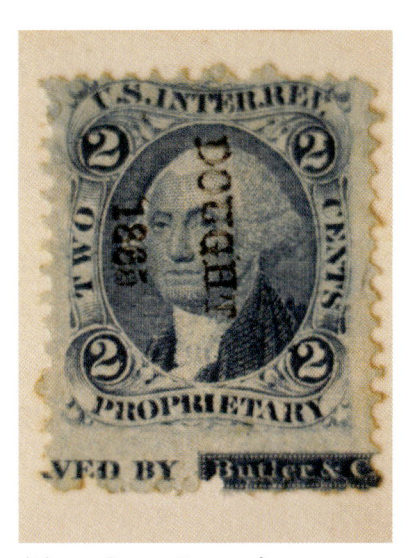

Two Cent Proprietary, Blue, Plate Imprint

Two Cent Bank Check, Orange, Plate Imprint

Three Cent Proprietary, Green, Plate Imprint

Two Cent Bank Check, Orange, Extra Row of Perforations

Three Cent Proprietary, Green, Extra Row of Perforations

Three Cent Telegraph, Green, Paper Fold

One-Quarter Centavo, Blue, Mexican Revenue 1883

127

Scarcity Charts and Graphs

Stamps Used on Photography

Some charts indicate 0%, however, this indicates that less than 1/2 of 1% is the actual percentage.

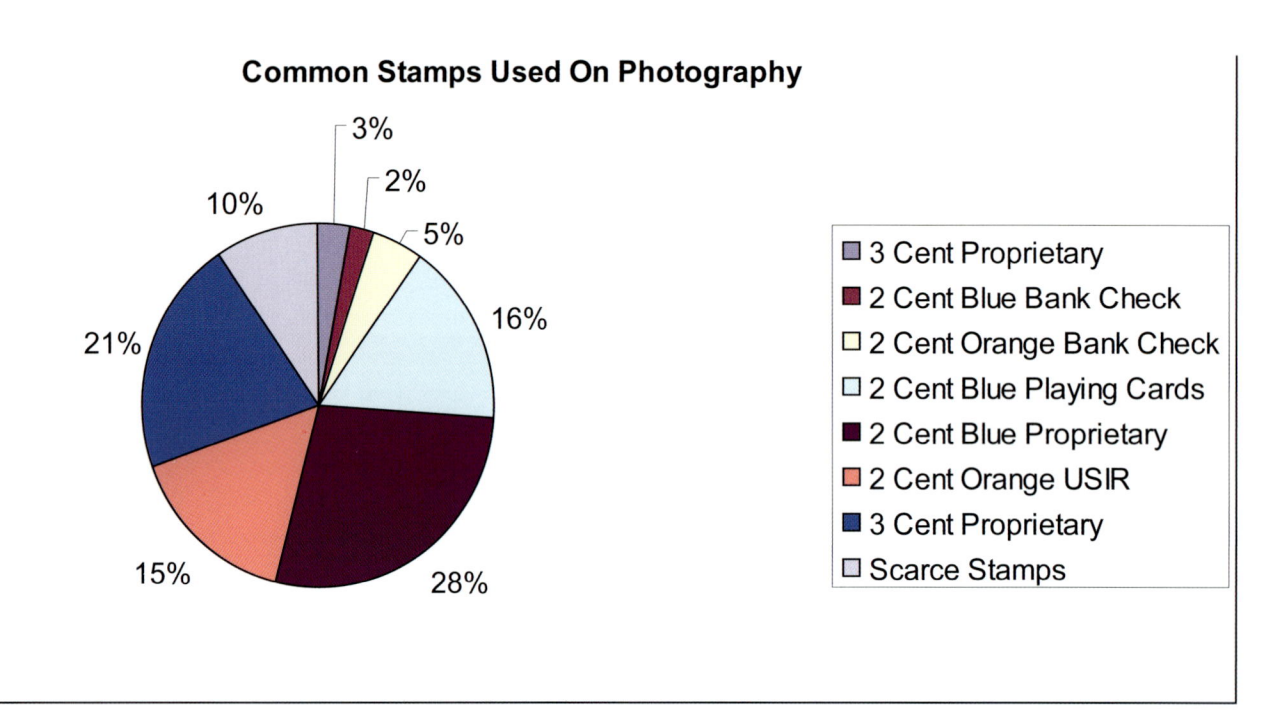

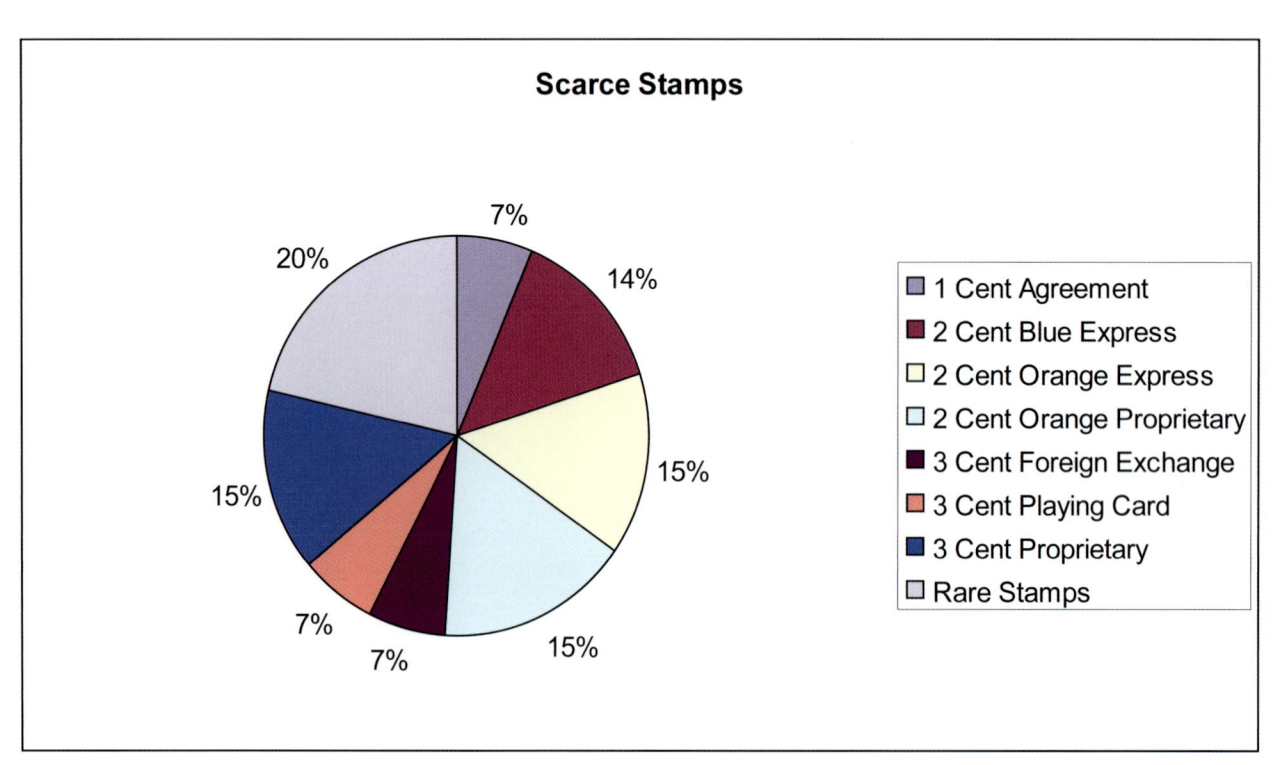

Common Stamps Used On Photography

- 3%
- 2%
- 5%
- 16%
- 28%
- 15%
- 21%
- 10%

Legend:
- 3 Cent Proprietary
- 2 Cent Blue Bank Check
- 2 Cent Orange Bank Check
- 2 Cent Blue Playing Cards
- 2 Cent Blue Proprietary
- 2 Cent Orange USIR
- 3 Cent Proprietary
- Scarce Stamps

Scarce Stamps

- 7%
- 14%
- 15%
- 15%
- 7%
- 7%
- 15%
- 20%

Legend:
- 1 Cent Agreement
- 2 Cent Blue Express
- 2 Cent Orange Express
- 2 Cent Orange Proprietary
- 3 Cent Foreign Exchange
- 3 Cent Playing Card
- 3 Cent Proprietary
- Rare Stamps

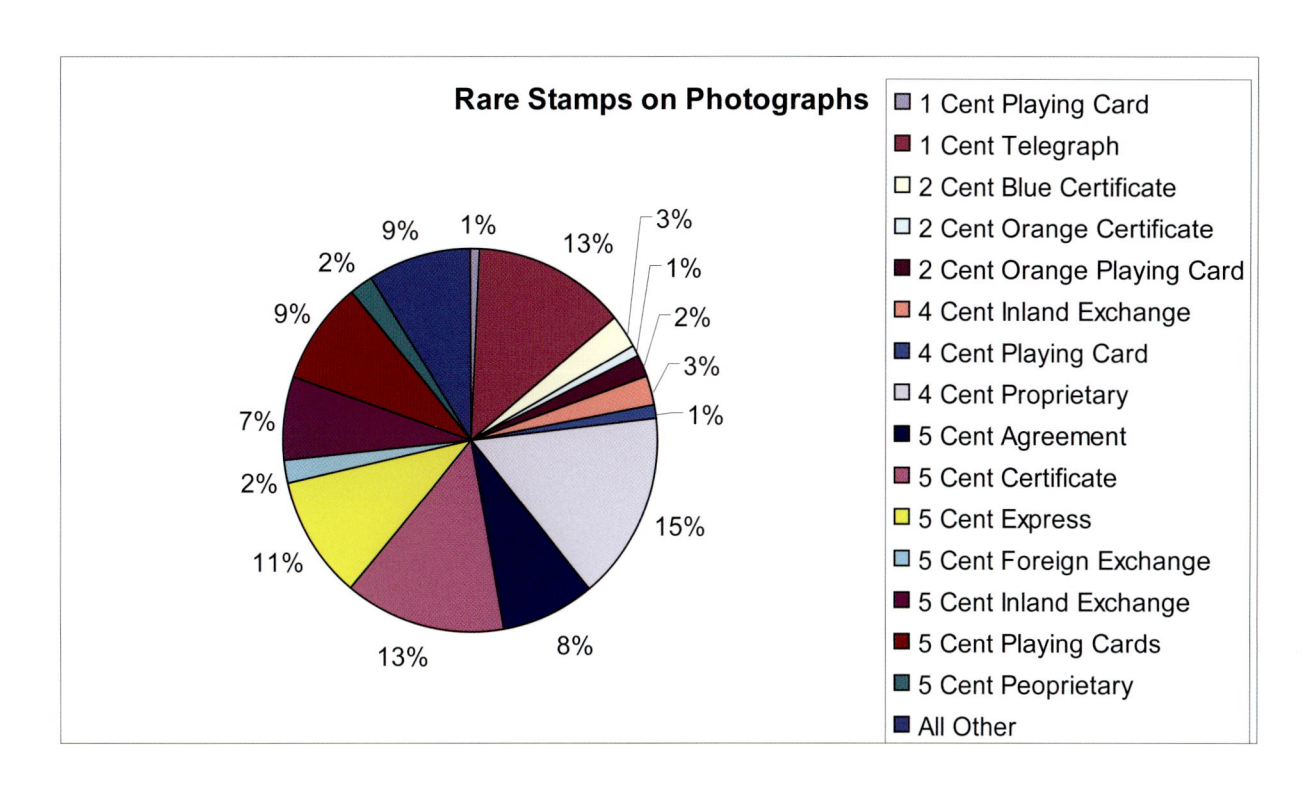

Rare Stamps on Photographs

- 1 Cent Playing Card
- 1 Cent Telegraph
- 2 Cent Blue Certificate
- 2 Cent Orange Certificate
- 2 Cent Orange Playing Card
- 4 Cent Inland Exchange
- 4 Cent Playing Card
- 4 Cent Proprietary
- 5 Cent Agreement
- 5 Cent Certificate
- 5 Cent Express
- 5 Cent Foreign Exchange
- 5 Cent Inland Exchange
- 5 Cent Playing Cards
- 5 Cent Peoprietary
- All Other

Values: 9%, 1%, 13%, 3%, 1%, 2%, 2%, 3%, 1%, 9%, 7%, 2%, 11%, 13%, 8%, 15%

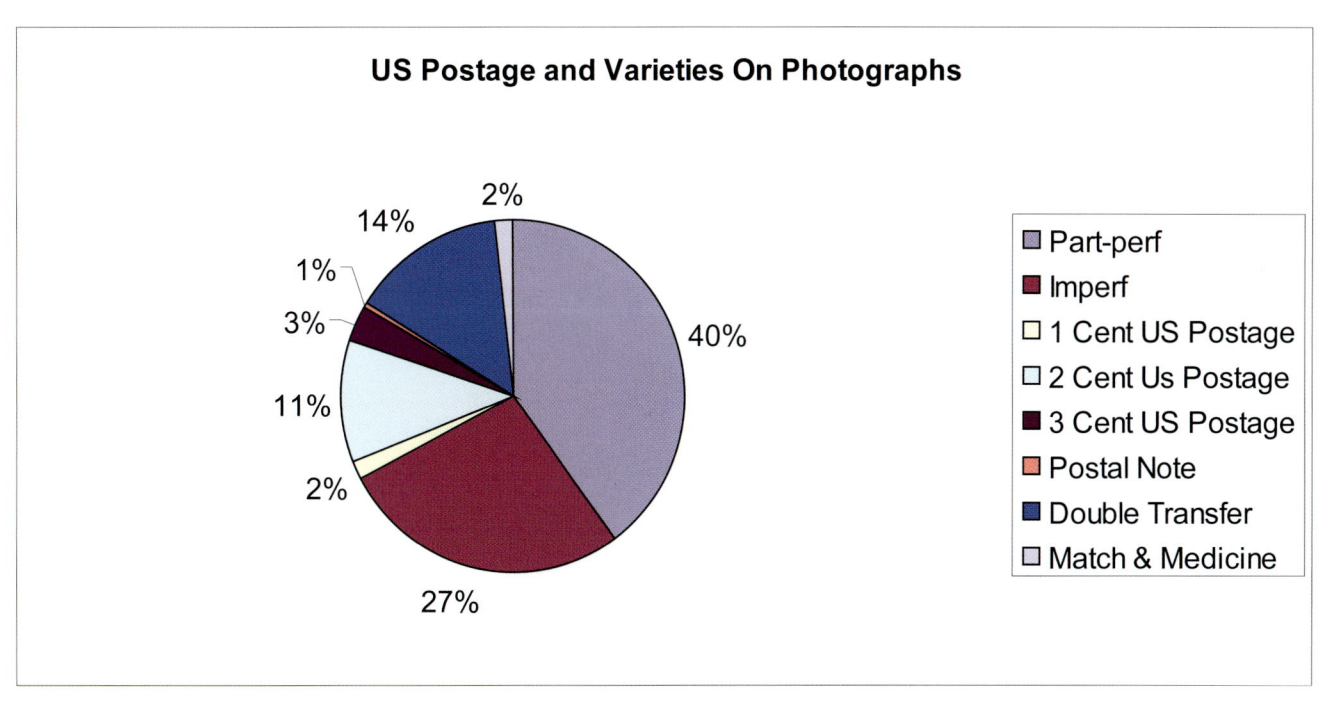

US Postage and Varieties On Photographs

- Part-perf
- Imperf
- 1 Cent US Postage
- 2 Cent Us Postage
- 3 Cent US Postage
- Postal Note
- Double Transfer
- Match & Medicine

Values: 2%, 14%, 1%, 3%, 11%, 2%, 27%, 40%

129

Image Scarcity by Geographic Area
with Tax Stamps

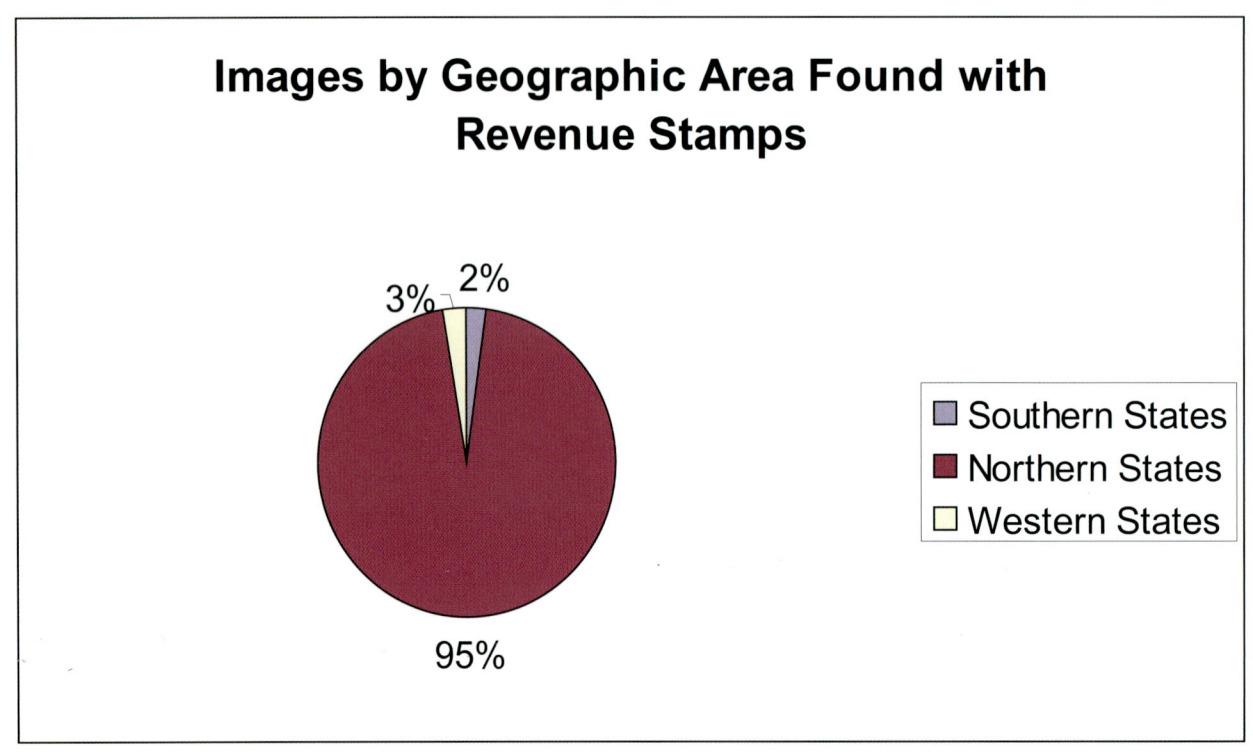

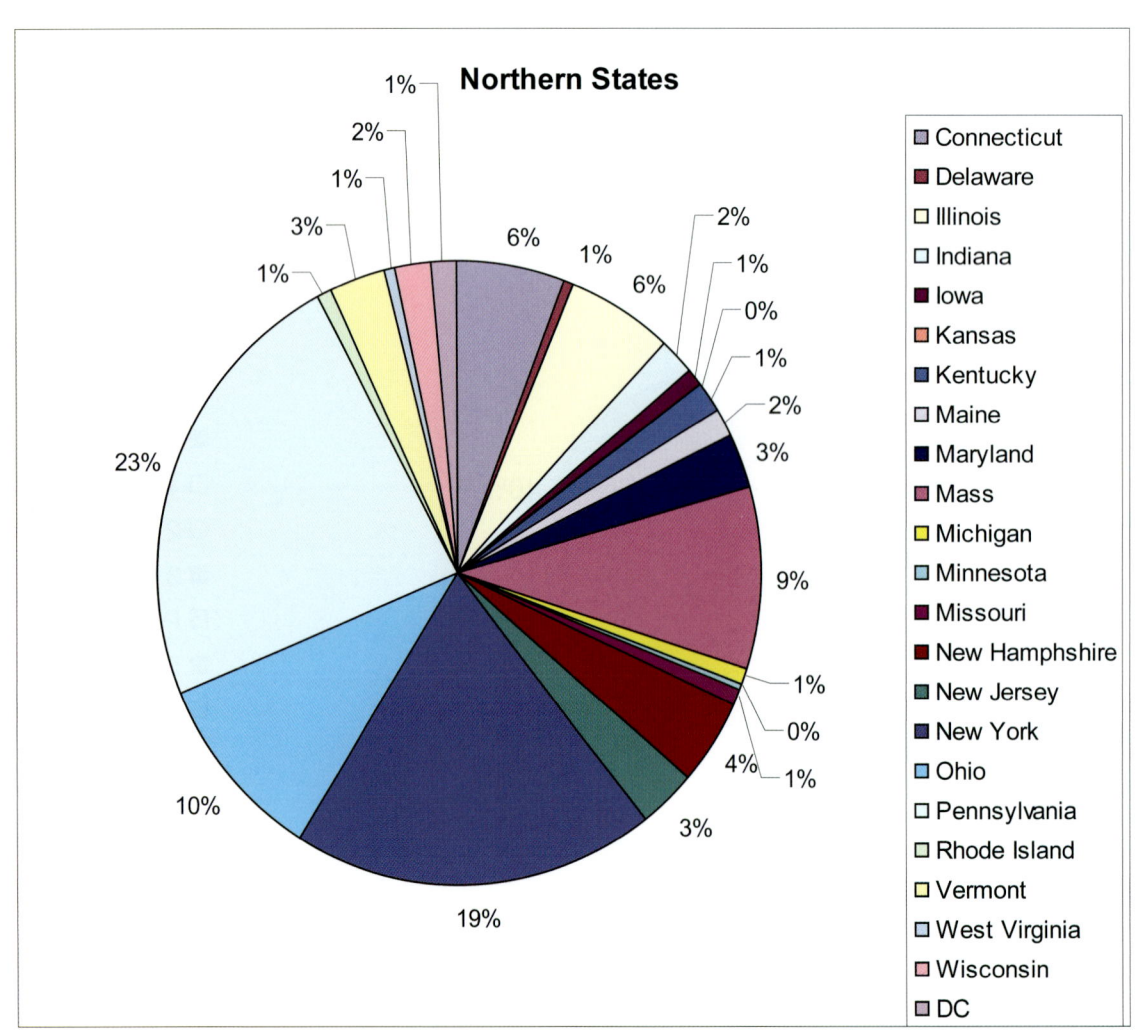

Images by Geographic Area Found with Revenue Stamps

- Southern States: 3%
- Northern States: 95%
- Western States: 2%

Northern States

- Connecticut: 6%
- Delaware: 1%
- Illinois: 6%
- Indiana: 2%
- Iowa: 1%
- Kansas: 0%
- Kentucky: 1%
- Maine: 2%
- Maryland: 3%
- Mass: 9%
- Michigan: 1%
- Minnesota: 0%
- Missouri: 1%
- New Hampshire: 4%
- New Jersey: 3%
- New York: 19%
- Ohio: 10%
- Pennsylvania: 23%
- Rhode Island: 1%
- Vermont: 3%
- West Virginia: 1%
- Wisconsin: 2%
- DC: 1%

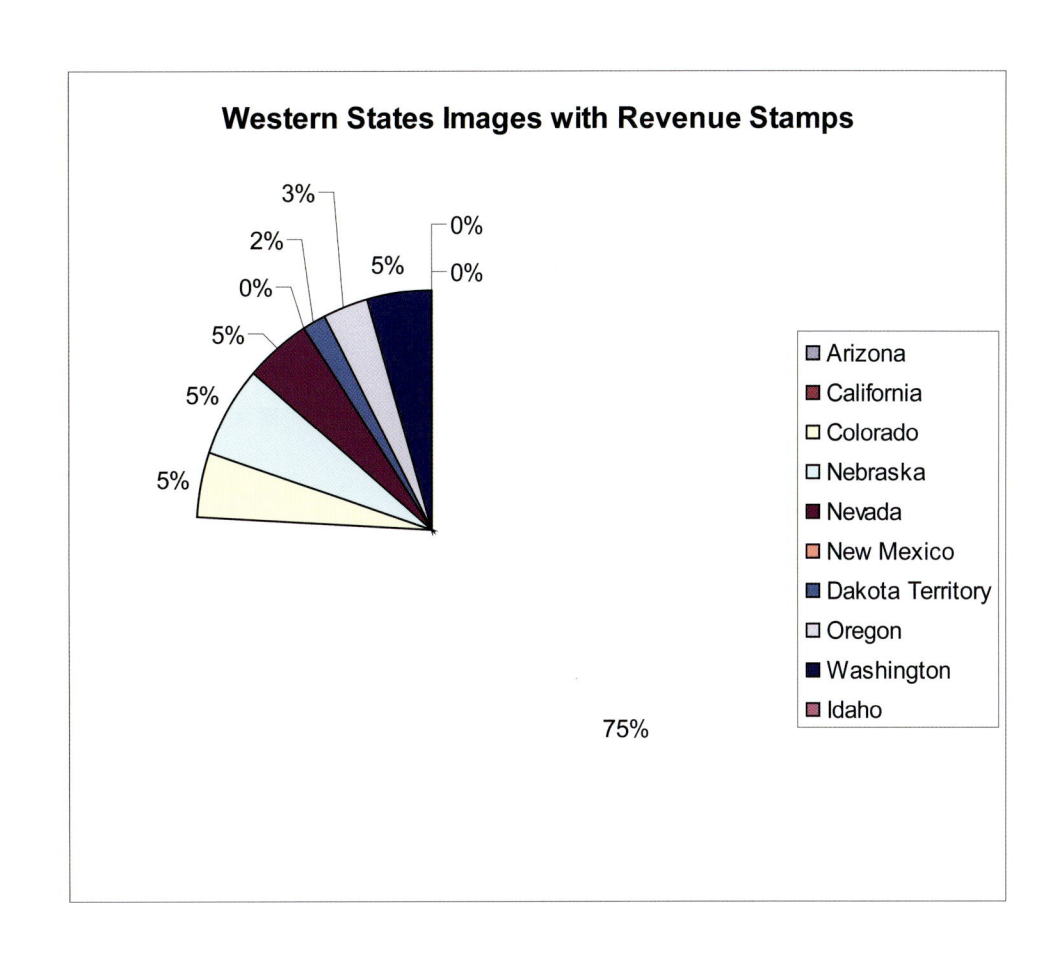

Western States Images with Revenue Stamps

- Arizona 0%
- California 5%
- Colorado 5%
- Nebraska 5%
- Nevada 5%
- New Mexico 0%
- Dakota Territory 2%
- Oregon 3%
- Washington 5%
- Idaho 0%
- (unlabeled) 75%

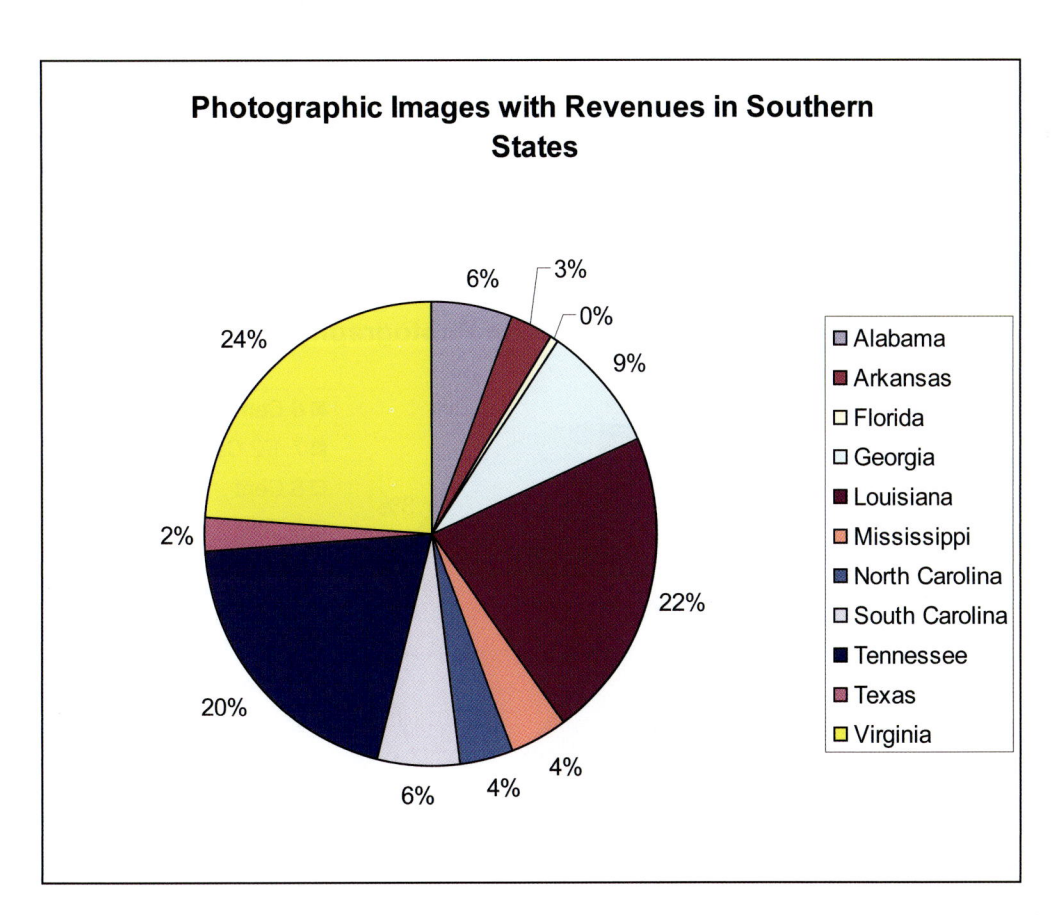

Photographic Images with Revenues in Southern States

- Alabama 6%
- Arkansas 3%
- Florida 0%
- Georgia 9%
- Louisiana 22%
- Mississippi 4%
- North Carolina 4%
- South Carolina 6%
- Tennessee 20%
- Texas 2%
- Virginia 24%

131

Rates Used on Photography

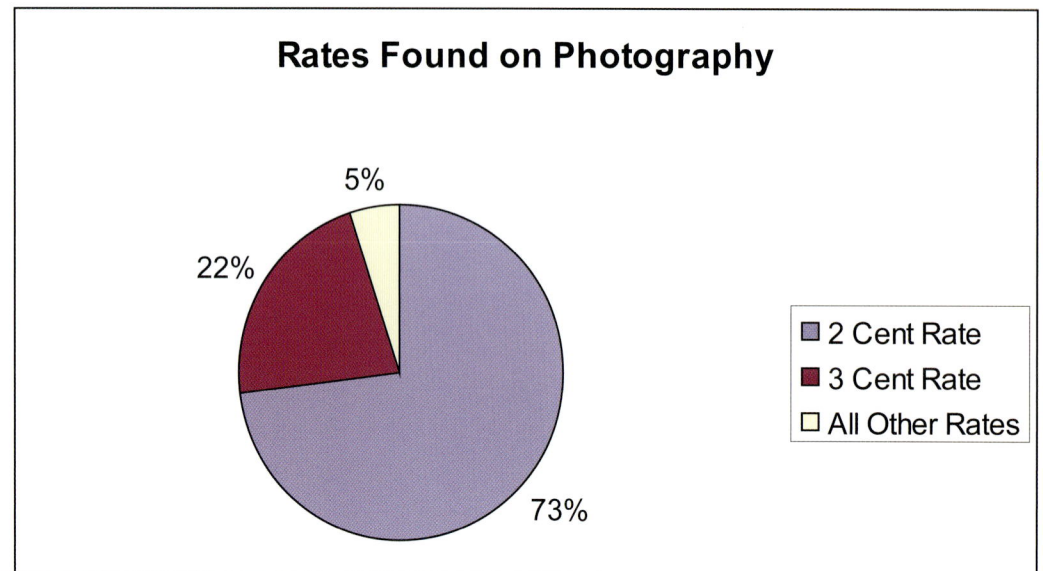

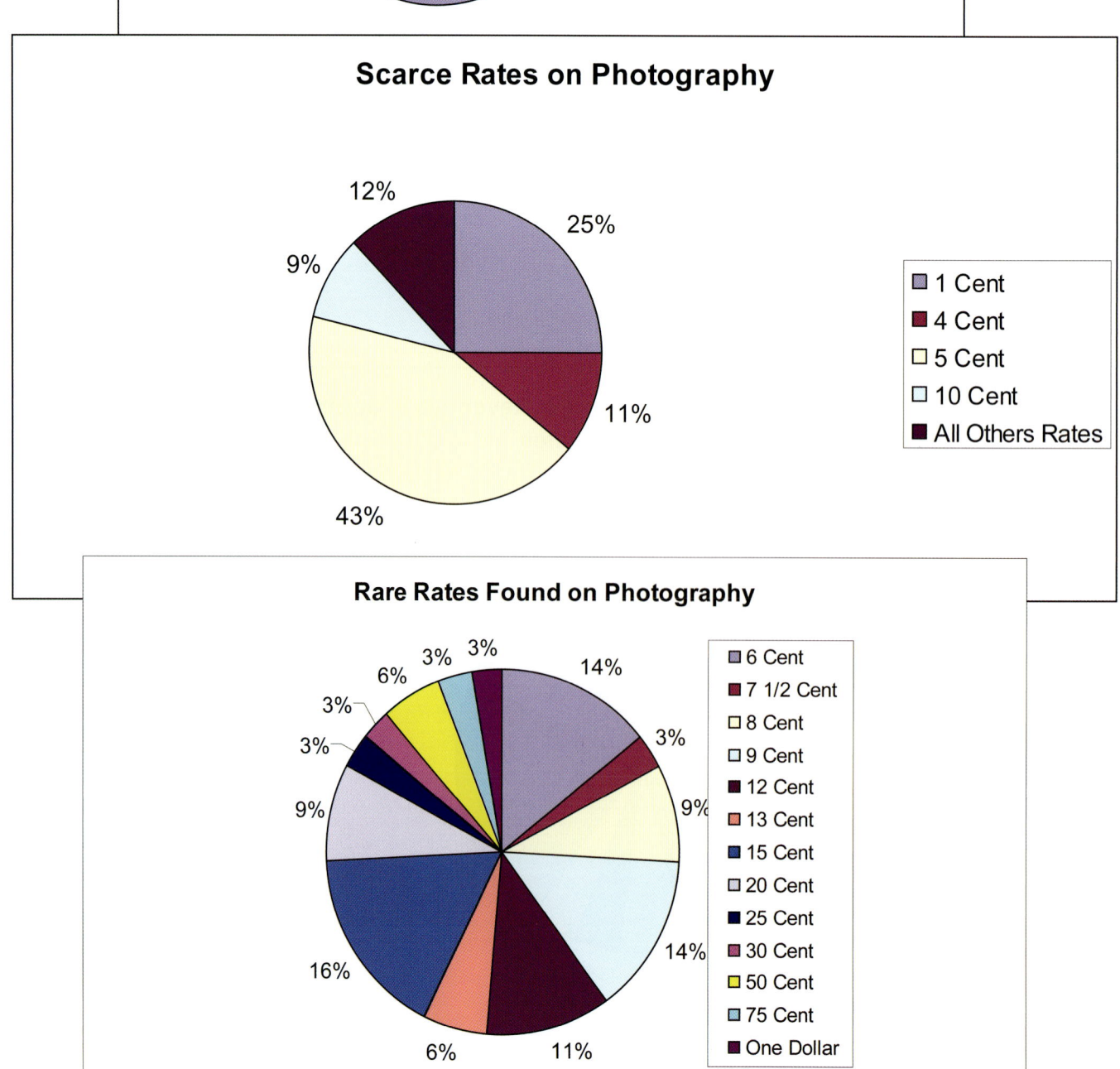

Rates Found on Photography

- 2 Cent Rate: 73%
- 3 Cent Rate: 22%
- All Other Rates: 5%

Scarce Rates on Photography

- 1 Cent: 25%
- 4 Cent: 11%
- 5 Cent: 43%
- 10 Cent: 9%
- All Others Rates: 12%

Rare Rates Found on Photography

- 6 Cent: 14%
- 7 1/2 Cent: 3%
- 8 Cent: 9%
- 9 Cent: 14%
- 12 Cent: 11%
- 13 Cent: 6%
- 15 Cent: 16%
- 20 Cent: 9%
- 25 Cent: 3%
- 30 Cent: 3%
- 50 Cent: 6%
- 75 Cent: 3%
- One Dollar: 3%

Fancy Cancels and Punch Cancels

Fancy cancels and punch cancels personify the photographer's entrepreneurial approach to the business of operating a studio. Some photographers, while technically proficient and artistically savvy, chose to make a statement. The statement was a further embellishment of the talent of the photographer. The variety of cancels and punches was limited only by the photographer's imagination. While some photographers cancelled stamps with simple ink strokes, technically an improper cancel, others chose a more colorful method of proclaiming their differences. Usually the fancy cancel was also an improper cancel.

Two Cent Bank Check, Orange, Perforated, Cork Cancel

Two Cent Internal Revenue, Orange, Perforated, Fancy Cancel

Two Cent Playing Cards, Blue, Perforated, Two Line Cancel

Two Cent Internal Revenue, Orange, Perforated, Circular Date Cancel

Circular Date Cancel on Card, Proof

Two Cent Internal Revenue, Orange, Perforated, Two Line Date Cancel

Two Cent Proprietary, Orange, Proof Cancel on Stamp

Two Cent Bank Check, Orange, Fancy Shield Cancel

Two Cent Bank Check, Orange, Fancy Shield Cancel with More Information

Two Cent Internal Revenue, Orange, Fancy Oval Cancel, Tied

Two Cent Bank Check, Orange, Barnum's Museum CDC Pre-Cancel

Two Cent Bank Check, Orange, Perforated, Fancy Cancel

Three Cent Proprietary, Green, Perforated, Fancy Cancel Letter B

One Cent Proprietary, Red, Perforated, Two Line Pre-Cancel

135

Alexander Gardner, Washington, D.C., Tied CDC

Two Cent Express, Orange, Perforated with Red Pre-Cancel

Brady's Imprint typical on Washington and NY Studio CDVs

Brady's New York Imprint

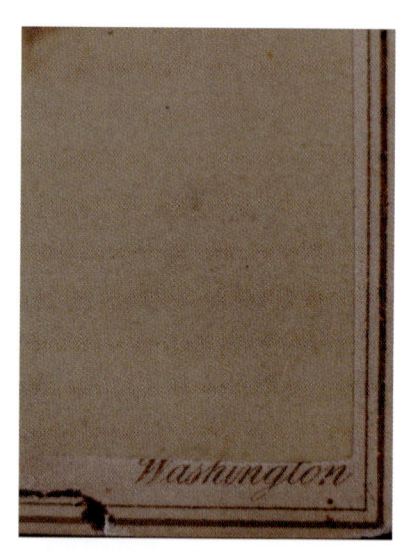

Brady's Washington, D.C. Imprint.

Three Cent Proprietary, Green, Brady Fancy Script, Washington, D.C.

Two Cent Bank Check, Orange, Brady NY CDC

Three Cent Proprietary, Green, Brady's Washington, D.C. Cancel Washington

Ferrand Photographic Strip Label

Two Cent Bank Check, Orange, Ferrand's Nevada, CA Cancel

Two cent Proprietary, Blue, B Punch Cancel

Two Cent Proprietary, Blue, Circular Punch Cancel

Three Cent Proprietary, Green, Pentagonal Punch Cancel

Two Cent Proprietary, Blue, JDP Punch Cancel

137

Chapter Four
The Photographer's Art

Mounted Tin-Types

Tin-types mounted on carte de visite cards are an unusual combination of formats. The tin-type, inside a brass frame similar to those found in cases, is attached to the card by inserting two flaps on the rear of the frame through two corresponding slots cut into the card. This bulky product was then inserted in the family album. The amount of damage done to the album and other images is surprisingly small, but the appearance of the product embellishes the album. It appears that this short lived new "gem" had some appeal due to the fact that different sizes were available. No examples are known outside the tax years.

Small size gem tin-type in a brass frame attached to a card.

Two cent orange Bank Check stamp.

Two cent blue Proprietary stamp.

Two cent orange Internal Revenue stamp.

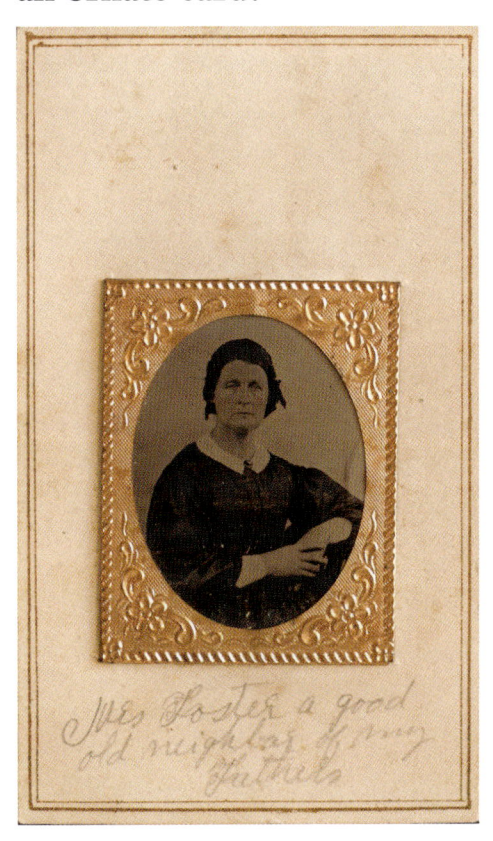

Medium size gem tin-type in a brass frame affixed to an ornate card.

Large size gem tin-type also in a brass frame, attached to a card.

139

Burgeoning Era of Victorian Women

The women of this era were standing on the precipice of change. During previous years, women were relegated to the tasks of keeping the social calendar, supervising the household, and bearing children. Prior to the war, the general opinion was that women didn't have the intelligence, stamina, or desire to do more. When the war began, women were left to run plantations and businesses in order for their families to survive. With such grievous loss of life, many women continued in those roles after the war. Women were no longer regarded as less valuable than slaves. They had shouldered the burdens handed to them when the first shot was fired. Most women succeeded at their new roles. America was on the brink of the Woman's Suffrage Movement. The following photographs reflect those new attitudes.

Vignette of a young lady. Smiles were uncommon in photographs during this period.

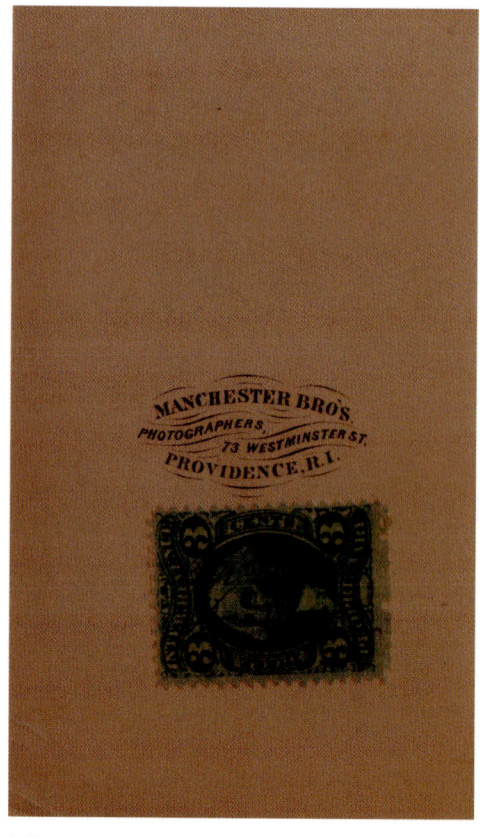

Three cent green Proprietary stamp.

140

Two cent orange Internal Revenue stamp.

Young woman raising her dress so that her ankle and petticoat are visible, a daring pose.

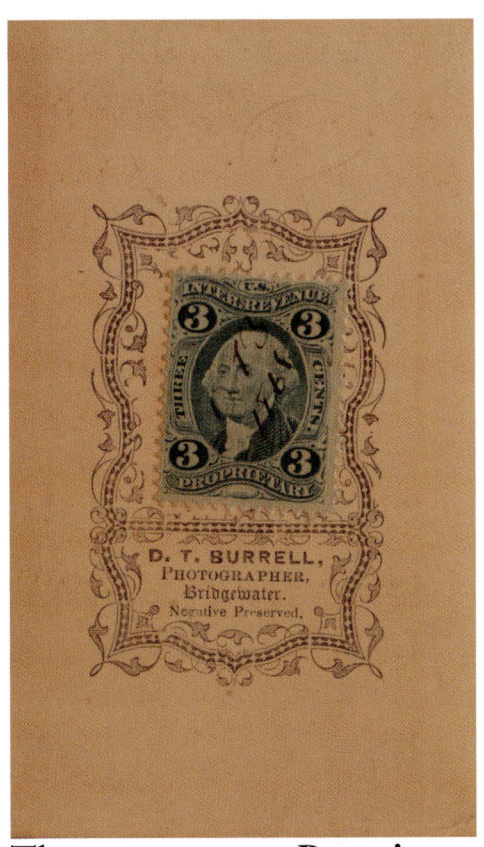

Three cent green Proprietary stamp in a block designed for the stamp.

Impish young girl posed on a stairway.

Group Images

Probably a group of scholars. Note detail of dog under chair.

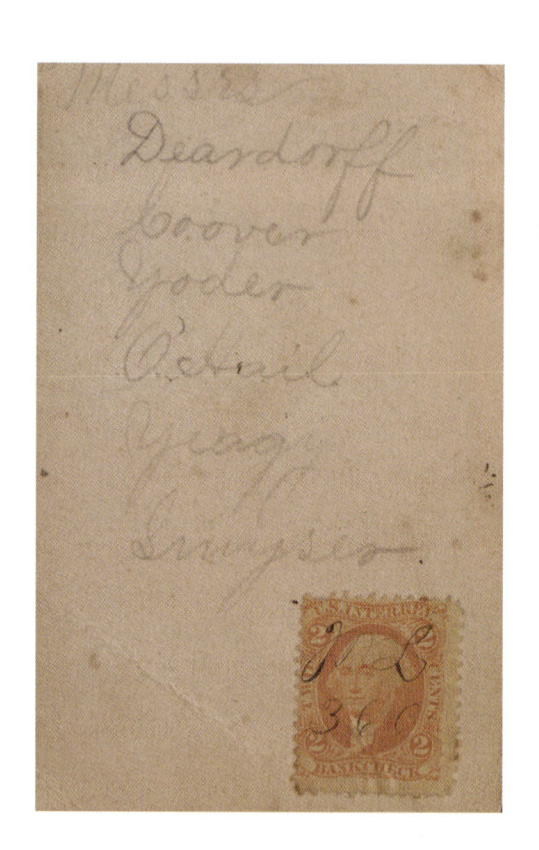

Two cent orange Bank Check stamp.

Group of husband, wife and four daughters.

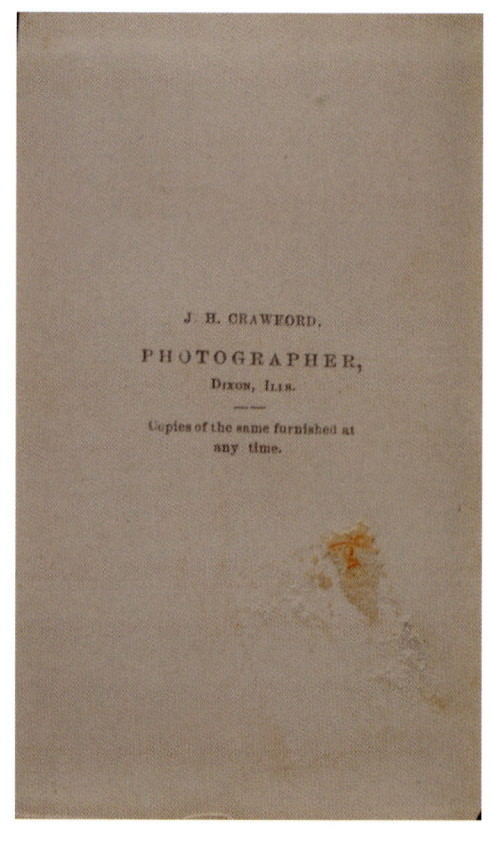

Prior "collector" removed most of the two cent orange Internal Revenue stamp.

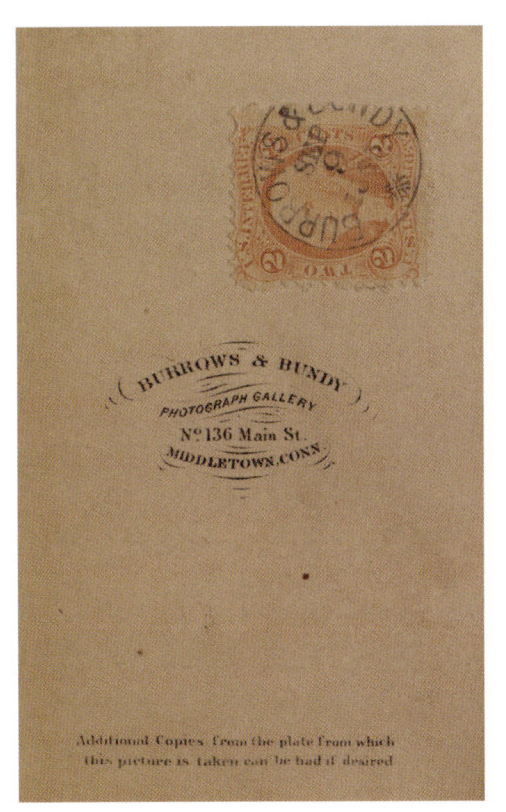

Two cent orange Internal Revenue stamp.

Group of three young ladies, probably sisters, reading what appears to be a letter from the war.

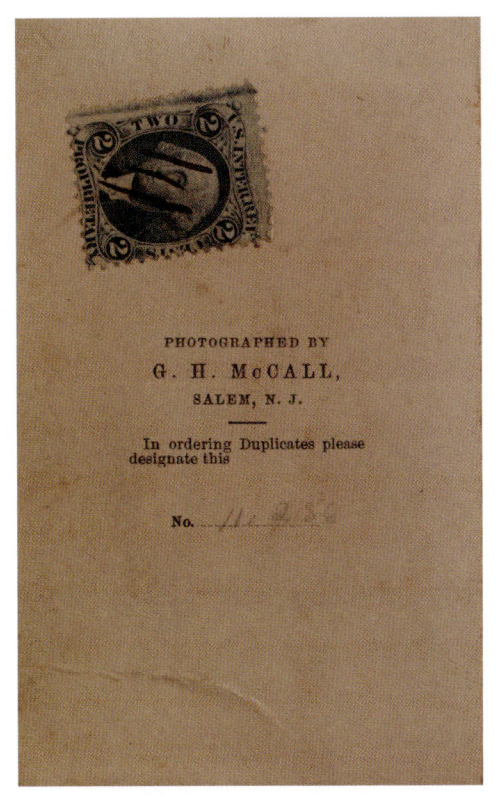

Two cent blue Proprietary stamp.

Group of four. Woman on right has face blackened as if to indicate her death.

143

Unusual horizontal portrait of four siblings. Portraiture didn't lend itself well to horizontal images.

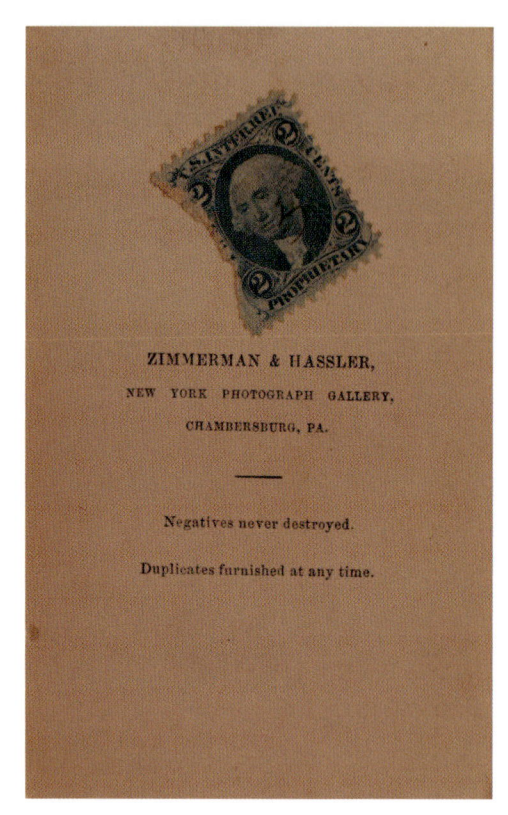

Two cent blue Proprietary stamp.

These eight men are Ordained Pastors of Burman Missions.

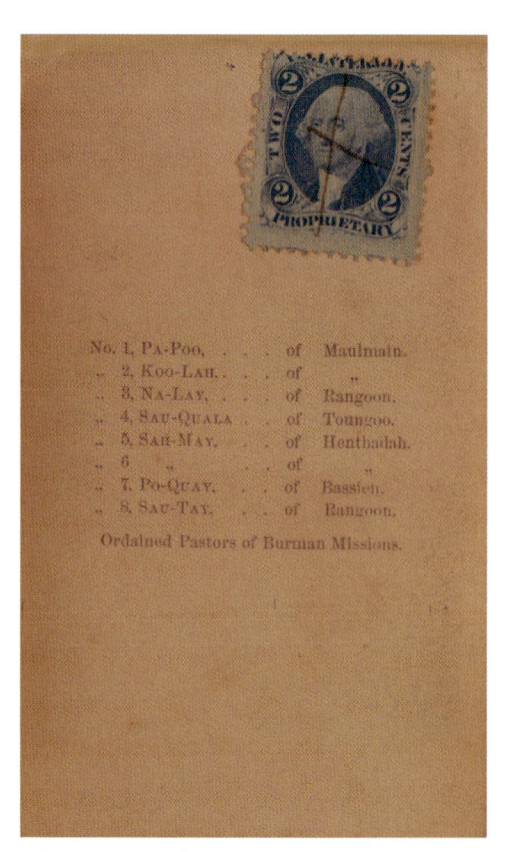

Two cent blue Proprietary stamp.

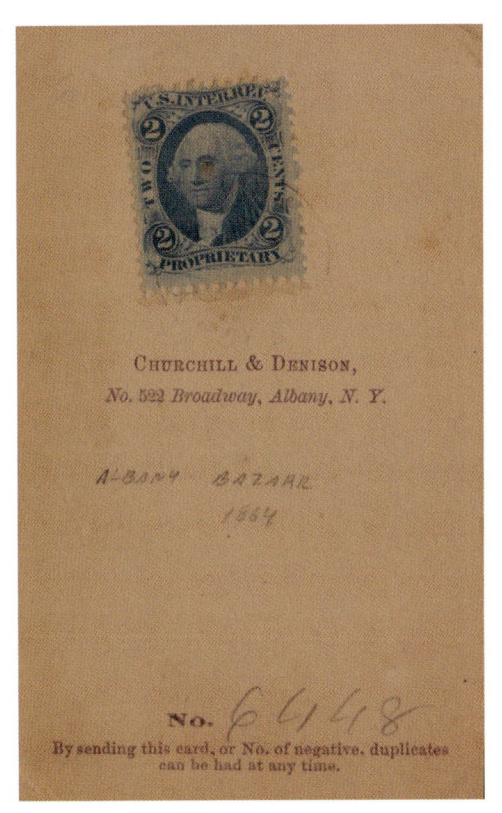

Two cent blue Proprietary stamp.

Probably a group of business men.

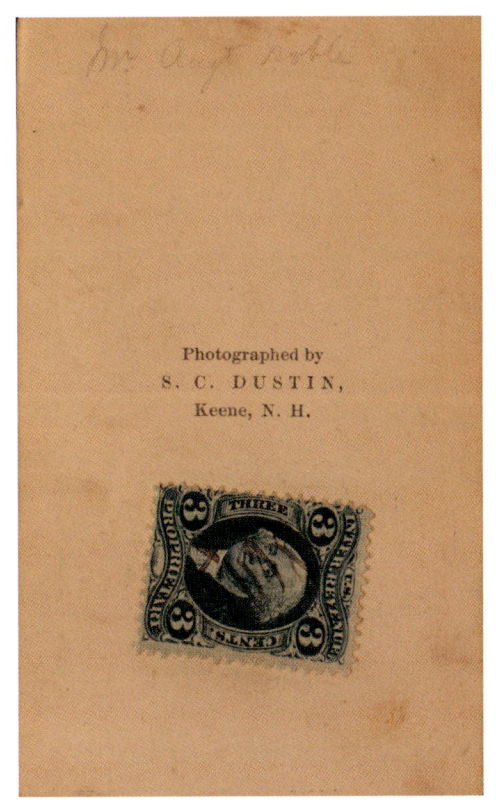

Three cent green Proprietary stamp.

Group of thirteen people. Large groups are unusual because of the failure rate due to someone moving during the long exposure.

145

Nice family image revealing their closeness.

Three cent green Proprietary stamp.

Unusual image where the photographer has manipulated six vignettes onto one card.

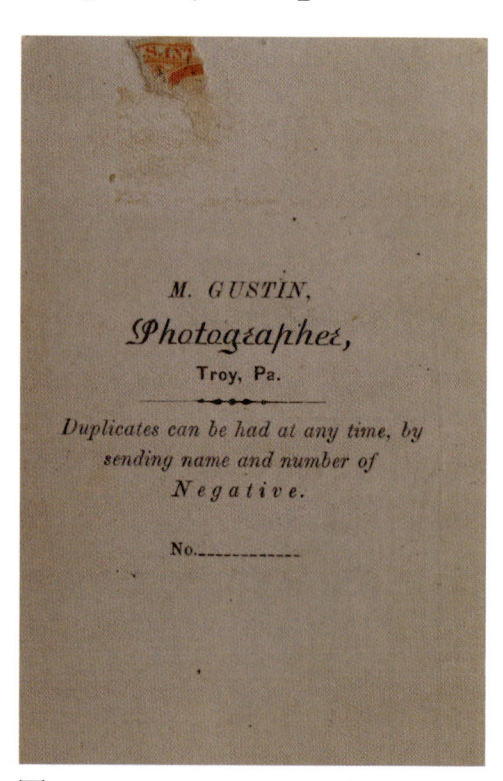

Two cent orange unknown title.

Fancy Vignettes

The vignette process was an extra step and desirable to the sitter. The photographer often would charge more for a vignetted photograph to compensate for the extra labor. The fancy vignette, known from as early as the Daguerrian era, again exemplifies the photographer's creativity and his willingness to give the patron a little extra. Following are several examples showing masking and negative manipulation.

Two cent orange Internal Revenue stamp.

Copy of an earlier painting that appears to be a vignette.

147

Ray vignette on a CDV. This technique is known from the daguerreotype era but very unusual on a CDV.

Two cent orange Internal Revenue stamp.

Unusual vignette with the perimeters darkened to highlight the subject.

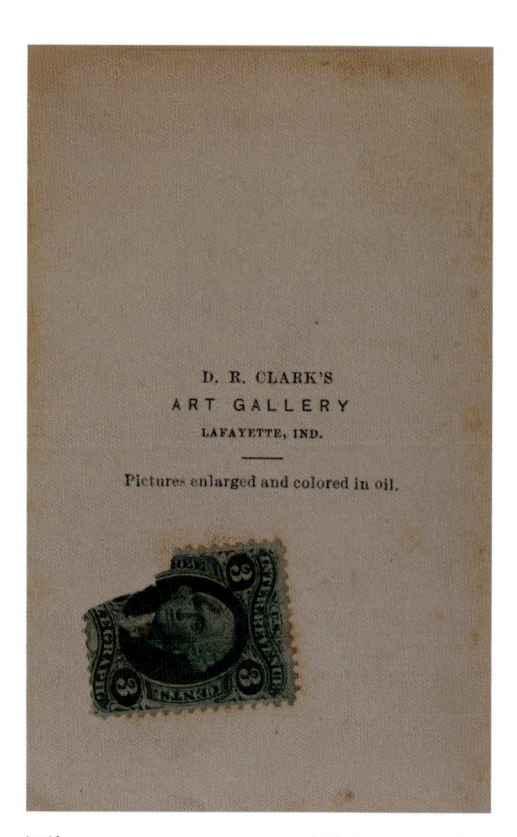

Three cent green Telegraph stamp.

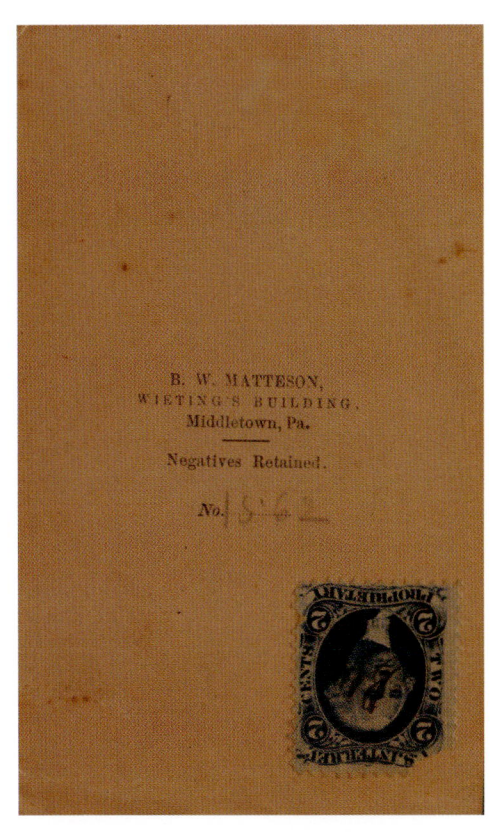

Two cent blue Proprietary stamp.

Saw-tooth vignette

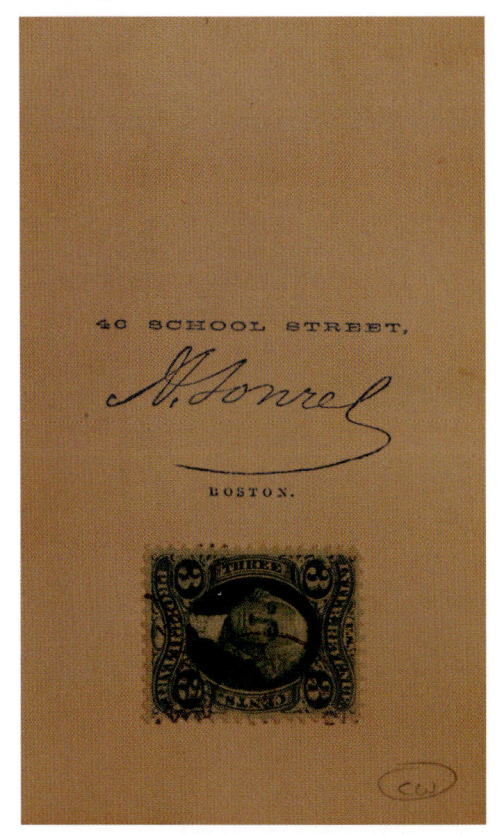

Three cent green Proprietary stamp.

Copy of a painted miniature appears to be a vignette. Note pin to hold the miniature on board while the image was taken.

149

Famous Photographers

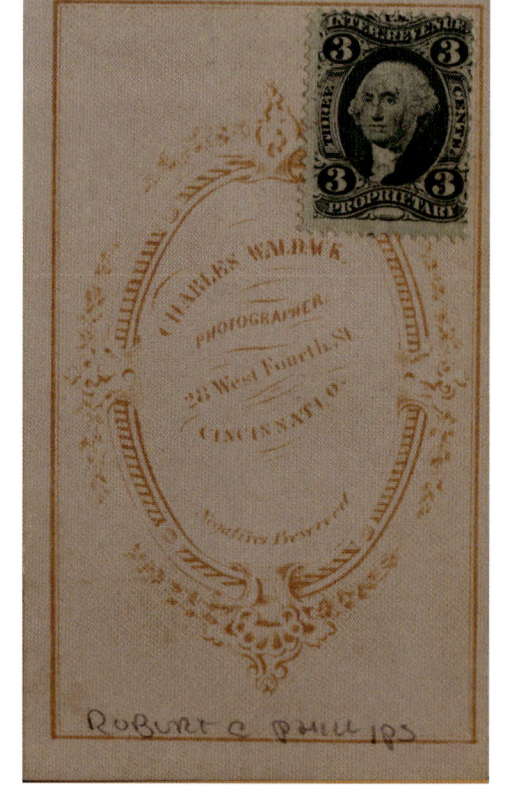

Image by Charles Waldack. He was the first photographer to successfully use flash photography, Mammoth Cave, KY August 1866.

Three cent green Proprietary stamp.

Image by A. F. Hawes of the famed Southworth and Hawes.

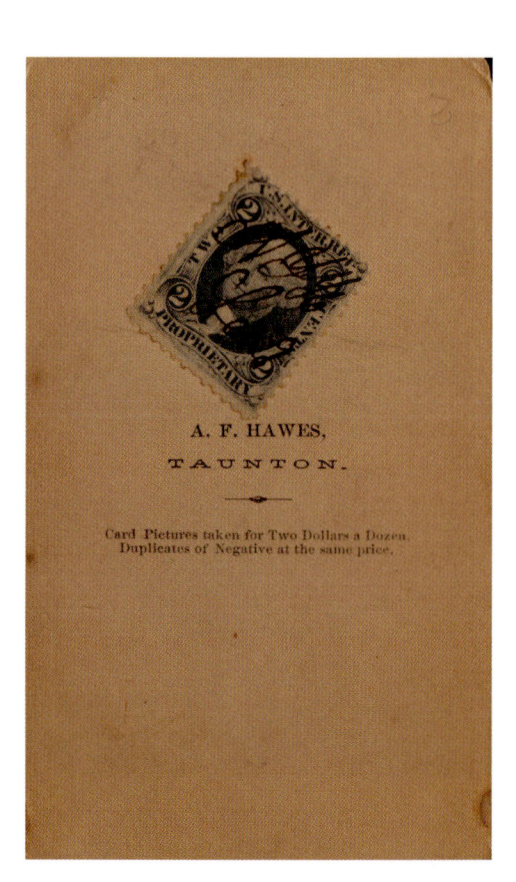

Two cent blue Proprietary stamp.

150

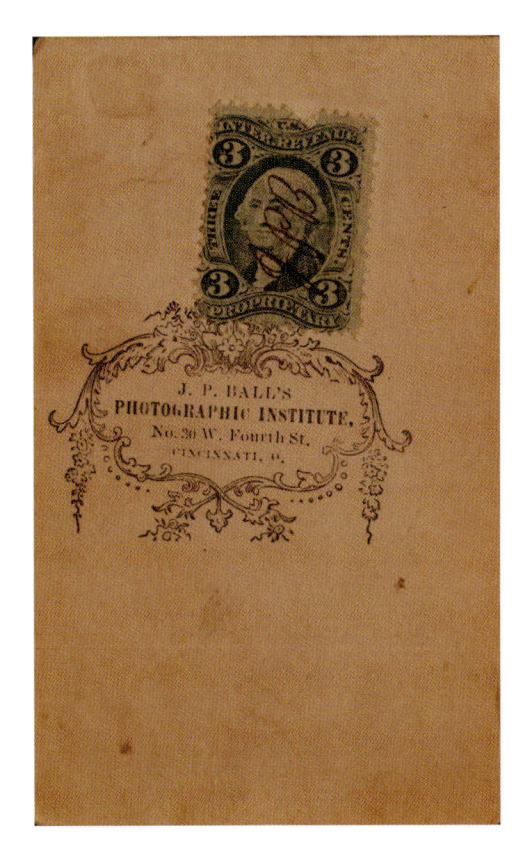

Three cent green Proprietary stamp.

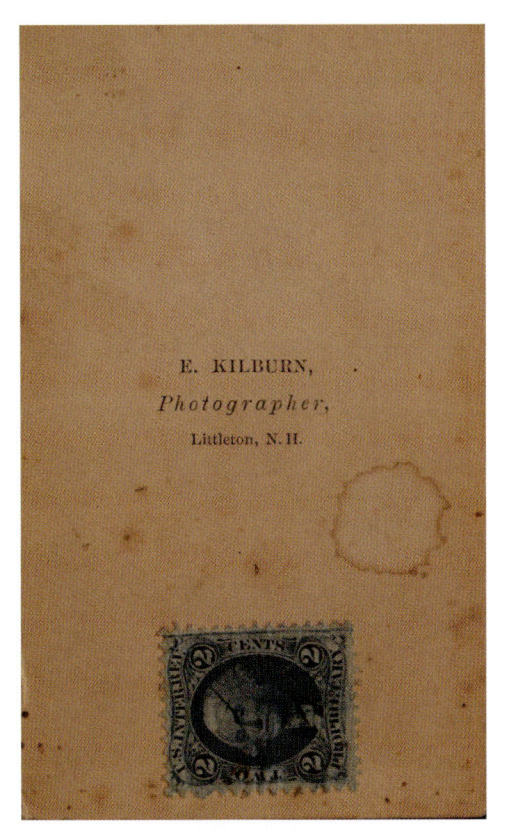

Two cent blue Proprietary stamp.

Image by noted black photographer J. P. Ball of Cincinnatti, OH.

Image by Edward Kilburn of the Kilburn Brothers. They became one of the most prolific manufacturers of stereo views.

Portrait by the Bennett Brothers who are well-known for their prolific views of the mid-west.

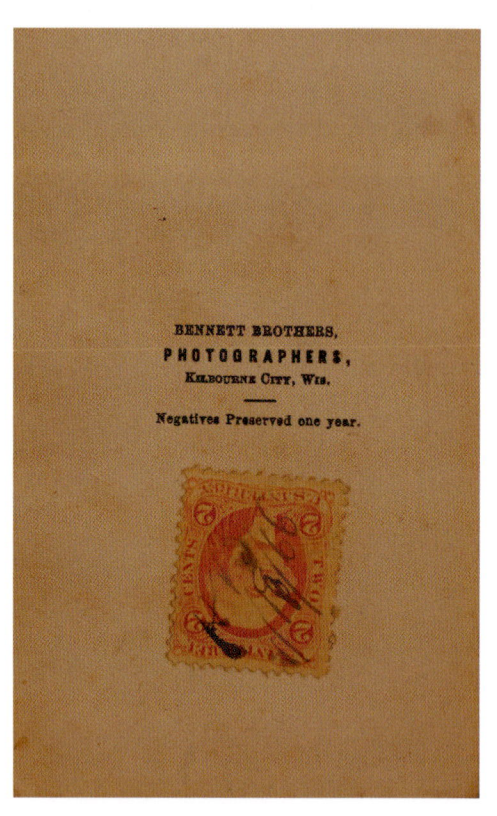

Two cent orange Internal Revenue stamp.

Image by S. A. King, the first American photographer to take photos from a balloon as depicted on the reverse backmark.

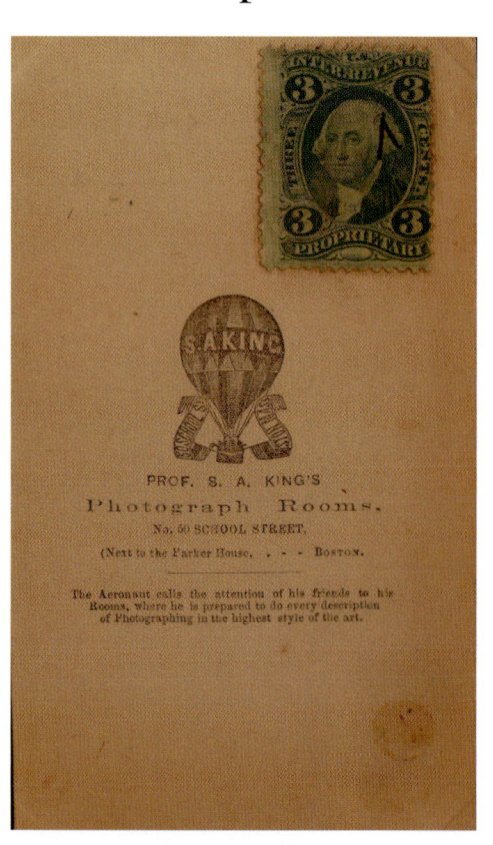

Three cent green Proprietary stamp.

152

Strip Labels

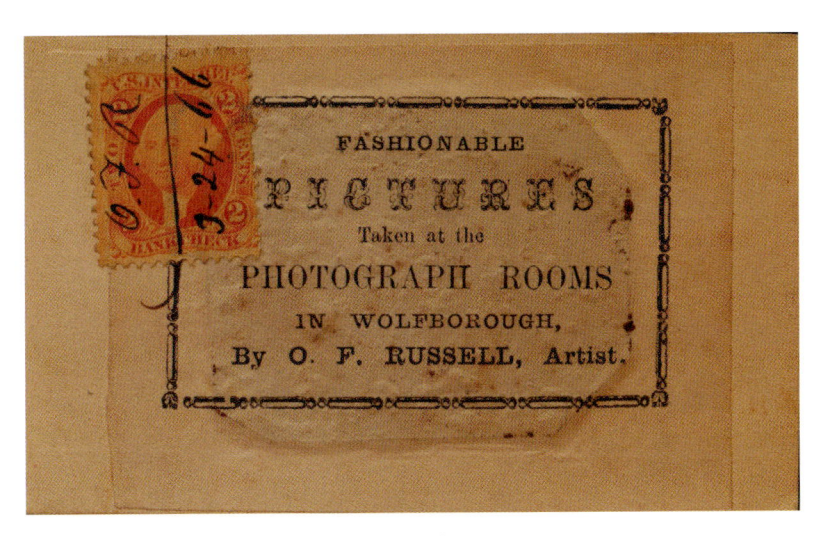

Two cent orange Bank Check stamp.

Tin-type with a strip label by O. F. Russell.

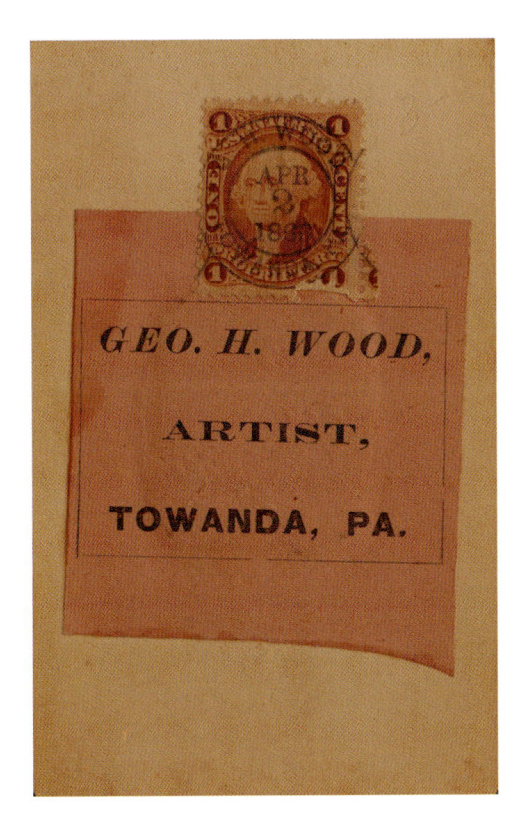

One cent red Proprietary stamp.

Tin-type with strip label by George H. Wood.

153

Common vignette portrait of a young woman.

Two cent orange Bank Check Stamp.

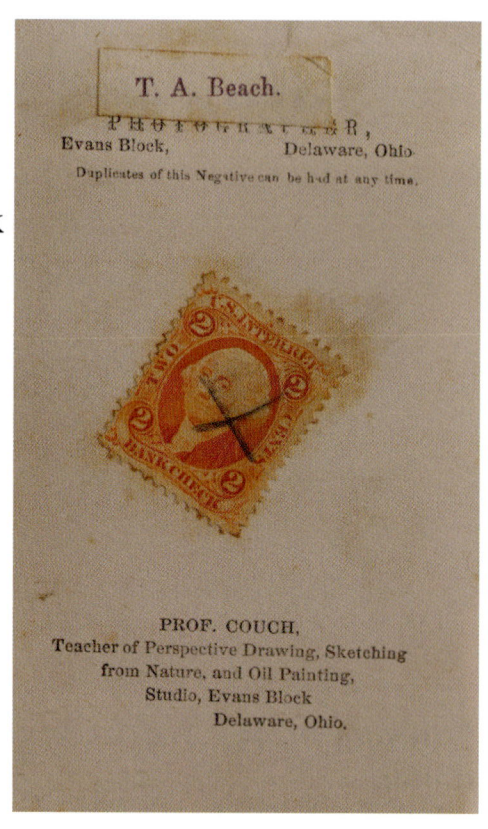

Strip label added to block the name of the previous studio owner.

Three-quarter seated portrait.

Two cent orange Bank Check stamp.

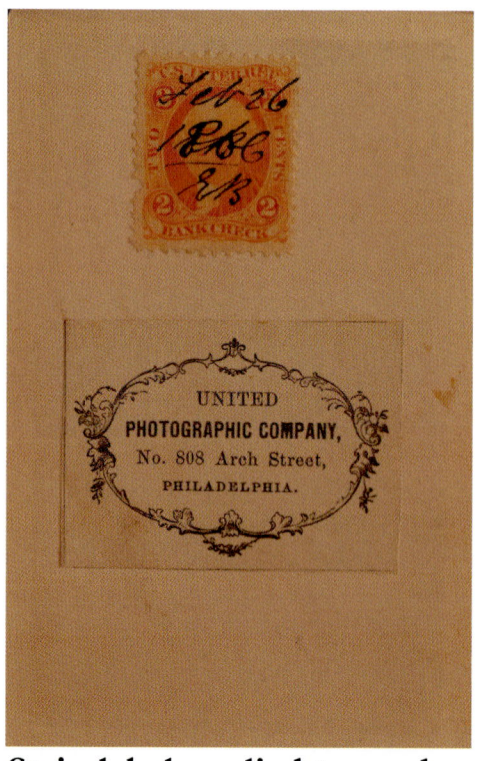

Strip label applied to card. United Photographic Company.

Studio Succession

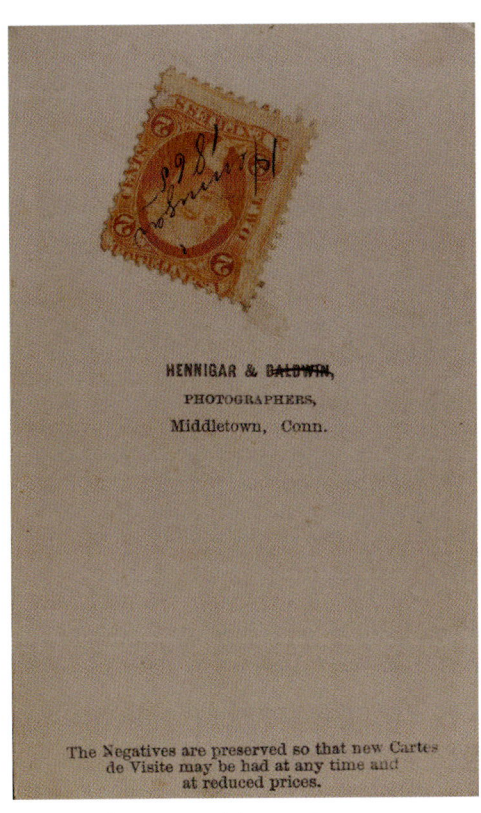

Two cent orange Express stamp.

Hennigar strikes the name of his partner and signs stamp in a studio succession.

Three-quarter seated portrait.

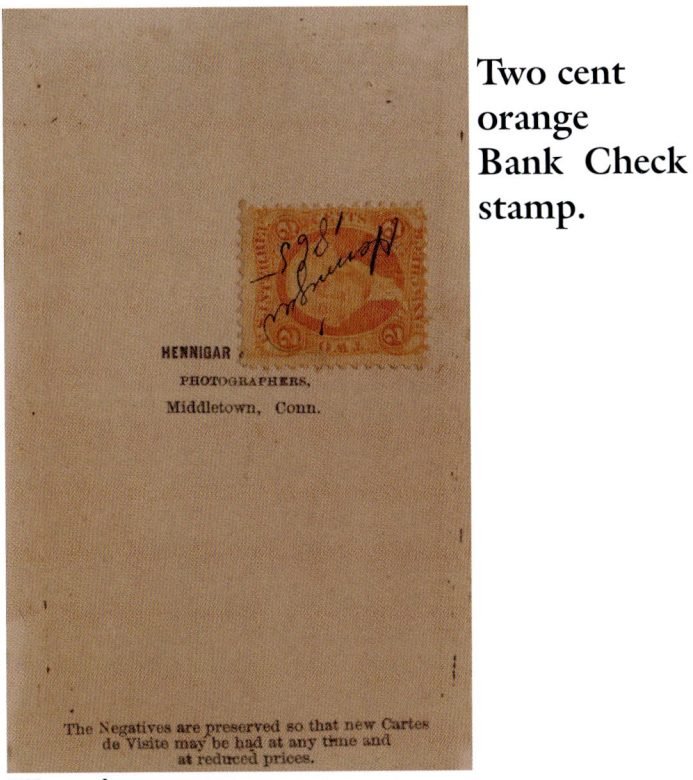

Two cent orange Bank Check stamp.

Hennigar uses a stamp to block the name of his ex-partner.

Three-quarter seated portrait of a woman.

Fancy Backs

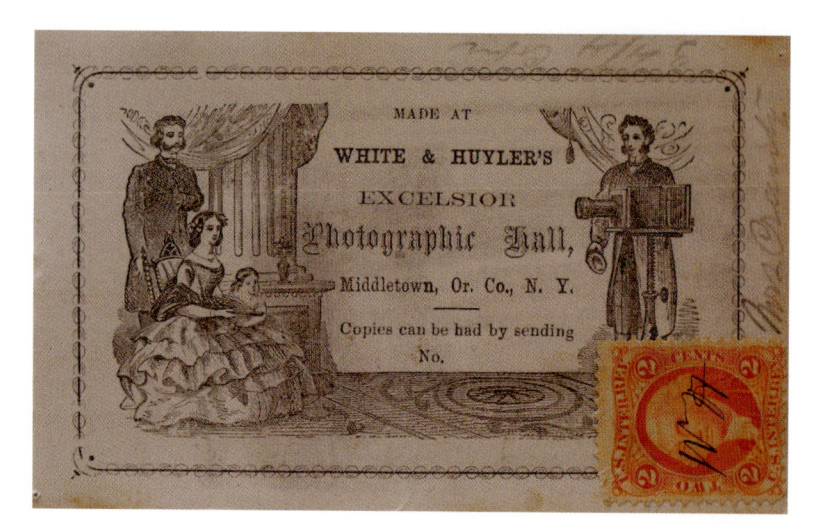

Three-Quarter seated portrait.

Fancy back showing the photographic camera and sitters at the studio. Two cent orange Internal Revenue stamp.

Three-quarter seated portrait.

Two cent blue Proprietary stamp.

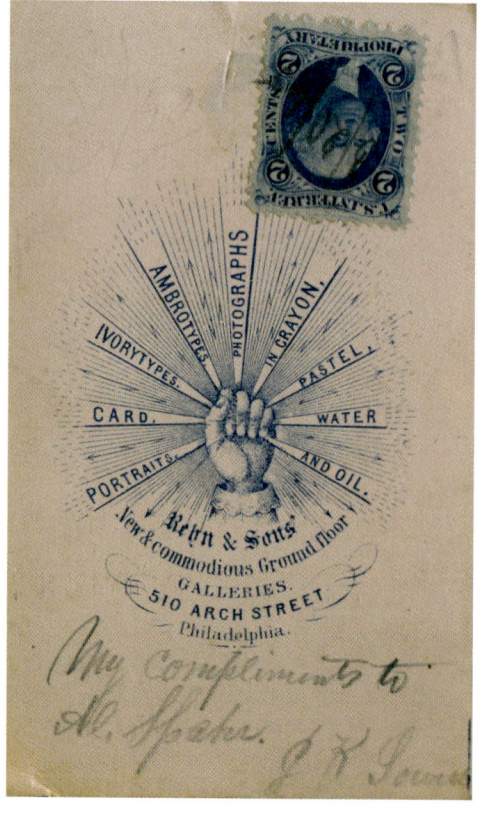

Fancy back depicts a hand holding light as if to control it.

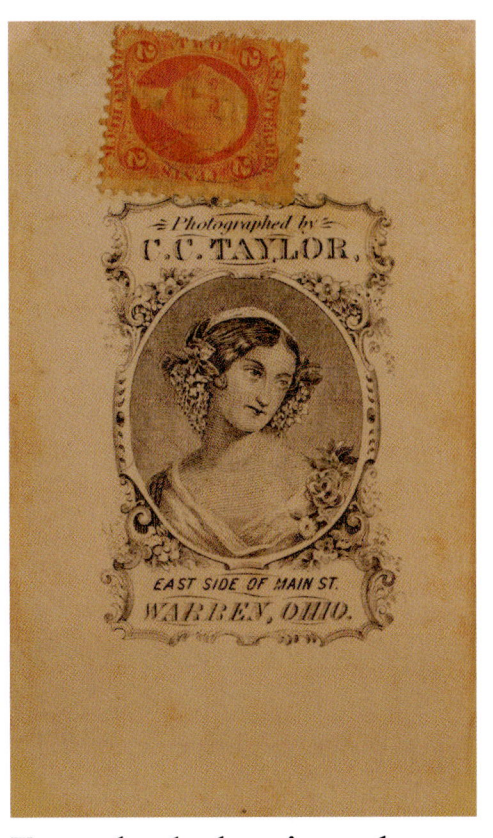

Two cent orange Bank Check stamp.

Fancy back showing what might be found on a bank note or printed on a check.

Vignette portrait

Three cent green Proprietary stamp.

Green printing of the carte is very unusual.

Bust vignette portrait.

157

Fancy front printed in two colors.

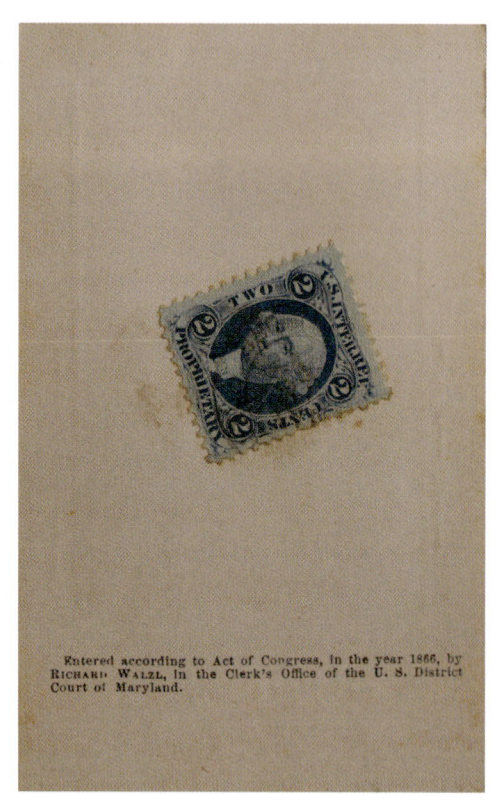

Two cent blue Proprietary stamp.

Another green card.

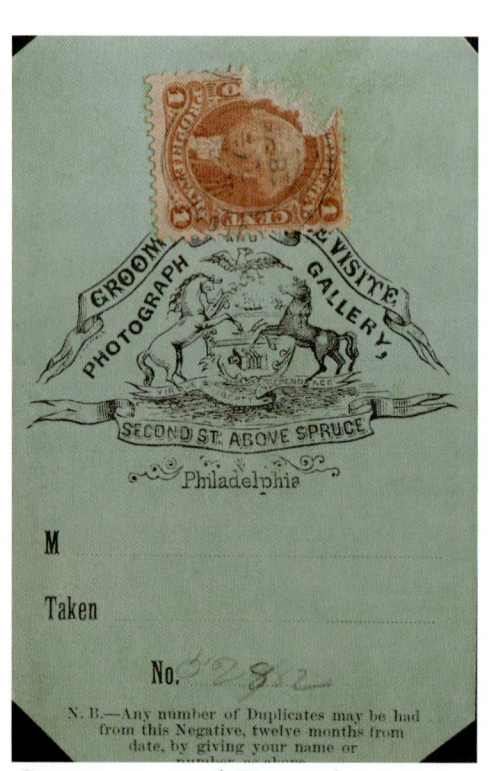

One cent red Proprietary stamp.

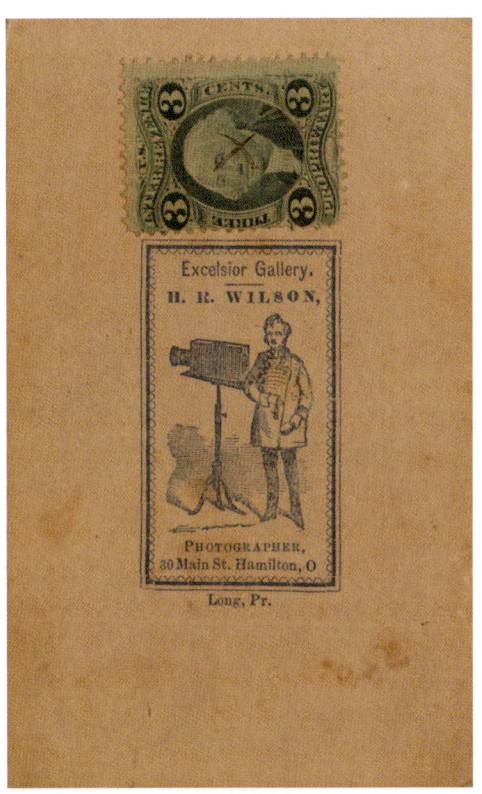

Fancy back showing the photographer and camera.

Three cent green Proprietary stamp.

Vignette portrait

Miss Liberty with Washington's head.

Three cent green Foreign Exchange.

Vignette portrait

159

Full-standing portrait.

Two cent orange Internal Revenue stamp

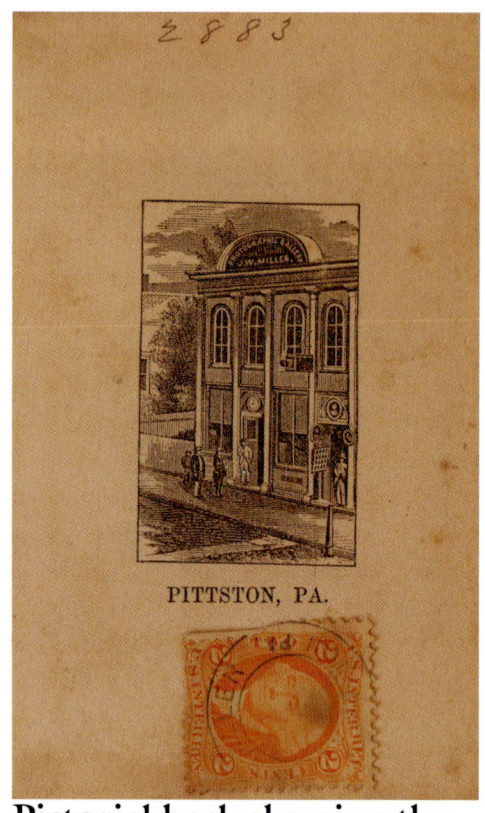

Pictorial back showing the photographer's studio street scene.

Full-standing portrait of a young lady.

Photo by Henry F. Warren with a fancy, patriotic back. Warren went to Washington to get an image of Abraham Lincoln. He was successful in gaining an audience with the president.

Three cent green Proprietary stamp.

160

Two cent orange Express stamp.

Warren befriended Tad, the president's son and asked to meet his father. Tad introduced them and Warren got the images of Lincoln he wanted. President Lincoln looks angry in both images. Note that Warren hired an engraver for his back, Jones of Waltham, MA.

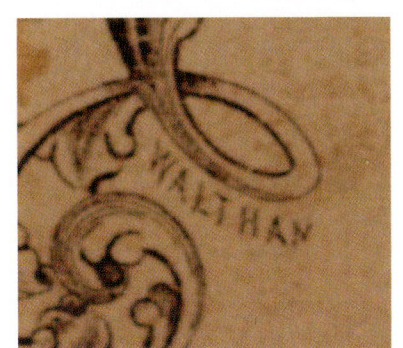

Three-quarter seated portrait.

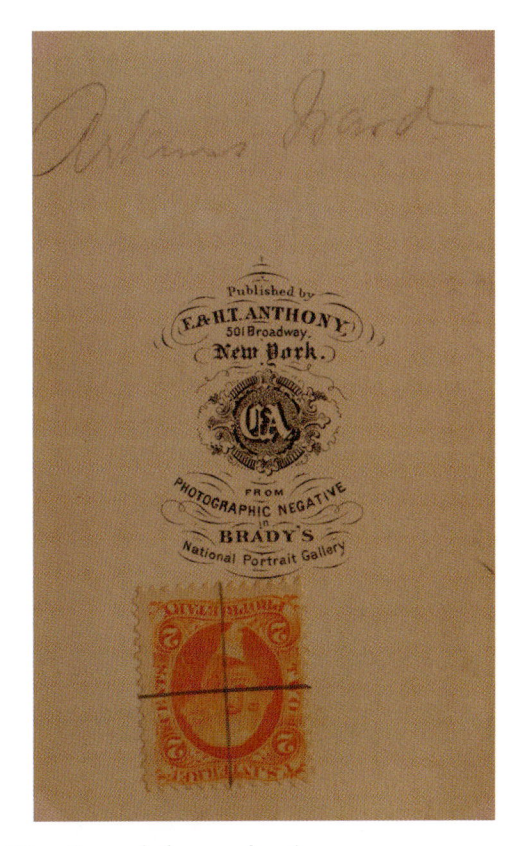

Portrait of Artemis Ward, Humorist, Author.

Back, with typical cross cancel on two cent Proprietary orange, of E & H.T. Anthony.

161

Vignette portrait.

Angel backmark from Mystic Bridge, CT. Two cent blue Bank Check stamp.

Three-quarter seated youth.

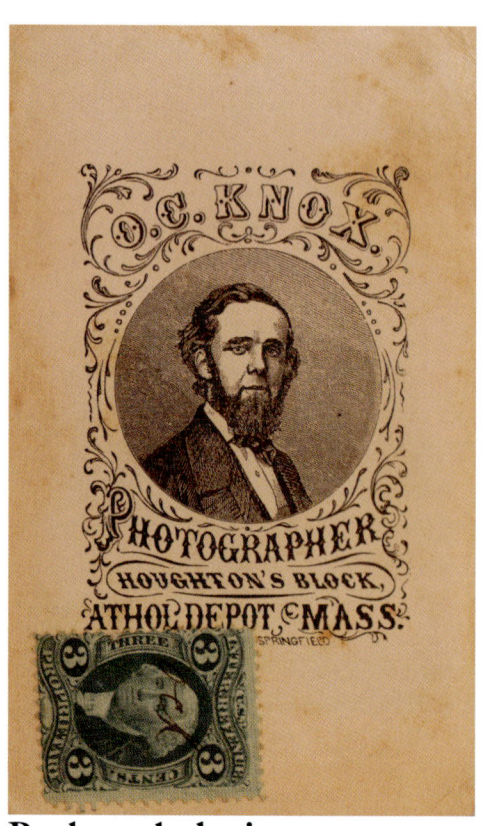

Backmark depicts photographer, O. C. Knox. Three cent green Proprietary stamp.

Fancy back showing two sailors and bales of cotton. Two cent blue Proprietary stamp.

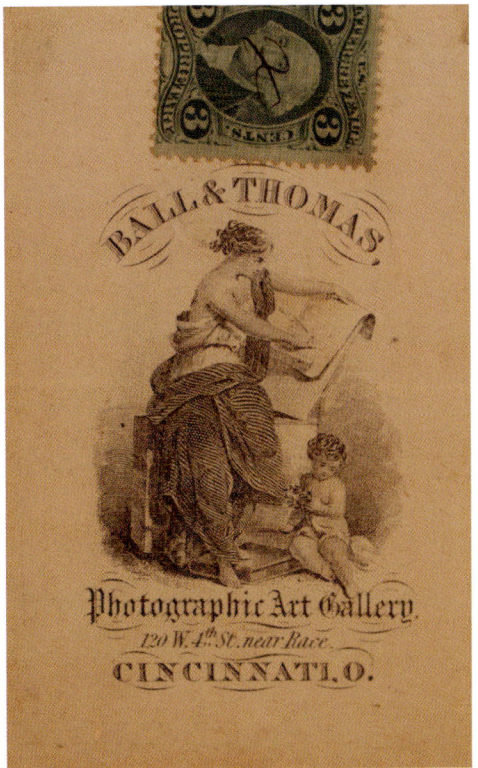

Three cent green Proprietary stamp.

Fancy back from studio succession of J. P. Ball, noted black photographer, and his partner, Thomas.

Three-quarter seated portrait.

Victoria and Albert pose.

163

Vignette portrait.

Three cent green Proprietary stamp.

Whimsical back of A. P. Hart. Note the palm tree in Elmira, NY.

Full-standing portrait.

Two cent blue Proprietary stamp.

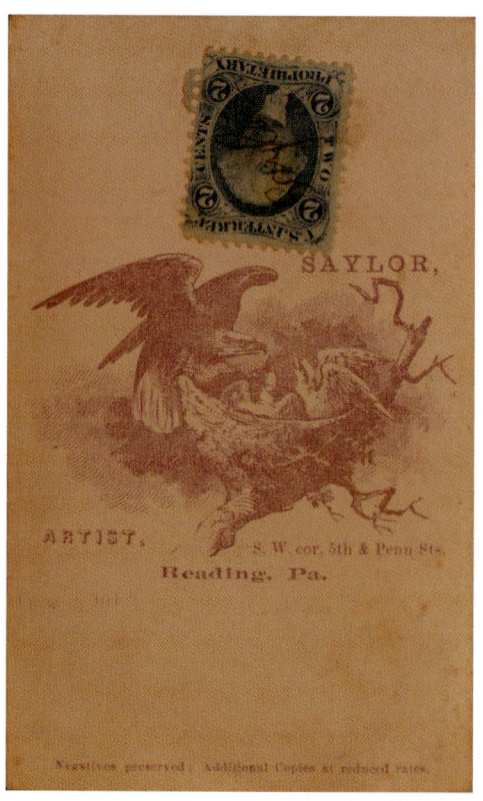

Purple patriotic back of an eagle feeding its young.

164

Patriotic back of an American flag.

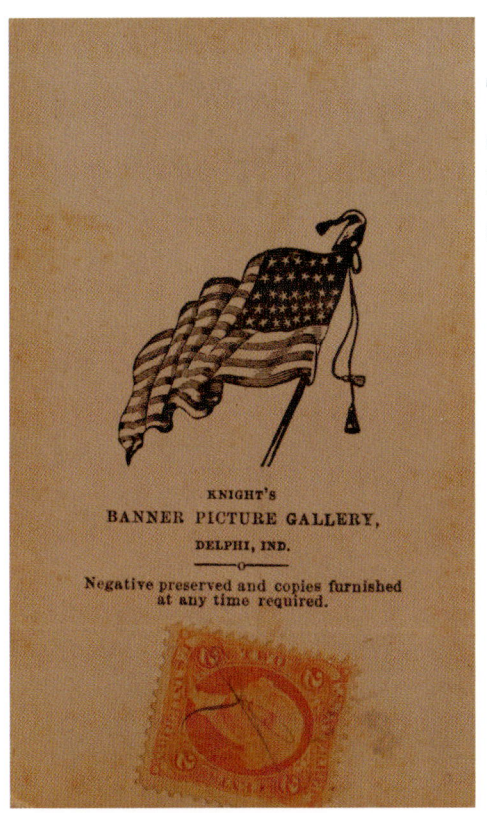

Two cent orange Internal Revenue stamp.

Unusual full seated vignette.

Patriotic backmark of an eagle over a shield.

Two cent orange Express stamp.

Full-standing portrait.

Three-quarter seated portrait.

Vignette portrait.

Two cent orange Bank Check stamp.

Patriotic backmark of an eagle surrounded by stars.

Two cent blue Playing Cards stamp.

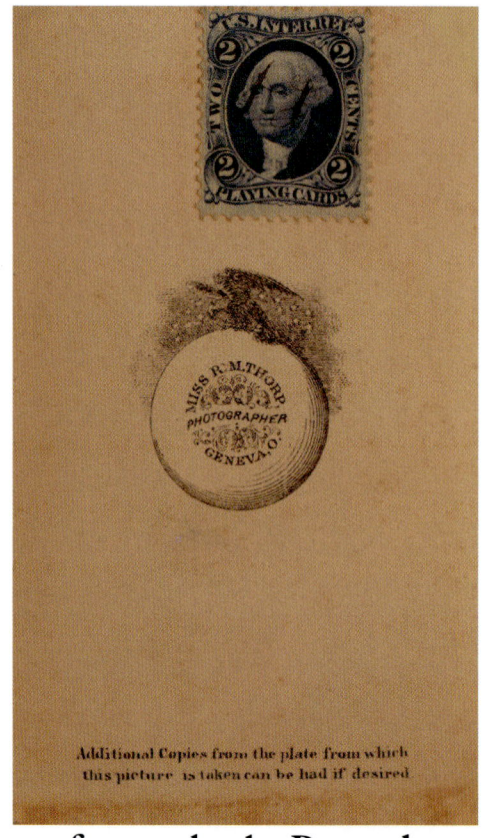

One of many backs Bogardus used. This patriotic backmark depicts an eagle.

166

Patriotic back in landscape orientation depicting flags, a drum and cannonballs. Two cent orange Internal Revenue stamp.

Oval-cut bust portrait.

Two two cent orange Express stamps.

Copy of a painting in an oval on a fancy green and gold printed card.

167

Southern Photographers

Young Union soldier in Key West, FL.

Two cent orange Bank Check stamp.

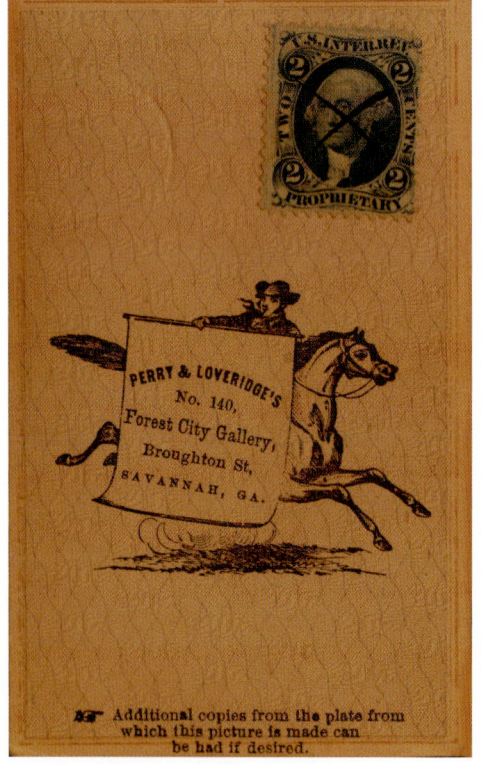

Two cent blue Proprietary stamp.

Fancy back of a rider and horse advertising the Savannah, GA photographer.

Pulaski monument in Savannah, GA.

168

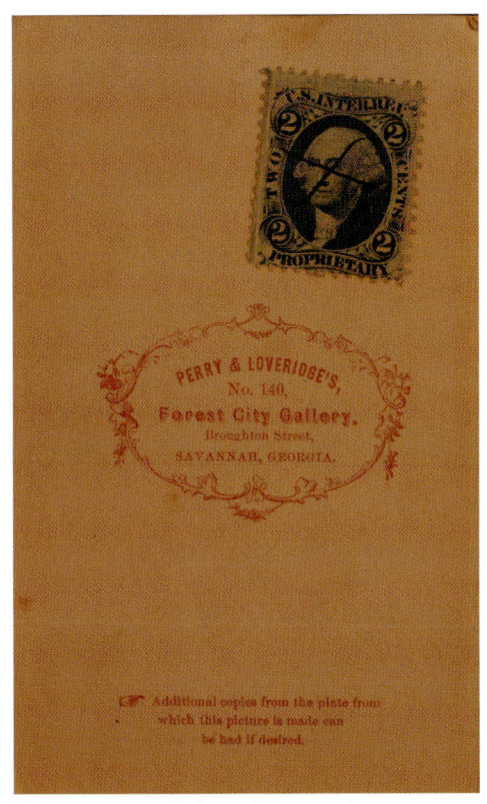

Two cent blue Proprietary stamp.

Street scene in Savannah, GA.

Image of same Pulaski monument by another Savannah, GA photographer. Note of interest: these two views, when viewed together, have some stereoscopic effect.

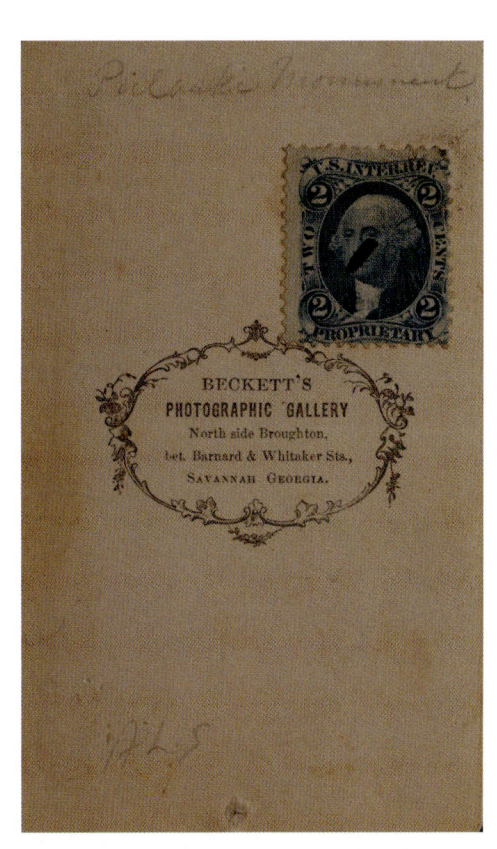

Two cent blue Proprietary stamp.

169

Image of Louis G. D'Russy, Major General of LA Militia from 1848-61 when he entered the Confederate Army.

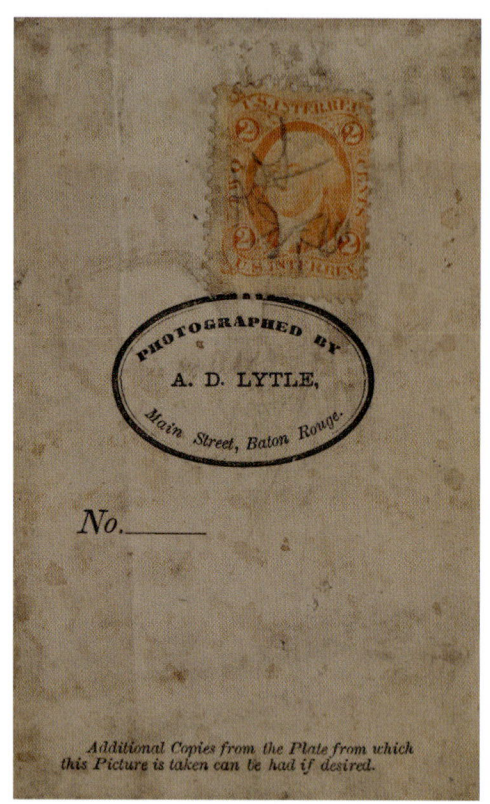

Two cent orange Internal Revenue stamp.

Copy of art of young mulatto girl looking through a hook as if seeing you and holding a small white dog in her other hand. From Jackson, MS.

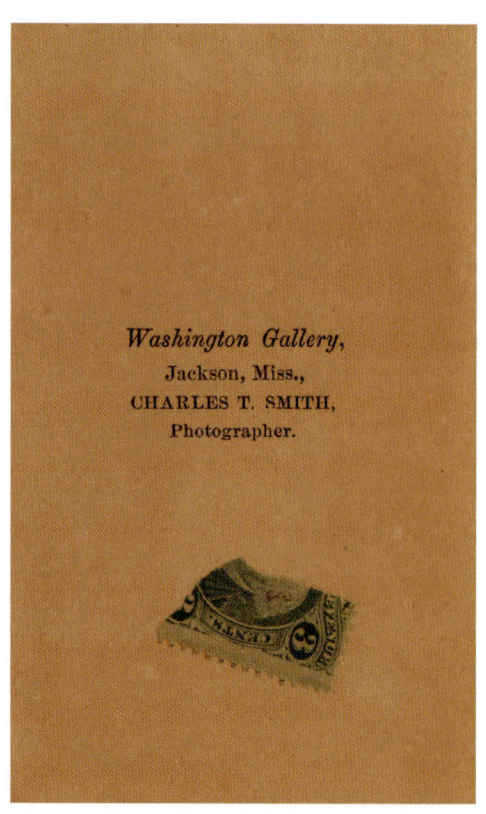

Questionable bisect paying one cent rate. Three cent green, unknown title.

170

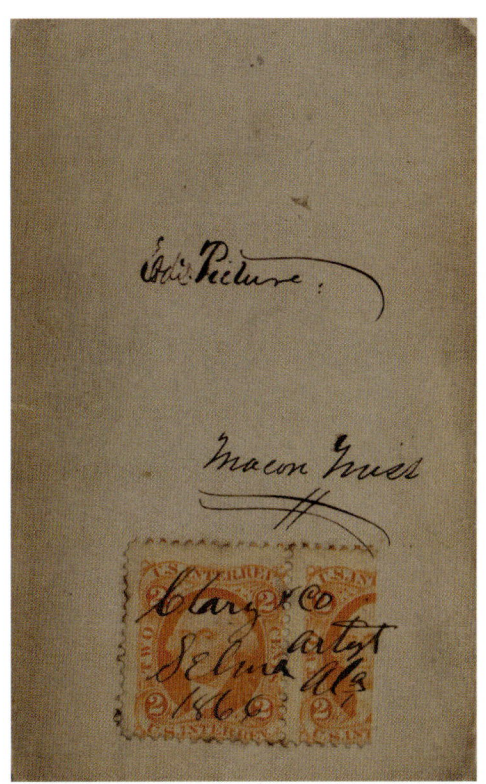

Two cent orange Internal Revenue stamps.

Photographer signed stamps from Selma, AL. Note the use of a bisect to pay the three cent rate.

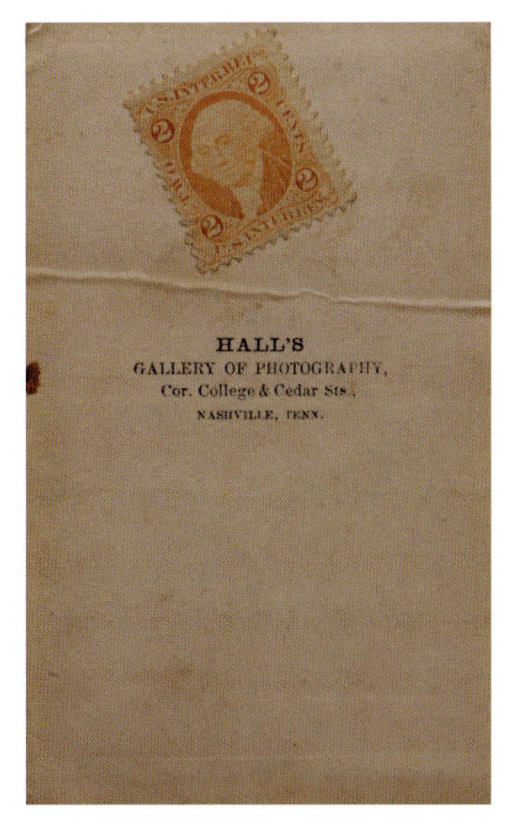

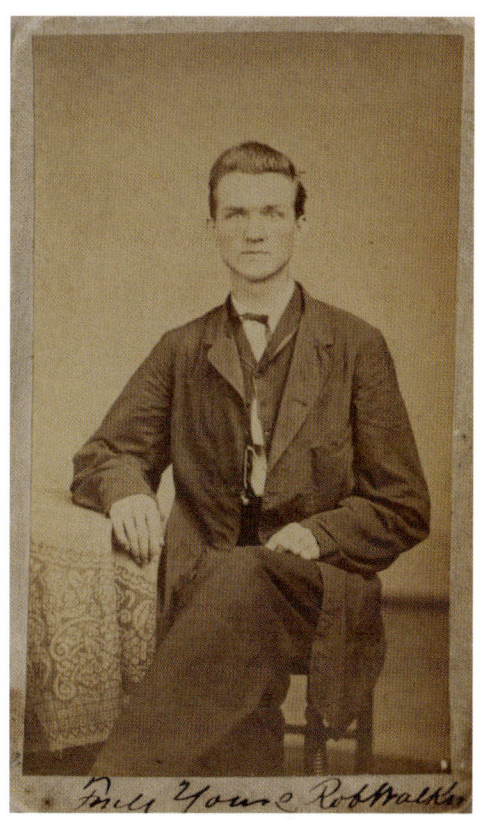

Three-quarter portrait.

Two cent orange Internal Revenue stamp.

Atypical pose of a Tennessee gentleman.

171

James King, Union officer, with note describing date of his assassination in Vicksburg, MS.

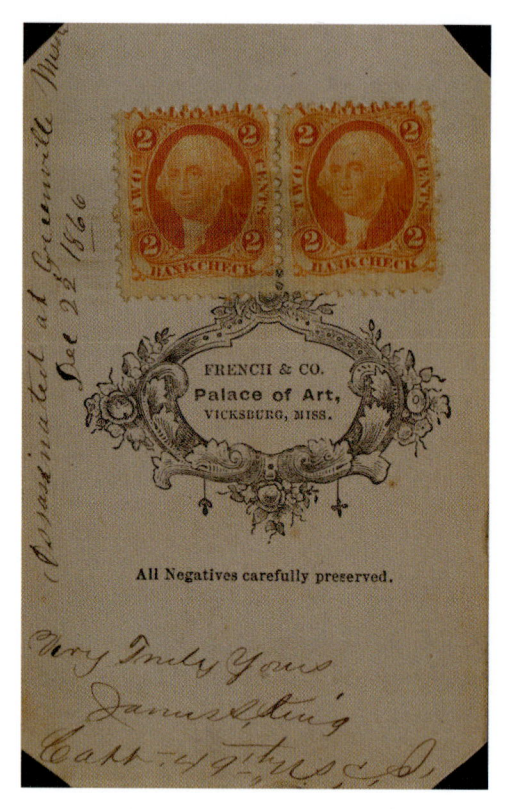

Two two cent orange Bank Check stamps paying the four cent rate.

Maysie Porter dated 1865 from Clarksville, TN. Interesting device on front more in keeping with Confederate motif than Union.

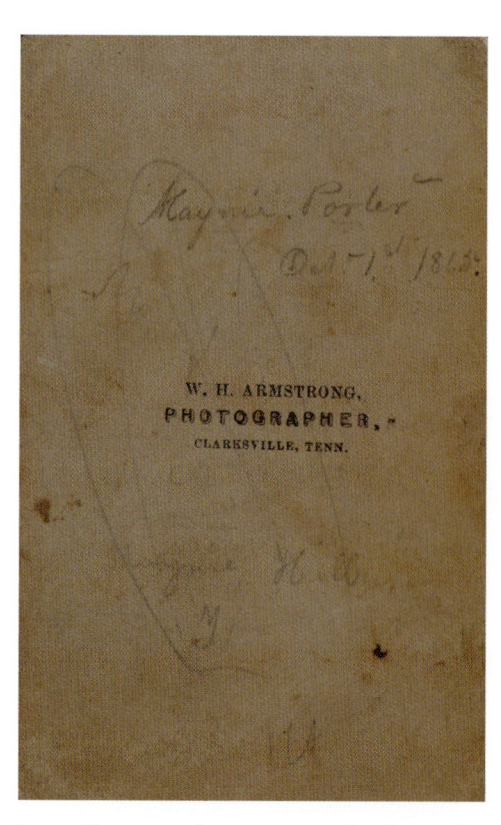

Southern photograph dated in the tax period, October 1, 1865 without stamp.

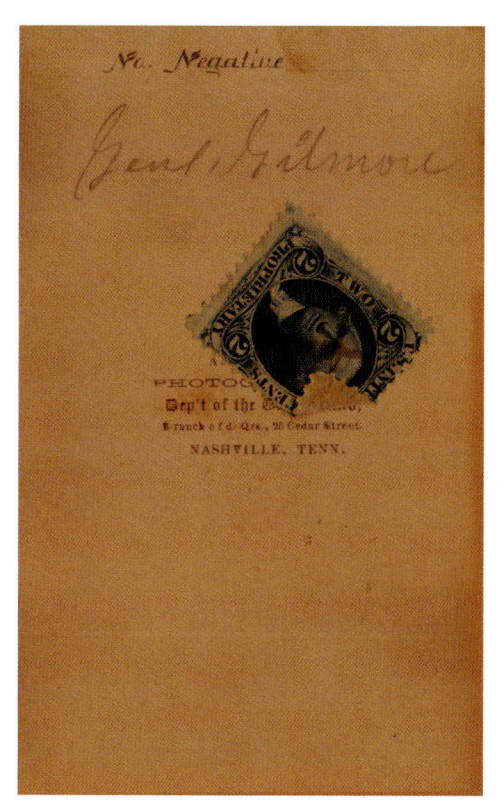

Two cent blue Proprietary stamp.

Image from life of Union General Q. A. Gilmore taken in Nashville, TN.

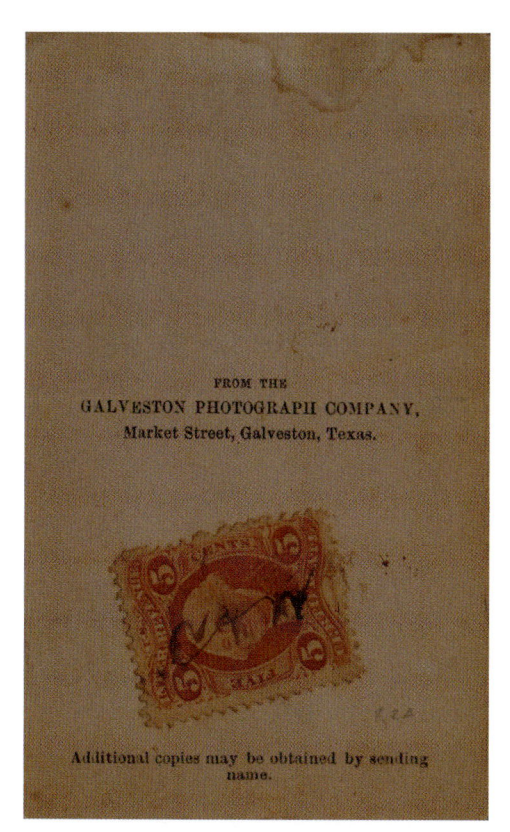

Five cent red Certificate stamp.

Union soldier A. N. Ballard, posted Galveston TX.

173

Young Southern belle taken at the Lone Star Gallery, Galveston, TX.

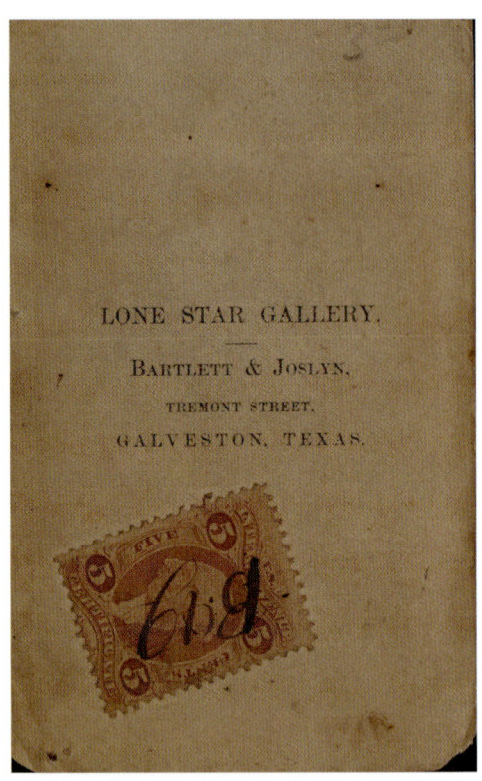

Five cent red Certificate stamp.

Image of a weathered young man, possibly wearing a Confederate battle shirt. Houston, TX.

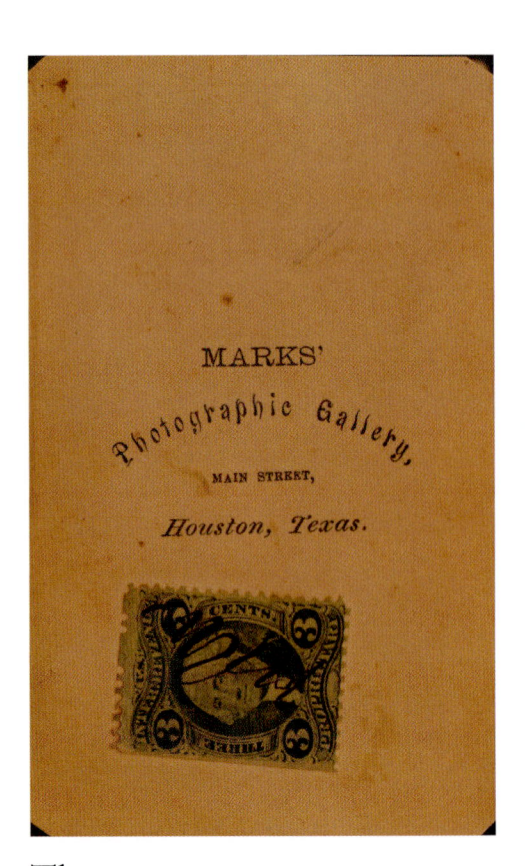

Three cent green Proprietary stamp.

Two cent blue Proprietary stamp.

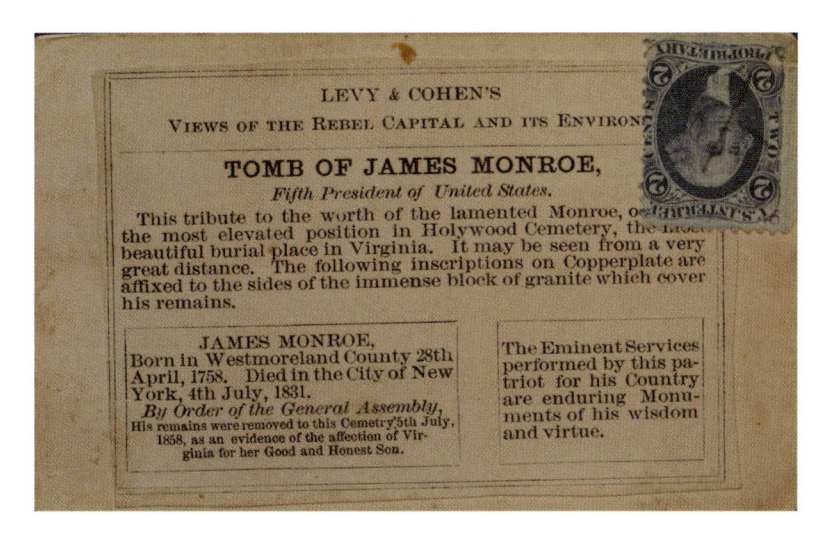

View of President James Monroe's tomb in Virginia. He served as president from 1817 to 1825.

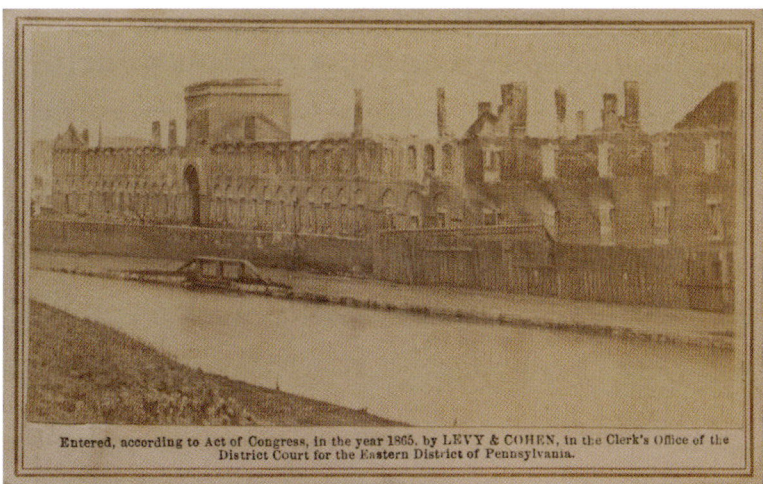

The Arsenal, Richmond, VA.

Two cent blue Proprietary stamp.

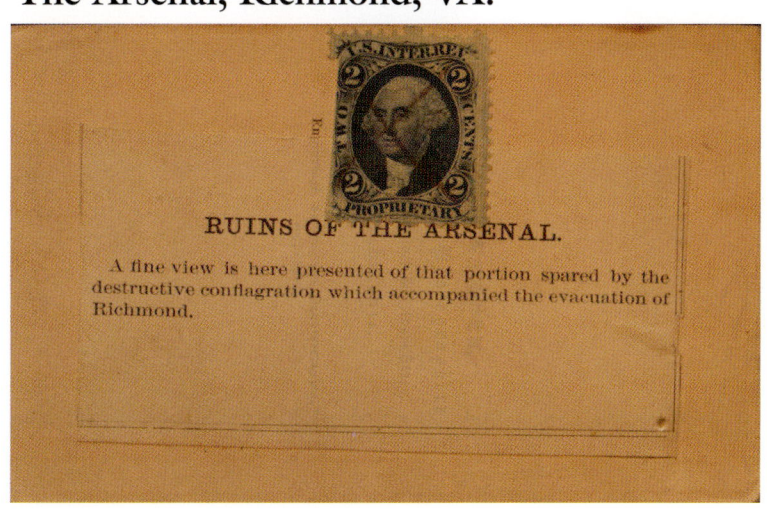

175

Western Photographers

Enlarged area showing two men and dogs on the point.

Two cent orange Internal Revenue stamp.

Views from the Nevada side of Lake Tahoe, NV by Lawrence & Houseworth.

Two cent orange Bank Check stamp.

176

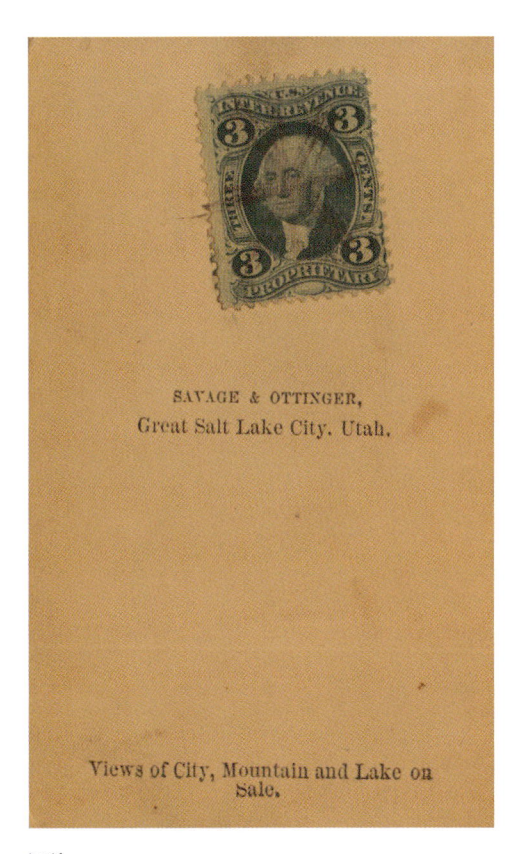

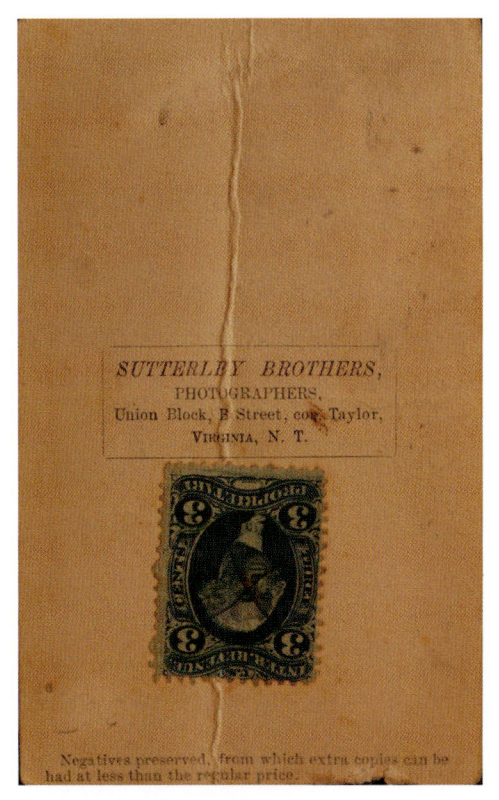

Three cent green Proprietary stamp.

Possibly a Masonic sect. Note green tinting on sash. From Great Salt Lake City, UT.

Three cent green Proprietary stamp.

Image by Sutterly Bros. Virginia City, NV, Nevada Territory.

177

Image Within An Image

This image is an enlargement from a section of the previous photograph. The lady on the right is pointing to one of five soldiers, probably her husband.

The original image of the three women, on page 178, holding a photograph is an example of photographic symbolism. The woman who points to one of the soldiers in the enlarged, transposed and stretched image on page 179 is probably pointing to her husband. She is using the image to symbolize her close relationship with the soldier.

Another example of photographic symbolism is the image of Sir Rowland Hill on page 17 where he is holding a quill. This probably indicates that the signature of the bottom of the card is from his hand.

Photography during this period is full of symbolism and is left open to the interpretation of the viewer.

Dual frank, three cent green Proprietary and five cent red Playing Cards stamps paying an eight cent rate.

Projection Views

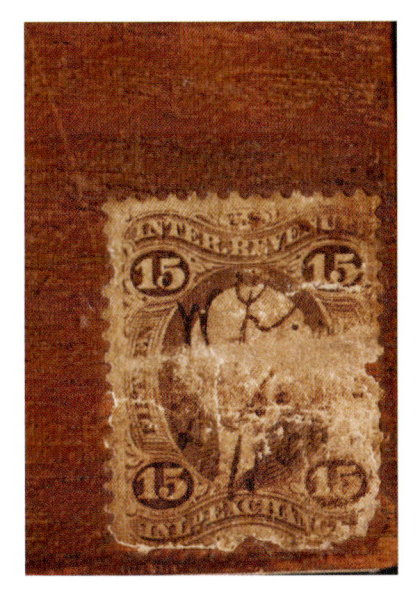

Tinted projection slide of Union General Phil Sheridan with a fifteen cent stamp paying the tax due.

Fifteen cent brown Inland Exchange stamp.

Holding a "Rocky Mountain cat," as indicated on the label, with fifteen cent stamp paying the tax due.

Fifteen cent brown Inland Exchange stamp.

181

Appendices

Table of Verified Photographers Working in the Tax Period

Huntsville, AL	Hubbard, O.
Huntsville, AL	Morse
Mobile, AL	Olwell & Gum
Mobile, AL	Titcomb, F.
Mobile, AL	Olwell, H.A.
Mobile, AL	Sancier, M.
Montgomery, AL	Hinton & Cleary's
Montgomery, AL	Lakin, J.H.
Montgomery, AL	Shaw & Town
Selma, AL	Clary, J.W. & Co.
Selma, AL	Wilde, Ino. T.
Little Rock, AR	Hasicht & Mealy (S.P. Hasicht)
Little Rock, AR	Millard, A.J.
Eureka, CA	Anderson, H. (Hugh); no state given
Forest Hill, CA	Jacobs, James M.
Grass Valley, CA	Cobb, David Cobb's Celebrated Photo Gallery
Grass Valley, CA	Rue, S.M.
Iowa Hill, CA	Jacobs, James M.
Marysville, CA	McCrary, S.
Marysville, CA	Stinson, L.J. (Lewis J.) note, signed Stinson, imprint Stinson
Nevada, CA	Ferrand, Charles
Oakland, CA	Ingersoll, William B.
Oroville, CA	Kusel, Edward A.
Petaluma, CA	Johnson, B.R.
Petaluma, CA	Ross, George
Redwood, CA	Somus, H.J.
Sacramento, CA	Beals & Walters
Sacramento, CA	Sherriff, T.B. for T. J. Higgins
Sacramento, CA	Todd, J.A.
San Francisco, CA	Addis & Koch (Addis, Robert W/Koch, John)
San Francisco, CA	Bayley & Cramer (Cramer, Charles L.)
San Francisco, CA	Bayley, Wilber F.
San Francisco, CA	Bradley & Rulofson
San Francisco, CA	Bryan, J.M.

San Francisco, CA	Bush's Photograph Gallery
San Francisco, CA	Edouart, Alexander
San Francisco, CA	Hamilton & Kellogg
San Francisco, CA	Higgins, T.J. (Thomas)
San Francisco, CA	Howland, B.F. & Co.
San Francisco, CA	Lawrence & Houseworth
San Francisco, CA	Nahl Bros. & Dickmann
San Francisco, CA	Olsen, H., Artist
San Francisco, CA	Perkins & Foss
San Francisco, CA	Pilliner, W.H.
San Francisco, CA	Selleck, Silas
San Francisco, CA	Shew, Jacob
San Francisco, CA	Shew, William
San Francisco, CA	Watkins, Carlton E.
San Francisco, CA	Wise & Prindle
San Jose, CA	Clayton, J.A.
San Jose, CA	Heering, John H.
Sonora, CA	Rulofson's Art Gallery, Daniel Sewell, ,Proprietor
Sonora, CA	Sewell, Daniel
Stockton, CA	Stuart, W. M.
Central City, CO	Garbanati, H.
Denver, CO	Allen, C.F.
Denver, CO	Chamberlain, Wm. (Denver Photograph Rooms)
Denver, CO	Wakely, Geo. D.
Birmingham, CT	Smith & Richardson
Birmingham, CT	Storrs, J.W.
Bridgeport, CT	Crandall & Barnum
Bridgeport, CT	Erekson & Lee
Bridgeport, CT	Erekson, O.
Bridgeport, CT	Horton & Wheeler
Bridgeport, CT	Mallon, M.M.
Bridgeport, CT	Naramore, R.C.
Bridgeport, CT	Partridge (G.L.)
Bristol, CT	Terry's Gallery
Colchester, CT	Lewis, L.R.
Collinsville, CT	Bigelow, S.
Danbury, CT	Ritton, E.D. (Ritton's Gallery)
Danbury, CT	Union Gallery
Danielsonville, CT	Dabis, S.P.
Daysville, CT	Aylsworth, F.B.
E. Meridian, CT	Everitt, E.B.
Hartford, CT	Bliss, J.W.
Hartford, CT	DeLamater, R.S.
Hartford, CT	Dexter
Hartford, CT	Gemmill, R.J.
Hartford, CT	Goodwin
Hartford, CT	Kellogg Brothers
Hartford, CT	Kellogg, E.P.
Hartford, CT	Miller, Sidney
Hartford, CT	Oldershaw, J.
Hartford, CT	Prescott
Hartford, CT	Prescott & Gage
Hartford, CT	Prescott & Gage, photog. D.W. Wilson
Hartford, CT	Waite, S.H.
Hartford, CT	Webster & Popkins
Hartford, CT	Wilson, D.W.
Hartford, CT	Wilson Bros.
Litchfield, CT	Judd, J.L.
Middletown, CT	Burrows & Bundy
Middletown, CT	Hennigar

Middletown, CT	Hennigar & Baldwin
Middletown, CT	Hennigar & Johnson
Middletown, CT	Hennigar, G.W.
Milford, CT	Wires
Meriden, CT	Wheeler, F.
Modus, CT	Russell, Mrs. B.H.
Mystic Bridge, CT	Angell, D.O.
New Bedford, CT	Hatch, Henry F.
New Bedford, CT	Jenney & Smith
New Britain, CT	Judson, W.A. (& Co.)
New Britain, CT	Kenyon, Wm. H.
New Haven, CT	Beers & Mansfield (National Gallery)
New Haven, CT	Bundy & Williams
New Haven, CT	Burwell & Homan
New Haven, CT	Filley & Gilbert
New Haven, CT	Homan, Chas.
New Haven, CT	Moulthrop
New Haven, CT	Peck Bros.
New Haven, CT	Peck, Henry S.
New Haven, CT	Rodgers, H.J.
New Haven, CT	Steiger, I.G.
New Haven, CT	Wells & Collins
New London, CT	Giles Bishop
New London, CT	Jordan's New Styles Pictures
New London, CT	Jordan, J.L. & H.A.
New London, CT	Morgan & Bolles (Kenyon, F.P.
New Milford, CT	Landon, S.C.
Norwalk, CT	Whitney & Beckwith
Norwich, CT	Jennings, W.H.
Norwich, CT	Thompson, L.
Norwich, CT	Vars, N.B.
Norwich, CT	Weeks or Weekes, J.
Plainville, CT	Allderige, W.
Stamford, CT	Crawford
Stamford, CT	Folsom Bros.
Waterbury, CT	Granniss, G.N.
Waterbury, CT	King, Wm.
West Meriden, CT	Everitt, E.B.
West Meriden, CT	Everitt, E.B. or Everitt
West Meriden, CT	Wheeler, F.
Willimantic, Ct	Lawton, Mrs. A.J.
Willimantic, Ct	Robbins, H.E.
Windsor Locks, CT	Parmalee, S.
Winstead, CT	Doughty, T.M.V. (also T.M.V. & E.V.)
Geortetown, DC	Cooper
Washington, DC	Addis Gallery
Washington, DC	Barnard, Geo. Norman & Bostwick, Chas. Oakley
Washington, DC	Baum & Burdine
Washington, DC	Bell & Brother
Washington, DC	Bell & Hall (Bell, F.H.)
Washington, DC	Brady, Mathew
Washington, DC	Crosbie, A.
Washington, DC	Gardner, Alexander
Washington, DC	Goldin, John & Co.
Washington, DC	Holyland, Jno.
Washington, DC	Loeb, R. Emory Hospital
Washington, DC	Marshall, Charles
Washington, DC	Marvin, Philomen B.
Washington, DC	Paige & Mills
washington, DC	Perkins, W. D.

Washington, DC	Solomon, Philip
Washington, DC	Slagle, Mrs. E.W.
Washington, DC	Snell, Wm. & Co.
Washington, DC	Starbuck, Thomas
Washington, DC	Ulke, Henry
Washington, DC	Wakely, G. D.
Washington, DC	Walker, Thomas
Washington, DC	Whitehurst Gallery
Washington, DC	Whitehurst Gallery, W. Snell Photographer & Partner
Washington, DC	Whitehurst Gallery, M. J. Powers, photographer
Wilmington, DE	Curry, Wm. H.
Wilmington, DE	Gawthrop, A. & Co.
Wilmington, DE	Jeanes, Joseph
Wilmington, DE	Sexton. T.E.
Wilmington, DE	Torbert, J.E.
Wilmington, DE	Webb, Miss Emily
Key West, FL	Moffatt
Athens, GA	Motes, C.W.
Atlanta, GA	Barnard, Geo. Norman
Atlanta, GA	Dill & Maier
Atlanta, GA	Kuhn, F.
Atlanta, GA	Lane, O.R.
Augusta, GA	Perkins Gallery
Macon, GA	Riddle, A.J.
Macon, GA	Lunquest, M.S.
Savannah, GA	Beckett
Savannah, GA	Brown, R.H.
Savannah, GA	Perry & Loveridge
Bloomfield, IA	Anderson & Dunlop
Burlington, IA	Twining's (H.N.) Gallery
Cedar Rapids, IA	Herbert, W.H.
Clinton, IA	Blackhall, J.
Davenport, IA	Balchmitteer
Davenport, IA	Cook & Foster
Davenport, IA	Foster & Atkinson
Davenport, IA	Nesbit, Wm. A.
Davenport, IA	Olmsted, P. (& Co.)
Davenport, IA	Shueller, J.
Decoach, IA	Adams & Shear
DeWitt, IA	Young, Wm.
Dubuque, IA	Cutter, E.
Dubuque, IA	Mills, N.A.
Dubuque, IA	Root, S.
Dubuque, IA	Samson, W.H.
Fairfield, IA	Gilchrist & Kyle
Ft. Madison, IA	Mourer, J.F.
Ft. Madison, IA	Phares, W.H.
Hesper, IA	Mrs. Worth
Hopkinton, IA	Warner, P.H.
Indianola, IA	Leach, J.A.
Iowa City, IA	Calkin, J.T.
Iowa City, IA	Wetherby, I.A.
Keokuk, IA	Blair, R.H.
Keokuk, IA	Booth & Stackhouse
Keokuk, IA	Emerson, W.H.
Keokuk, IA	Hamill
Keokuk, IA	Sellers', C. Photographic Gallery
Keokuk, IA	Van Grieken, S.
McGregor, IA	Kricks, N.
Manchester, IA	Libby, E.P.

185

Maquokita, IA	Gardner & Willey
Maquokita, IA	Gardner, R.G.
Marshalltown, IA	Datesman, P.
Merron, IA	Stone, J.B.
Montezuma, IA	Bowen, W.N.
Morrison, IA	Seaman, J.B.
Mt. Pleasant, IA	Leisening, J.R.
Mt. Pleasant, IA	Leisening Bros.
Mount Vernon, IA	Eberhart, M.H.
Oskalossa, IA	Bird, J.M.
Oskalossa, IA	Miles, Wm.
Sabula, IA	Esmay, John
Washington, IA	Kracaw's, A.
Waterloo, IA	J.L. St.Clair
West Union, IA	White, A.P.
Abingdon, IL	Johnston's
Alton, IL	Breath, E.M., Proprietor (Alton Photograph Gallery)
Amboy, IL	Andrus, Mrs. W.B.
Atlanta, IL	Neal & Crihfield
Aurora, IL	Pratt, D.C.
Aurora, IL	Weld, D.T.
Batavia, IL	Whitney & Kendig
Beardstown, IL	Carter, E.S.
Belleville, IL	Deeke & Krebs
Belleville, IL	Neff
Belleville, IL	Ryan J.
Belleville, IL	Sargent, A.J.
Belleville, IL	Weinal & Schubert
Belvidere, IL	Bishop, C.W.
Belvidere, IL	Bishop's & W. & F.H.
Belvidere, IL	Cross, A.M.
Belvidere, IL	Herren, A.
Bloomington, IL	Anderson, W.
Bloomington, IL	Fullerton's Art Union Gallery
Bloomington, IL	Scibird Bros. & Co.
Bloomington, IL	Scibird, Joe H.
Cairo, IL	Parker's Gallery
Camp Point, IL	Gaunt, W.H.
Canton, IL	Barker, A.W.
Canton, IL	Bays & Bullard
Canton, IL	Seavey
Carlinville ,IL	Stewart, John G.
Carrollton, IL	Tandy & Gledhill
Carthage, IL	Philpot, T & Co.
Champaign, IL	Sanderson
Charleston, IL	Paris & Co.
Chicago, IL	Mrs. E. Aldridge
Chicago, IL	Apfel, Henry, Jr.
Chicago, IL	Battersby, J.
Chicago, IL	Brand's Art Gallery
Chicago, IL	Carbutt, J.
Chicago, IL	City Photograph Gallery, L.D. Patton, Agent
Chicago, IL	Crater, Issac, Union Photographic Gallery
Chicago, IL	Cunningham, Robert
Chicago, IL	Crater & Bill
Chicago, IL	Dillon, John
Chicago, IL	Fassett, Samuel M.
Chicago, IL	Gard, E.R. Wood's (Col.) Museum and Gallery
Chicago, IL	Gard, E.R.
Chicago, IL	Green, Frank

Location	Name
Chicago, IL	Green, G.B.
Chicago, IL	Hesler, A. (Green, G.B.)
Chicago, IL	Hine,. T.
Chicago, IL	Mosher's, Charlie
Chicago, IL	National Copying (strip label over stamp by Even & Clow,)
Chicago, IL	Pattiani, A.
Chicago, IL	Patton, L.D., Agent, City Photograph Gallery
Chicago, IL	Rocher, Henry
Chicago, IL	Rider, B.L.
Chicago, IL	Schneider, G. & Co.
Chicago, IL	Shaw, William
Chicago, IL	Van Vlack, Jay (Jay E.)
Chicago, IL	Wallis & Abbott
Chicago, IL	Wallis Bro.
Chicago, IL	Wuensche, C.
Clinton, IL	Payne, Jas. L.
Cortland Station, IL	Webb, R. J.
DeKalb, IL	Flinn, James W.
DeKalb, IL	Hartwell, S.M.
Decatur, IL	Barnwell & Pitner
Dixon, IL	Crawford, J.H.
Elgin, IL	Adams, J.M.
Elgin, IL	Anderson, Mrs. L.S.
Elgin, IL	Dawson, R. W.
Elgin, IL	Cummings, E.
Elmwood, IL	Blakeslee,W.
Farmington, IL	Forbes, J.
Franklin-Grove, IL	Mrs. C.T. Bridgeman
Freeport, IL	Hoerichs, A.R.
Freeport, IL	Halrihs, A.R.
Freeport, IL	McHenry, Wm.
Fulton, IL	Roberts, C.
Galena, IL	Lamberson & James
Galena, IL	Peirce, E.W.
Galesburg, IL	Briggs, N. Photographic Art Gallery
Galesburg, IL	Linstett & Throlson
Galesburg, IL	McMillen, Z.P.
Geneva, IL	Kindblade, B.
Greenville, IL	Pogue, J.N.
Jacksonville, IL	Merine & Williams
Jacksonville, IL	Merine, J.C. & Co.
Jacksonville, IL	Tandy's Art Gallery
Jerseyville, IL	Lee, D.A.
Jerseyville, IL	Strong & Lipscomb
Jerseyville, IL	Strong, J.C.
LaHarpe, IL	Goodwin, J.E.
LaSalle, IL	Mapstone, R.
Lincoln, IL	Erinfield, Dr.
Lincoln, IL	Judy, G.W. & Co.
Lincoln, IL	Judy & Miller
Mackinaw, IL	Payne, J.E.
Macomb, IL	Ragan & Wood
Malcomb, IL	Edouart
Malcomb, IL	Hawkins & Philpot
Malcomb, IL	Ragan, W.O.
McHenry, IL	Ford
Mendota, IL	Hogan & Ensminger
Mendota, IL	Smith
Morris, IL	Even & Clow
Morris, IL	Even, Joseph

Morris, IL	Field, W.B. (Star Gallery)
Morrison, IL	Brown, J.R.
Mound City, IL	Leonard, J.B.
Mt.Carroll, IL	Bitner & Robinson
Napierville, IL	Kendig, C.
Napierville, IL	Metzler's
Olney, IL	Rush, Jacob
Ottawa, IL	Alschuler's
Ottawa, IL	LaSalle & Peru, Bowman & Rawson
Ottawa, IL	Butt, Geo.
Ottawa, IL	Gibbs, L.E. National Gallery
Paris, IL	Martin, I.R. First National Gallery
Pekin, IL	Parker, J.C.
Pekin, IL	Williams
Peoria, IL	Cole's Photographic Gallery
Peoria, IL	Luccock, T.J.
Peoria, IL	Mills
Peoria, IL	Thurlow, J.
Pittsfield, IL	Obst, C.L.
Polo, IL	Johnston, S.S.
Polo, IL	Wagoner, J.H.
Princeton, IL	Endsley, T.E.
Princeton, IL	Hogman, R.
Princeton, IL	Masters, W.H.
Quincy, IL	Bradshaw, J.T. & Co. Eclipse Gallery
Quincy, IL	Moses, G & A
Quincy, IL	Moses, G.
Quincy, IL	Reed, Mrs. W.A.
Quincy, IL	Simons, J.
Rochelle, (Ogle Co.) IL	Pierce & Cogswell
Rock Island Barracks, IL	Smith, Josh
Rock Island, IL	Gayford & Speidel
Rock Island, IL	Newberry & Solanders
Rockford, IL	Anderson, J.S.
Rockford, IL	Barnes, G.W. or Geo.
Rockford, IL	Brown
Rockford, IL	Rhodes, Mrs. A. A.
Rockford, IL	Wakeman, J.H.
St.Charles, IL	Cropper, Samuel
Sandwich, IL	Thompson, R.
Shelbyville, IL	Hannaman, G.
Springfield, IL	German, C.S.
Springfield, IL	Hall, C.H.
Springfield, IL	Ingmire, F.W.
Springfield, IL	Townsend, A.C. Enterprise Gal.
Springfield, IL	Tresize, J.Q.A.
Sterling, IL	Cavert, W.
Sycamore, IL	Dowe & Co.
Sycamore, IL	Dowe, L.
Sycamore, IL	Dowe & Colton
Taylorsville, IL	Squier, Jno.
Tonica, IL	Culver, D.M.
Warsaw, IL	Oliver, E.W.
Washington, IL	Sickler, R.F.
Waukegan, IL	Kellogg
Waukegan, IL	Thurston, E. Q & J.S.
Wenona, IL	Clark, L.H.
West Aurora, IL	Giles, Wm.
Woodstock, IL	Medlar, J.S.
Woodstock, IL	Dawson, R. W.

Location	Name
Attica, IN	Chapman, M.V.
Attica, IN	Chapman & Ennis
Aurora, IN	Tuck, N.H.
Bloomington, IN	Allison
Cambridge City, IN	Hunt, D.W.
Cambridge City, IN	Rinker, C.P. & Bro.
Connersville, IN	Tatman, J.H.
Crown Point, IN	Up the Grove, H.A.
Delphi, IN	Knight's Banner Picture Gallery
Delphi, IN	Eversole, S.P.
Delphi, IN	Peckham & Dingle
Elkhart, IN	Clark, P.K.
Elkhart, IN	Maury
Evansville, IN	Pakhill, H.H.
Evansville, IN	Parhill, H.H.
Fort Wayne, IN	Dunckleburg, Wm.
Fort Wayne, IN	Saunders
Fort Wayne, IN	Shoaff, J.A.
Franklin, IN	Mangrum, C.W.
Green Castle, IN	Spurgin, D.M. (& Son)
Greensburg, IN	House & Faries
Greensburg, IN	Ridener & Farris
Indianapolis, IN	Barnes, A.A.
Indianapolis, IN	Apple, G.W., National Gallery
Indianapolis, IN	Bruening, E. & J.
Indianapolis, IN	Runnion's Gallery of Art
Indianapolis, IN	Swain Brothers
Indianapolis, IN	Treadwell & Peaslee
Jeffersonville, IN	Switzer, O.S.
Kendallville, IN	Cole & Adams
Kendallville, IN	Parrish, Geo.
Lafayette, IN	Claflin, D.B.
Lafayette, IN	Claflin & Eaton
Lafayette, IN	Clark, D.R.
Lafayette, IN	Cornell, C.G.
Lafayette, IN	Erb, Frederick
Lafayette, IN	Evernden, Wm.
Lafayette, IN	Pickerill, O.F.
Lafayette, IN	Wolever
Lagrange, IN	Cornell, C.G.
Laporte, IN	Stark, C.M.
Logansport, IN	Longwell & Bottenberg
Logansport, IN	Longwells' Gallery
Madison, IN	Gorgas & Mulvey's
Mount Vernon, IN	Willis, A.
Muncie, IN	Darracott
New Albany, IN	Wilson, J.A.
Orleans, IN	Kemp, W.C.R
Pendleton, IN	Roberts, D. H.
Peru, IN	Fetter
Raporte, IN	Stark, C.M.
Richmond, IN	Addleman, J.P.
Richmond, IN	Maxwell & Estell
Rockport, IN	Randall & Littlepage
Seymour, IN	Jackson, T.M.
Shelbyville, IN	Bowman, Alfred
South Bend, IN	Bonney, James
Terra Haute, IN	Eppert, C.
Terra Haute, IN	Husher, J.W.
Terra Haute, IN	Wright, D.H.

Terra Haute, IN	Wright & Prescott's
Valparaiso, IN	Mandeville, L.H.
Vevay, IN	Ruggles, Wm. H.
Wabash, IN	Rhodes, R.K.
Warsaw, IN	Milice, H.C. & Bro. Empire Gallery
Williamsport, IN	Cavanaugh, John
Winamac, IN	Rhodes, B.K.
Fort Scott, KS	Parker & Tomlinson
Lawrence, KS	Lamon, W.H.
Leavenworth, KS	Babbitt, J.P.
Leavenworth, KS	Kimball, R.H.
Leavenworth, KS	Stevenson, R. & Co.
Bowling Green, KY	Edwards, C.
Camp Nelson, KY	Rodecker, Wm. W.
Carlisle, KY	Henry's Gallery
Danville, KY	Finley, G.W.
Lexington, KY	Carpenter & Mullen
Lexington, KY	Elrod, D.B.
Lexington, KY	Marrs, W.R.
Lexington, KY	Phipps, W.R.
Louisville, KY	Allan & Gorbutt
Louisville, KY	Campbell & Ecker's
Louisville, KY	Cooper's
Louisville, KY	Cooper (different address)
Louisville, KY	Doerr, H.
Louisville, KY	Elrod, J.C.
Louisville, KY	Elrod, W.M. Excelsior Gallery
Louisville, KY	Excelsior Gallery
Louisville, KY	Hebel, Chas.
Louisville, KY	Heineman & Co.
Louisville, KY	Heineman & Flexner
Louisville, KY	Hoyt's, W.W.
Louisville, KY	Smith & Wybrant
Louisville, KY	Stowe, H.D.
Louisville, KY	Stuber, Daniel
Louisville, KY	Whitelock, W.
Louisville, KY	Van Aken
Mammoth Cave, KY	Waldack, Chas.
Newport, KY	Scherer, Geo. J.
Paducah, KY	Barr, D.P.
Russellville, Ky	Bryan, Wm.
Baton Rouge, LA	Lytle, A.D.
New Orleans, LA	Anderson & Turner
New Orleans, LA	Anderson's
New Orleans, LA	Edwards
New Orleans, LA	Guay, Wm.
New Orleans, LA	Harvey
New Orleans, LA	Leeson, W.H.
New Orleans, LA	Lilienthal, T. (Theo)
New Orleans, LA	McPherson & Oliver
New Orleans, LA	McPherson, W.D.
New Orleans, LA	Mealy, E.W.
New Orleans, LA	Moses & Piffitt
New Orleans, LA	Moses, B.
New Orleans, LA	Moses, Moses & Son
New Orleans, LA	New Orleans Photographic Co. (Turner, A.A.)
New Orleans, LA	Piffet, Eugene A.
New Orleans, LA	Prince, L. I.
New Orleans, LA	Turner & Cohen
New Orleans, LA	Turner, A.A.

Location	Name
New Orleans, LA	Washburn, Will
?MA	Richardson, L.A. "At His Traveling Saloon" MA?
Amesbury, MA	Clarkson & Jones
Amesbury, MA	Currier
Amherst, MA	Lovell, J.L.
Athol Depot, MA	Knox, O.C.
Athol Depot, MA	Smith, D.
Ayer, MA	Putnam, A.H.
Boston, MA	Allen, (E.L.)
Boston, MA	Allen@ No. 6 Temple Plaza
Boston, MA	Barbour. T
Boston, MA	Banister
Boston, MA	Black & Case
Boston, MA	Black, J.W.
Boston, MA	Burnham, T.R.
Boston, MA	Chapman, A.F.
Boston, MA	Chessman & McCosker
Boston, MA	Chute, R.J.
Boston, MA	Clifford & Shapleigh
Boston, MA	Cobb, Cyrus, Jr.
Boston, MA	Collard & Annible
Boston, MA	Davis & Co. Andrews, artist
Boston, MA	Day & Dean
Boston, MA	Foss & Richardson
Boston, MA	Hardy, A.N.
Boston, MA	Hatstate, A. J.
Boston, MA	Hawes, J.J.
Boston, MA	Hazelton, B.C.
Boston, MA	Heard, John A.
Boston, MA	Heywood
Boston, MA	Horton,
Boston, MA	Hussey (William)
Boston, MA	Jones, Evan R.
Boston, MA	King, S. A. (Prof.)
Boston, MA	Kingman, S.
Boston, MA	Lasselle, G.P.
Boston, MA	Lay's, F.L.
Boston, MA	Lincoln
Boston, MA	Loomis, G.H.
Boston, MA	Marshall, A.
Boston, MA	Measury, S.
Boston, MA	Miller & Rowell
Boston, MA	Miller, R.A.
Boston, MA	Richardson & Co.
Boston, MA	Richardson, J.C.
Boston, MA	Rowell, Frank
Boston, MA	Russell, G.D. (publisher)
Boston, MA	Samuels, E.
Boston, MA	Seaver, C.
Boston, MA	Sonrel, A.
Boston, MA	Soule, John P. (also a publisher)
Boston, MA	Southworth Co.
Boston, MA	Stimpson
Boston, MA	Stuart, Mrs.
Boston, MA	Trott, A.
Boston, MA	Turner, J.W.
Boston, MA	Wardwell, Wm. H.
Boston, MA	Whipple
Boston, MA	Wyman & Co.
Bridgewater, MA	Burrell, D.T.

Cambridgeport, MA	Danforth, Charles H.
Cambridgeport, MA	Warren
Charlestown, MA	Bryant
Charlestown, MA	Doane, R.N.
Charlestown, MA	Freeman
Charlestown, MA	Triller & Freeman
Charlestown, MA	Venner, G.W.
Chicopee, MA	Knox & Brazer
Clinton, MA	Boynton, J.J.
East Boston, MA	Hawhes, W.R.
Edgartown, MA	Chute, Chas. H. & Son
Fall River, MA	Crittenden, J.H.
Fall River, MA	Nichols & Warren
Fall River, MA	Warren, Joseph W.
Feltonville, MA	Lewis, R.B.
Fitchburg, MA	Gott, C.O.
Fitchburg, MA	Moulton, J.C.
Fonda, MA	Boozer, R.W.
Foxboro, MA	Plimpton, G.H.
Globe Village, MA	Knapp, H.J.
Gloucester, MA	Elwell, W.A.
Great Barrington, MA	Buell, O.B.
Great Barrington, MA	Clark, E.H.
Greenfield, MA	Cushing. H.
Greenfield, MA	Ely, E.C.
Greenfield, MA	Kingman & Bradford
Greenfield, MA	Taylor, D.B.
Groton Junction, MA	Ross. H.
Haverhill, MA	Anderson, A.W.
Haverhill, MA	Judkins
Haverhill, MA	Lane, W.H.
Haverhill, MA	Robinson, G.C. (& O.B.)
Hingham, MA	Chandler, M.
Holmes Hole, MA	Conant, J.F.
Holyoke, MA	Haskins & Sweetser
Hyannis, MA	Elllis & Stiff
Lawrence, MA	Cook, E.T.
Lawrence, MA	Hall
Lawrence, MA	Judkins, L.D.
Lawrence, MA	Judkins & Rolllins
Lawrence, MA	Potter & Reed
Lawrence, MA	Reed Brothers
Lawrence, MA	Robie & Potter
Lawrence, MA	Yeaw & Lufkin (Yeaw & Co) Yeaw, A./Lufkin, F.M.
Leominster, MA	Allen, W.T.
Leominster, MA	Pierce, C.M.
Lowell, MA	Eaton, A.B.
Lowell, MA	Brigham
Lowell, MA	Gilchrist
Lowell, MA	Gilchrist, Geo.
Lowell, MA	Mitchell, G.E.
Lowell, MA	Sanborn, N.C.
Lowell, MA	Shattuck, S.
Lowell, MA	Simpson, A.J.
Lowell, MA	Towle, S.
Lowell, MA	Washburn
Lowell, MA	Yeaw & Co.
Lynn, MA	Bushby & Hart
Lynn, MA	Whiting & Ellis
Marlboro, MA	Marshall, F.A.

Medford, MA	Wilkinson, O.R.
Middleboro, MA	Stiff Brothers
Middleboro, MA	Cornwall, H.F.
Milford, MA	Willis & Hastings
Milford, MA	Willis, E.L.
Monson, MA	Cross, H.G.
Nantucket, MA	Freeman & Coffin
Natick, MA	Barrett, Henry
New Bedford, MA	Bierstadt Bros.
New Bedford, MA	Cook, C.
New Bedford, MA	Cook & Christian
New Bedford, MA	Cook, C. & S.
New Bedford, MA	Howard, (J.S.) Parisian Photographer
New Bedford, MA	Smith, M.
New Bedford, MA	Howland & Crowell
New Bedford, MA	Ward, Jenney
New Bedford, MA	Knowles & Hillman
New Bedford, MA	Parlow, Geo. F.
Newburyport, MA	Mosely & Meinerth
No. Bridgewater, MA	Howard Bros.
Northampton, MA	Ingraham Bros
Northampton, MA	Murlles, D.
Northampton, MA	O'Neil & Kidder
North Brookfield, MA	Carey, C.H.
North Brookfield, MA	Cary, C.H.
Pittsfield, MA	Dewey, R.H.
Plymouth, MA	Locke, A.H.
Plymouth, MA	Whiting Gallery
Roxbury, MA	Cole's, C.
Roxbury, MA	Ruggles & Matthews
Roxbury, MA	Miller
Salem, MA	Bowdoin, D.W.
Salem, MA	Moulton, J.W.
Salem, MA	Proctor, G.K.
Salem, MA	Perkins, E.R.
Shelburne Falls, MA	Patch, J.K.
South Adams, MA	Hurd, L.F.
South Boston, MA	Gilbert, F.A.
South Brookfield, MA	Townsend, P.P.
South Danvers, MA	Knowlton, W.F.
South Handley, MA	Baldwin, E.A.
South Weymouth, MA	Rogers, Charles E.
Southbridge, MA	Lamb, C.F.
Springfield, MA	Moore Brothers
Springfield, MA	Nelson, L.
Springfield, MA	Spooner's, J.C.
Springfield, MA	Spooner, D.B. & Co.
Springfield, MA	Warren, R.
Stoneham, MA	Barrett, J.W.
Taunton, MA	Child, R.H.
Taunton, MA	Hawes, A.F.
Taunton, MA	King, H.B.
Taunton, MA	Read, P.R.
Waltham, MA	Warren, H.F.
Warren, MA	Brown, J.M.
Webster, MA	Bennett
West Lynn, MA	Whiting, B.
Westboro, MA	Rice, Geo. M.
Westfield, MA	Collins, T.P.
Westfield, MA	Miller & Willard

Weymouth Landing, MA	Cook, L.W.
Williamstown, MA	Earl & Hill
Winchendon, MA	Allen, W. F.
Winchendon, MA	Alger, I.F.
Winchendon, MA	Porter, K.S.
Woburn, MA	Knowlton, F.S.
Woburn, MA	Wyman, S. Webster
Worcester, MA	Adams Gallery Walker, S.L.
Worcester, MA	Beal, H.L.
Worcester, MA	Carter, (Milton T.)
Worcester, MA	Clafin's
Worcester, MA	Collins, I.A. & Adams
Worcester, MA	Critcherson & Leland
Worcester, MA	Daniels, A.F.
Worcester, MA	Reed's, H.J.
Annapolis, MD	Hopkins
Baltimore, MD	Bassford & Co.
Baltimore, MD	Baumgarten & Son
Baltimore, MD	Bendann Bros.
Baltimore, MD	Brackland, Ben
Baltimore, MD	Cowen, Wm & Co.
Baltimore, MD	Culpepper, Daniel W.
Baltimore, MD	Edkins' Gallery
Baltimore, MD	Fischer & Bro.
Baltimore, MD	Hewitt, G.W. & Co.
Baltimore, MD	Hohlweg, V.
Baltimore, MD	Israel & Co.
Baltimore, MD	Leach, William
Baltimore, MD	Moltz, Henry
Baltimore, MD	Perkins, P.L.
Baltimore, MD	Pope's, J.H.
Baltimore, MD	Ridgely's, R.D. (& Co.)
Baltimore, MD	Ridgely's, R.D.
Baltimore, MD	Shorey, W.F.
Baltimore, MD	Stanton & Butler
Baltimore, MD	Taylor, G.W. H.
Baltimore, MD	Van Ness, W.
Baltimore, MD	Walzl, Richard
Baltimore, MD	Whitehurst, Passano
Baltimore, MD	Young, J.H.
Cumberland, MD	Park, H.A.S.
Elkton, MD	Lodore, Ben E.
Emmitsburg, MD	Rowe, Joshua
Federalsburg, MD	Murray, C.
Frederick, MD	Byerly, J. & Son
Frederick, MD	Byerly, J.
Frederick, MD	Marken's, J.R.
Hagerstown, MD	Phreaner, B.W.T.
Hagerstown, MD	Recher, E.M.
Uniontown, MD	Christ, D.E.
Westminster, MD	Grammer, B.
Auburn, ME	Dresser
Augusta, ME	Bender, J.S.
Augusta, ME	Rideout, N.R.
Bangor, ME	Burnham, A.M.
Bangor, ME	Dirigo
Bangor, ME	Hardy, J.R. & F.W.
Bangor, ME	Marston, C.L.
Bangor, ME	Nash, R.C.
Bangor, ME	Sawyer, S.W.

Bath, ME	Butler, George W.
Bath, ME	Stearns, Wm. B. (W.B.)
Biddeford, ME	McKenney, E.H.
Brunswick, ME	Pierce, Wm.
Eastport, ME	Loring
Ellsworth, ME	Peek, J.M.
Farmington, ME	Merrill & Crosby
Farmington, ME	Merrill, G.D.
Lewiston, ME	Crosby, A.B.
Lewiston, ME	Smith, Wingfield
Lewiston, ME	Sprague, A.W.
Lewiston, ME	Sanderson, C.S.
N. Vasselboro, ME	Hinds, B.W.
North Anson, ME	Blunt, Wm. F.
Norway, ME	Crockett, A.B.
Oldtown, ME	Averill, M.L.
Portland, ME	Burnham, J.U.P.
Portland, ME	Lewis, A.C.
Portland, ME	McKenney, A.M.
Portland, ME	Smith, B.F. & Son
Rockland, ME	Crockett, E.
Skowhegan, ME	Gordon, E.G.
Thomaston, ME	Tuttle, G.W.
Waterville, ME	Carleton, C.G.
Weymouth Landing, ME	Cook, L.W.
Yarmouth, ME	Durgan, J.O.
Adrian, MI	Aldrich, A.W.
Adrian, MI	Cathcart, N.H.
Adrian, MI	Morris, J.W.
Albion, MI	Nye, S.S.
Anarbor, MI	Foster, E.C., Miss
Ann Arbor, MI	Gillett, G.C.
Battle Creek, MI	Loring, G.W.
Battle Creek, MI	S.C. Wright
Constantine, MI	Edmiston, J.A.
Detroit, MI	Bowring, Thos. D.
Detroit, MI	Grelling, G.
Detroit, MI	Millis, Millis' Gallery
Detroit, MI	Randall, J.J.
Detroit, MI	Roberts, J.H.
Detroit, MI	St. Alary & Watson
Detroit, MI	Van Deusen & Houghton
Dowagiac, MI	Dunning's, O.B.
Dowagiac, MI	Leckenby, H.
East Saginaw. MI	Eastman & Randall
East Saginaw. MI	Goodridge Brothers
Fentonville, MI	Phipps Bros.
Grand Haven, MI	Cass, Wm.
Grand Rapids, MI	Horton, O.W.
Grand Rapids, MI	Merrill, L.A.
Grand Rapids, MI	Wykes, W.
Hillsdale, MI	Andrew, R.L.
Hillsdale, MI	Clark
Hillsdale, MI	Hummel, J.H.
Hillsdale, MI	Wheeler & Sherman
Hudson, MI	Rowley, Mrs. N.L.
Hudson, MI	Spencer, D.H.
Jackson, MI	Cookingham, J.V.
Jackson, MI	Excell, J.W.
Jackson, MI	Higgins & Terrill

Jonesville, MI	Griffin, A.J.
Kalamazoo, MI	Boughton, E.A.
Kalamazoo, MI	Porter, M.H.
Kalamazoo, MI	Shafer, J.M.
Lansing, MI	Chenney, A.M.
Monroe, MI	Bowlsby, W.H.
Monroe, MI	McClellan, W.
Niles, MI	Faulknor, M.M.
Niles, MI	Westervelt & Conley
New Baltimore, MI	Randall, Wm.
Pontiac, MI	Benson, J.H.
Romeo, MI	Horton, L.E.
Saline, MI	Gillett, Miss
St. Johns, MI	Pruden, P.W.
Sturgis, MI	Hutchinson, L.N.
Tecumseh, MI	Bissel, Mrs. C.R.
Tecumseh, MI	Hoag, A.J.
Three Rivers, MI	Frary, F.L.
Ypsilanti, MI	Baker, E.P. & H.W.
Ypsilanti, MI	Clark, A.J.
Ypsilanti, MI	Ormsby, E.D.
__?__ont, MI	Hallock, D.W.
Red Wing, MN	Fisher, George
Red Wing, MN	Washburn & Bennett
St. Anthony, MN	Upton, B.F.
St. Paul, MN	Carpenter, C.E. & Co., successors to M. Watkins
St. Paul, MN	Falkenshilde, A.
St. Paul, MN	Martin's Photographic Gallery (J.E. Martin)
St. Paul, MN	Whitney & Zimmerman
St. Paul, MN	Whitney's
Winona, MN	Wiggins, S.T.
Canton, MO	Detwiler, A.R. & Co.
Canton, MO	Morton, J.G.
Carondelet, MO	Cramer, G.
Chilicothe, MO	Moberly, L.
Fulton, MO	Manchester, E.T.
Hannibal, MO	Shockley, J.R.
Kansas City, MIO	Christy, A.C.
Macon, MO	Wells, Geo.
Palmyra, MO	Shannon, John
St. Joseph, MO	Ulhmann & Rippel
St. Joseph, MO	Adams, R.F.
St. Louis, MO	Brown, N. & Sons
St. Louis, MO	Brown, William
St. Louis, MO	Brown, Williams & Co.
St. Louis, MO	Butts, A.R.
St. Louis, MO	Fox, A.J.
St. Louis, MO	Gross & Co.
St. Louis, MO	Heald & Stiff
St. Louis, MO	Hoelke & Benecke
St. Louis, MO	Mansfield & Cornwell
St. Louis, MO	Mansfield, E.S.
St. Louis, MO	McConnell, G.H.
St. Louis, MO	Nichols & Bros.
St. Louis, MO	Nichols & Howard
St. Louis, MO	Outley's Photographic Palace of Art
St. Louis, MO	Palmer, Justus W.
St. Louis, MO	Phillips, J.H.
St. Louis, MO	Pittman & Wolfrom (card lists primary studio @ Trenton, TN)
St. Louis, MO	Rino, A.

St. Louis, MO	Rivers & Evans
St. Louis, MO	Rivers Gallery
St. Louis, MO	Saettle, Max
St. Louis, MO	Scholten, J.A.
St. Louis, MO	Wood, A.W.
Corinth, MS	Griswold & White
Jackson, MS	Smith, Charles T. (Washington Gallery)
Vicksburg, MS	Barr & Young
Vicksburg, MS	Barr, D.P.
_____, MS	Taylor & Seavey
Vicksburg, MS	French & Co.
Vicksburg, MS	Joslyn & Smith
Nebraska City, (NB) NT	Smith, A.M.
Nebraska City, NB	Batcheller & Wall
Nebraska City, NB	Bridenstine & Young
Omaha City, NT	Hamilton, J.
Omaha, NY (NB)	Hamilton, J.
Omaha, NB	Adams, L.
New Bern, NC	Smith, O.J.
Raleigh, NC	Watson's, J.W.
Wilmington, NC	Vanorsdell, C.M.
Andover, NH	Keniston, J.F.
Claremont, NH	Allen, Charles
Claremont, NH	Johnson, J.H.
Concord, NH	Carr, Benjamin
Concord, NH	Hoit, William P.
Concord, NH	Hunt, E.J.
Concord, NH	Kimball & Son(s)
Concord, NH	Morgan, J.
Dover, NH	Brigham
Dover, NH	Drew, A.P.
Dover, NH	Hall & Dean
Dover, NH	Legg, James A.
Dover, NH	Libbey's Photographic Gallery
Dover, NH	Sanderson, C.S.
Exeter, NH	Davis Brothers
Fisherville, NH	Currier, Herman J.
Franconia Notch, NH	Fifield, H.S.
Franklin, NH	Poor, B.N.
Great Falls, NH	Bracy, W.L.
Great Falls, NH	Foster, J.R.
Hanover, NH	Bly, H.O.
Haverhill, NH	Morrison, Frank M. & Co,
Keene, NH	Allen's Co.
Keene, NH	Dustin, S.C.
Keene, NH	French & Sawyer
Laconia, NH	Ladd & Co.
Laconia, NH	Wilder, W.L.
Lancaster, NH	White, F.
Lebanon, NH	Billings & Hough
Littleton, NH	Kilburn, E.
Manchester, NH	Bean
Manchester, NH	Farrar, E. Y.
Manchester, NH	Furnald, D.O.
Manchester, NH	Kimball, A.W.
Manchester, NH	Piper, S.
Manchester, NH	Simons, D.A.
Manchester, NH	Wilson, O.P.
Milford, NH	Masseck, J.S.
Milford, NH	Wires

Nashua, NH	Andrews & Lawrence
Nashua, NH	Andrews, Charles O.
Nashua, NH	Hamilton, S.C.
Nashua, NH	Jewell, J. B(yron).
Nashua, NH	Johnson, E.W.
Nashua, NH	Miles & Co. (Mammoth Saloon)
Nashua, NH	Miles, A.O.
Nashua, NH	Perry, J.M.
Newport, NH	Baston, O.P.
Newport, NH	Billings & Hough
Newport, NH	Rowell, C.C.
Peterboro, NH	Scripture, G.H.
Pittsfield, NH	Nutter, J.P.
Pittsfield, NH	Oswood, H.W.
Portsmouth, NH	Davis Brothers
Portsmouth, NH	Meinerth, Carl
Salmon Falls, NH	Brookings, G.W.
Sanbornton Bridge, NH	Allen, Jesse L.
Walpole, NH	Ball, H.
Warren, NH	Clough, A.F.
Winchester, NH	Algere, I.F.
?, NJ	Haines, E.C. Travelling Gallery
Belvidere, NJ	Teel's, S.S.
Bridgeton, NJ	Edwards & Ogden
Bridgeton, NJ	Edwards, Charles E.
Burlington, NJ	Torr & Jeffries
Camden, NJ	Hinkley, A.S.
Camden, NJ	Sims, Andrews
Clinton, NJ	Terabery, E.
Elizabeth, NJ	Price, Frank H.
Flemington, NJ	Sherwood, W.K.
Freehold, NJ	Roth, John
Frenchtown, NJ	Rockafellow, B.T.
Glouchestere City, NJ	Hepburn
Hackensack, NJ	Terhune, J.D.
Hackettstown, NJ	Owen, I.G.
Hightstown, NJ	Priest, R.R.
Jersey City, NJ	Green's, J.T.
Jersey City, NJ	Gubelman, T.
Jersey City, NJ	Hinkley, A.S.
Jersey City, NJ	Piard, Victor
Lambertville, NJ	Reeve, J.C.
Long Branch, NJ	Lane, C.
Millville, NJ	Hartman, John
Mount Holly, NJ	Colton
Morristown, NJ	Alexander & Stevens
New Brunswick, NJ	Boggs, R.M.
New Brunswick, NJ	Clark, D.
Newark, NJ	Bedford, Geo. O.
Newark, NJ	Benjamin, O.C.
Newark, NJ	Decamp & Crane
Newark, NJ	Decamp, G.W.
Newark, NJ	Douglas, A.H.
Newark, NJ	Hurlburt
Newark, NJ	Kirk, J.
Newark, NJ	Newton Gallery
Newark, NJ	Park
Newark, NJ	Park Gallery, Bedford, Geo., artist
Newark, NJ	Stoutenburgh & Rolf
Newark, NJ	Stoutenburgh & Rose

Newark, NJ	Woods, H.T.
Newton, NJ	Edwards, L. (E.) & Son(s)
Newton, NJ	Owen, I.G.
Patterson, NJ	Doremus
Patterson, NJ	Jenks, J.B.
Rahway, NJ	LaForge, John E.
Red Bank, NJ	Sherwood, W.K.
Salem, NJ	Garrett's, C.A.
Salem, NJ	McCall, G.H.
Salem, NJ	Simkins, J.H.
Somerville, NJ	Alt, John
Trenton, NJ	Brown
Trenton, NJ	Cheeseman, L.B.
Trenton, NJ	Good, J.
Trenton, NJ	Moses
Washington, NJ	Brotzman, Wm. L.
Woodstown, NJ	Crouse, Charles E.
Austin, NV	Krause
Virginia (City), NV NT	Sutterley Bros.
?, NY	Stacy
Adams, Jefferson Co., NY	Armsbury, Stiles, P.
Albany, NY	Abbott, J.H.
Albany, NY	Abbott, J.H. & J.L.
Albany, NY	Churchill & Denison
Albany, NY	Churchill, H.W. (Bonton Gallery)
Albany, NY	Haines & Wickes
Albany, NY	Harter
Albany, NY	Huested, E.
Albany, NY	Thompson Gal. Jeffers, T.C.
Albany, NY	Wood & Brother
Albany, NY	Woodworth, D.
Albion, NY	Hopkins, Geo. P.
Antwerp, NY	Hayne & Fairbank
Antwerp, NY	Stone, N.L.
Auburn, NY	Bartholomew, C.G., also Martholomew
Auburn, NY	Fowler Upham, S.L.
Auburn, NY	Gibbs, Geo. E.
Auburn, NY	Harters' Fine Art Gallery
Auburn, NY	Morris, S. Hall Union Picture Gallery
Auburn, NY	Upham, L.S.
Auburn, NY	Wilber, A.D.
Baldwinsville, NY	Whitney's, C.H. Gallery
Ballston (Spa), NY	Bronk, L.R.
Batavia, NY	Buckley, C.L. (C.C.)
Batavia, NY	Eales & Longmier
Batavia, NY	Knight & Eales
Batavia, NY	Knight, Q.P.
Batavia, NY	Philo, T.L.
Bath, NY	Rutherford, T.R.
Bath, NY	Vickery, J.D.
Binghampton, NY	Hickcox, A.
Binghampton, NY	Murphy, E. & Bro.
Binghampton, NY	Pierce, Z.B.
Binghampton, NY	Webster & Battery
Binghampton, NY	Webster, C.W.
Binghampton, NY	Webster, C.H.
Binghampton, NY	Woodbridge, E.S.
Boonville, NY	Jenks, N.
Brookfield, NY	Quivey, M.S.
Brooklyn, NY	Douglas, E.M.

Brooklyn, NY	Gross & Becher
Brooklyn, NY	Gurney, J. & Son
Brooklyn, NY	Howard & Marsh
Brooklyn, NY	Jackson, Andrew
Brooklyn, NY	James, W.E.
Brooklyn, NY	Mead
Brooklyn, NY	Morand, Augustus
Brooklyn, NY	Sherman, S. J.
Brooklyn, NY	Shipman, John S.
Brooklyn, NY	Stevenson
Brooklyn, NY	Spitzer, S.
Brooklyn, NY	Troxell, W.L.
Brooklyn, NY	Van Doorn
Brooklyn, NY	Wasson, W.R.
Brooklyn, NY	Williamson's, C.H.
Brooklyn, E.D., NY	Mead
Brooklyn, E.D., NY	Stevenson's Photograph Gallery
Buffalo, NY	Bliss, H.L.
Buffalo, NY	Beyer's
Buffalo, NY	Clive, R.H.
Buffalo, NY	Douglass & Co.
Buffalo, NY	Knight, W.M.
Buffalo, NY	Lothrop
Buffalo, NY	Powelson, B.F.
Buffalo, NY	Upson & Simson
Butternuts, NY	Smith, W. (Randolph)
Cambridge, NY	Wells, H.M.
Camden, NY	Babcock & Van Valkenburgh
Camden, NY	Copeland
Camden, NY	Hinckley & Wood
Camden, NY	Sears, Mrs. D.
Canandaigua, NY	Finley & Sons
Canandaigua, NY	Marsh, C.M.
Carthage, NY	Porter & Rulison
Carthage, NY	Rulison, C.M.
Catskill, NY	Walden, William B.
Cazanovia, NY	Weld, E.G. & Son
Chitteango, NY	Palmer
Cincinnatus, NY	French, F.
Clayton, Jefferson Co., NY	Johnson, O.T. & Bro.
Clayton, Jefferson Co., NY	Johnson, O.T.
Cooperstown, NY	Bolles', L.M. (N.Y. Photograph Gallery)
Cooperstown, NY	Delong & Robie
Cooperstown, NY	Delongs, J.L.
Cooperstown, NY	Smith, W.G. New Photograph Gallery
Copenhagen, NY	Parsons, G.D.
Corning, NY	Sagar, J.
Cortland, NY	Edwards, T.
Cortland, NY	Lyon, J.E.
Cortland, NY	Lynde, M.T.
Cortland, NY	Newton, A.G.
Cuba, NY	Otis, C.
Cuba, NY	Page, W.F.
Cuba, NY	Tomlinson & King
Cuba, NY	Tomlinson, Charles
Dan(s)ville, NY	Betts & Prusia's
Delhi, NY	Gilbert, B.F.
Delhi, NY	Van Kleek
Dundee, NY	Hooker, F. Smith
Dunkirk, NY	Monroe, O.

East Randolph, NY	White, J.M.
Ellenville, NY	Tice, A. Wurtz or Wurts
Elmira, NY	Hart, A.P.
Elmira, NY	Knowlton, W. (Chase, W.P.)
Elmira, NY	Larkin, J.E.
Elmira, NY	Moulton & Larkin
Elmira, NY	Moulton, W.J.
Elmira, NY	Whitley, J.H. & Co.
Elmira, NY	Whitley, J.W. & Co.
Flushing, L.I., NY	Roe, Silvester
Friendship, NY	Parish, Julius
Ft. Edwards, NY	Nims, Wm.
Fulton, NY	Skinner, H.
Geneva, NY	Vail, J.G.
Glen Falls, NY	Carpenter, J.H.
Glen Falls, NY	Crandell & Conkey
Glen Falls, NY	Hathaway
Gloversville, NY	Scidmore & Brother
Goshen, NY	Edsall, Frank
Gouverneur, NY	Rhodes, A.S.
Gowanda, NY	Starr, J.S.
Gowanda, NY	Stiles, A.J.
Greene, NY	Baker, G.W.
Greene, NY	Wood, F.D.
Greenwich Station, NY	Tait, W.J.
Groton, NY	Adam's Bros.
Hamilton, NY	Abbott, S.C.
Havana, NY	Freeman, R.B.
Homer, NY	Barker, L.E.
Hornellsville, NY	Newman, W.L.
Hornellsville, NY	Sutton & Newman
Horse Head, NY	House, J.W.
Hudson, NY	Becker, C.
Hudson, NY	Forshew, F.
Ilion, NY	Caspares, H.S.
Ilion, NY	Orfendorf, P.
Ithaca, NY	Beardsley Bros.
Ithaca, NY	Beardsley, Young & Schenck
Ithaca, NY	Burritt, J.C.
Ithaca, NY	Granger & Young
Ithaca, NY	Sedgwick & Lewis
Ithaca, NY	Tolles & Seely
Jamestown, NY	Howe's Photograph Rowe Malin, H., Artist
Jamestown, NY	Phillips & Frear
Jordan, NY	Dygert, Geo. H.
Keeseville, NHY	Beach, A.
Keeseville, NHY	Tousley, H.S.
Lansingburgh, NY	Bronk, L.R.
Lansingburgh, NY	Sterry, E.S.
Lenyard, NY	Boughton, E.H.
Lima, NY	Miller & Upton
Little Falls, NY	Goetchius, G.H.
Lockport, NY	Bennett, G.W.
Lockport, NY	Clench, F.B.
Lockport, NY	Craves, Mrs.
Lockport, NY	Gantt's New Sunlight Gallery
Lockport, NY	Graves, Mr. & Mrs.
Lockport, NY	LeClear, J.M.
Lockport, NY	Vickery & Clench
Lockport, NY	Wymen, D.D.

Long Island, Riverhead, NY	Raynor, Edge
Lowville, NY	Van Aken, (E.M.)
Lyons, NY	Ravell, C.H.
Lyons, NY	Tuttle, C.M.
Madison, NY	Wales, H.P.
Malone, NY	Fay & Barney's
McGrawville, NY	Holden, G.L.
Marion, NY	Parks', D.N.
Mexico, NY	Muth, J.
Mexico, NY	Severance, H.W.
Middletown, NY	Baird & Jessup
Middletown, NY	Huyler, J.J.
Moravia, NY	Alley, E.H.
Moravia, NY	Brown, R.
Mount Morris, NY	Sutphen, D.
New Berlin, NY	Smyth, W.J.
New York, NY	Aitken, J.F.
New York, NY	Anson's
New York, NY	Anthony, E. & H.T.
New York, NY	Baab, Peter
New York, NY	Balch, E.
New York, NY	Barcalow, R.
New York, NY	Barnum's Museum
New York, NY	Barnum
New York, NY	Beniczky, H.W.
New York, NY	Bills, Charles K.
New York, NY	Bogardus
New York, NY	Brady, Mathew
New York, NY	Brill, Julius
New York, NY	Brinkerhoff
New York, NY	Burrough, A.M.
New York, NY	Clarke
New York, NY	Dessaur, Fernando
New York, NY	Duchochois & Klauser
New York, NY	Duchochois
New York, NY	Faris, T.
New York, NY	Frederick(s, C.D.) & Co.
New York, NY	Fredericks & Co., O'neal Jr.
New York, NY	Gardner, J.B.
New York, NY	Gibbon, H.E.
New York, NY	Gibbon, H.E. & Co.
New York, NY	Glosser, H.
New York, NY	Goodrich, M.P. & Hough…
New York, NY	Gray, T.A.
New York, NY	Greer, Henry
New York, NY	Grotecloss, William G.
New York, NY	Gurney, J. & Son
New York, NY	Hallett, S..J. (Hallett & B…..)
New York, NY	Hamilton
New York, NY	C.H. Heimburgh's
New York, NY	Herron, Jos. M.
New York, NY	Hope
New York, NY	Hopper, A.D.
New York, NY	Hopper, L. Banta, artist
New York, NY	Howland, B.F.
New York, NY	Johnson, Williams & Co.
New York, NY	Jordan & Co. Late of Bogardus
New York, NY	Keller, J.
New York, NY	Klauser, Wm.
New York, NY	L.S. & P.

New York, NY	Lape, G.T.
New York, NY	Lewis, R.A.
New York, NY	Lord, R.A.
New York, NY (Bowery)	Loud, G.W.
New York, NY	Martin, Thomas H.
New York, NY	Mason
New York, NY	Mayer, J.S.
New York, NY	Miller, M.
New York, NY	N.Y. Photographic Co., The
New York, NY	Ormsbee, M.
New York, NY	Pasquet, A. & Co.
New York, NY	Paxton, Chas.
New York, NY	Pendleton, W.S.
New York, NY	Roche, Thos. C.
New York, NY	Rockwood, (Geo. C.) & Co.
New York, NY	Roger's, H.M.
New York, NY	Schuberth, J & Co.
New York, NY	Semsey, C.
New York, NY	Stacy, G. (George)
New York, NY	Stadtfeld
New York, NY	W.J. Tait
New York, NY	Taylor, J.
New York, NY	Thwaites & Co.
New York, NY	Wagner, F.W. & Co.
New York, NY	Warner, Jas. L. or L S & P Co.
New York, NY	Whitney & Paradise
New York, NY	Williams, J.H., Jr. Pub.
New York, NY	Winslow & Slocum, also @ Ft. Shuyler, David's Island, Willetts Point .
New York, NY	Wood, Sidney A.
Newark, NY	Hurlburt
Newark, NY	Tooker, T.D.
Newburgh, NY	Lawrence
Newburgh, NY	Le Roy's Gem Gallery
Newburgh, NY	Palmer, C.A.
Newburgh, NY	Pope (Bros.)
Newburgh, NY	Pope
Newburgh, NY	Remillard
Newburgh, NY	Whiddit, W.W.
Niagra Falls, NY	Barnum, David
Niagra Falls, NY	Mason, Samuel
Norwich, NY	Brown, H.C.
Norwich, NY	Chamberlain
Nyack on the Hudson, NY	Nesbit, Wm. B.
Ogdensburg, NY	Dow, Jas. M.
Olean, NY	Cranston, W.H.
Olean, NY	Miner & Allen
Oneida, NY	Hall, E.
Oneida, NY	Hollenbeck, O.A.
Oneida, NY	Hollenbeck, M.A.
Oswego, NY	Austen, J.
Oswego, NY	Austen, S.
Oswego, NY	Lazier
Oswego, NY	Rundell, R.R.
Owego (as printed), NY	Coburn & Co.
Ovid, NY	Everett, W.
Oxford, NY	Farnham & Hull
Oxford, NY	Farnham, S.H.
Palmyra, NY	Elton, Mrs. E & Gue, Mrs. E.
Palmyra, NY	Vail, J.P.
Penn Yan, NY	Crum, W.C.

Penn Yan, NY	Francis, L.G.
Penn Yan, NY	Mills, Dr. (J.C.)
Penn Yan, NY	Mills, H.F.
Penn Yan, NY	Mills & Son
Perry, NY	Crocker, M.N.
Perry, NY	Thayer, J.H.
Pheonix, NY	Sparrow, W.E.
Plattsburgh, NY	Averill, H.K., Jr.
Plattsburgh, NY	Howard & Co.
Plattsburgh, NY	Rees, M.A.
Poland, NY	Franklin, O.
Port Jervis, NY	Masterson's (E.P.)
Potsdam, NY	Van Alstine
Potsdam, NY	Wagner, J.K.
Poughkeepsie, NY	Biddle, J.E.
Poughkeepsie, NY	Gullmann, C.
Poughkeepsie, NY	Slee Bros.
Poughkeepsie, NY	Southworth, H.B.
Poughkeepsie, NY	Townsend & Broas
Pulaski, NY	Grout, D.W.
Rhinebeck, NY	Myers, John S.
Rhinebeck, NY	Woodbridge
Richfield Springs, NY	Getman & Bowdish
River Head, L.I., NY	Raynor, Edgar
Rochester, NY	Dunshee Bros., Greig & Co., also Powelson
Rochester, NY	Dunshee, E.S.
Rochester, NY	Fox, J. Marsden & Gates, Menzo E.
Rochester, NY	Hartman & Taylor
Rochester, NY	Kempe
Rochester, NY	Kempe & Gates
Rochester, NY	Maser, J.W. Monroe, M.H.
Rochester, NY	Masterson & Wood's
Rochester, NY	Monroe & Bert....
Rochester, NY	Powelson
Rochester, NY	Rice, D.E.
Rochester, NY	Roberts, J.B.
Rochester, NY	Squiers, G.W.
Rochester, NY	Taylor & Bacon
Rome, NY	Hovey, J.S.
Rome, NY	Moulton & Dopp
Rome, NY	Oliver, H.W.
Rondout, NY	Decker, G.M.
Rushville, NY	Beers, A.E.
Saratoga Springs, NY	Alden, A.
Saratoga Springs, NY	McKernon, P.H.
Saratoga Springs, NY	Peirce, D.S.
Saratoga Springs, NY	Thomalen, E.A.
Saugerties, NY	Jernegan's
Schenectady, NY	Taber, C.A.M.
Seneca Falls, NY	Boardman's, B.D.
Seneca Falls, NY	Rutherford & Boardman
Sherburne, NY	Parker, H.R.
Silver Creek, NY	Wells, A.F.
Sinclearsville, NY	Young, Charles
Sing Sing, NY	Havens, O. Pierre
Sing Sing, NY	Sherwood's Photograph Rooms
Sodus, NY	Almy & Tufts
Syracuse, NY	Abbott, R. R. In Mrs. Gloves Studio
Syracuse, NY	Bonta & Curtiss Howland, B.F.
Syracuse, NY	Collins, E.M.

Syracuse, NY	Glover, Mrs.
Syracuse, NY	Howland, B.F. (& Co.)
Syracuse, NY	Knapp, Geo. K. (& Co.)
Syracuse, NY	Lazier
Syracuse, NY	Winter
Syracuse, NY	Wood, G.J.
Tompkinsville, S.I., NY	Loeffler's, J. Photographic Gallery
Trenton Falls, NY	Moore, J.R. (John R.)
Troy, NY	Alden, A.E.
Troy, NY	Cobden, A.
Troy, NY	Schoonmaker
Union Springs, NY	Tuthill
Utica, NY	Baker, W.J.
Utica, NY	Mundy & Williams
Utica, NY	North, W.C.
Utica, NY	Pilkins & Hall
Utica, NY	Rounds, S.S.
Utica, NY	Smith, F.B.(Smith's Gallery of Art: Cancel)
Wappingers Falls, NY	McGregor, P.
Warrenburg, NY	Fuller, James
Waterford, NY	Tarbell, W.H.
Waterford, NY	Sterry, E.S.
Watertown, NY	Hart's Gallery, Poor & Leady
Watertown, NY	Hart's
Watertown, NY	Hose's Art Gallery (Washington Hall)
Waterville, NY	Nolan, J.H.
Watkins, NY	Crum & Sharp
Watkins, NY	Crum, R.D.
Watkins, NY	Gates Bros.
Wellsville, NY	Orvis, D.H.
Waverly, NY	Mead, M.
White Corners, NY	Schwent, M.
White Corners, NY	Young, William
White Plains, NY	Greer & Maynard
White Plains, NY	Maynard, W.P.
Whitehall, NY	La Barre, I.D.
Williamsburgh, NY	Biffar Photographic Gallery
Williamsburgh, L.I., NY	Moseley, Charles H.
Williamsburgh, L.I., NY	Richardson
Williamson, NY	Almy & Tufts
Wolcott, NY	Ravell, C.H.
Akron, OH	Battels, B.F.
Akron, OH	Gilbert Bros.
Akron, OH	Manley, G.W.
Alliance, OH	Crew's, E.
Alliance, OH	Excelsior Gallery
Ashtabula, OH	Harvey & Blakeslee
Athens, OH	Ball's Gallery
Athens, OH	Coffee, D.G.
Bellefontaine, OH	Rudy & Bros.
Bucyrus, OH	Dougherty, J.
Canal Dover, OH	Robb's Gallery
Canton, OH	Smith, Edwin
Carrollton, OH	Gould, A.R.
Chagrin Falls, OH	Shaw, Thos.
Chillicothe, OH	Simonds, (F.A.)
Cincinnati, OH	Ball's, J.P.
Cincinnati, OH	Bankes, T.W. Sp. Var. Banks
Cincinnati, OH	Blondin, Charles L.
Cincinnati, OH	Closs, J.

Cincinnati, OH	Dewey's
Cincinnati, OH	Doan, J.S.
Cincinnati, OH	Gulick
Cincinnati, OH	Hoag & Quick's
Cincinnati, OH	Howland
Cincinnati, OH	Keenan
Cincinnati, OH	Landy
Cincinnati, OH	M'card or M'cord, D.A.
Cincinnati, OH	Reinhold, J.H.
Cincinnati, OH	Schoenberg, A.
Cincinnati, OH	Stein, J.V.
Cincinnati, OH	Sweet, C.
Cincinnati, OH	Sweet & Morgan
Cincinnati, OH	Tilse, C.C.
Cincinnati, OH	Van Loo, Leon
Cincinnati, OH	Walton & Adams
Cincinnati, OH	Walter & Heuck
Cincinnati, OH	Watson, J.
Cincinnati, OH	Winder, J.W. (& Co.) National Art Palace
Cincinnati, OH	Ball & Thomas
Cincinnati, OH	Cowan's
Circleville, OH	Buchwalter, C.
Circleville, OH	Haddock, Wm.
Circleville, OH	Haddock & Collier
Circleville, OH	Marshall, M.K.
Circleville, OH	Spencer
Circleville, OH	Thomas, A.W.
Cleveland, OH	Beckwith, M.E.
Cleveland, OH	Decker
Cleveland, OH	Folijambe Bros.
Cleveland, OH	Greene
Cleveland, OH	Lewis, M.L.
Cleveland, OH	Nock, E.B.
Cleveland, OH	Payan Bros.
Cleveland, OH	Ryder, J.F.
Clyde, OH	Benham, L.W.
Columbus, OH	Baldwin, A.S.
Columbus, OH	Baldwin & Stephens
Columbus, OH	Davis & Baker
Columbus, OH	Davis, G.W.
Columbus, OH	Elliott & Heyl
Columbus, OH	Nason's
Columbus, OH	Reeve & Watts
Columbus, OH	Reeve, Charles E. & Co.
Columbus, OH	Smith, A.F. & Co.
Columbus, OH	Walker's, E.S.
Columbus, OH	Warner, (&) Elliott
Columbus, OH	Witt, M.
Conneaut, OH	Hawk, W.W,
Conneaut, OH	Willcox, S.L.
Coshocton, OH	McDonald, G.A.
Crestline, OH	Nason
Dayton, OH	Boehme, E.H.
Dayton, OH	Cridland's
Dayton, OH	Cross
Dayton, OH	Gross, James B.
Dayton, OH	Seebohm, Louis
Dayton, OH	Young, W.K.
Dayton, OH	Yount's, A.
Delaware, OH	Beach, T.A., Couch…..

Location	Name
Delaware, OH	Goodridge, G. & Co.
Eaton, OH	Rhea, Johnb
Elyria, OH	Potter, J.C.
Findlay, OH	Findlay Photograph Rooms Twining & Zay
Findlay, OH	Zay, F.B.
Fostoria, OH	Curtis, F.B.
Fredricktown, OH	Crowell, Fred S.
Fredricktown, OH	Weider, J.S.
Fremont, OH	Wiles, A.D.
Gambier, OH	Payne, H.H.
Geneva, OH	Thorp, Miss R.M.
Granville, OH	Melone, T.L.
Greenfield, OH	Morrow, J.P.
Greenville, OH	Harper & Brother
Greenville, OH	Horton & ….
Hamilton, OH	Jones, Alonzo
Hamilton, OH	Rogers, Ed. B.
Hamilton, OH	Stephenson & Williams
Hamilton, OH	Stevenson & Wilson
Hamilton, OH	Wilson, H.R.
Harveysburg, OH	Thornton, E.C.
Hillsboro, OH	Roan, Wm. M.
Hudson, OH	Markille, J.
Jackson Courthouse, OH	Reasoner, Milton
Kelloggsville, OH	Hawkins, Chas. S.
Kenton, OH	Deck, P.W.
Lancaster, OH	Fellers, A.L.
Lima, OH	Denison, Mrs. S.A.
Lima, OH	Krebs, A.R.
Logan, OH	Oaks, W.M.
London, OH	Nason
London, OH	Witt, M.
Mansfield, OH	Christmas' New Photograph Gallery
Mansfield, OH	Ruth
Mansfield, OH	Ruth & O'Keson
Mansfield, OH	Whissemore, A.
Marietta, OH	Bennett, W.P.
Marietta, OH	Cadwallader & Tappen
Marietta, OH	Kelly, Henry
Marietta, OH	Marshall & Pearce
Marietta, OH	Racer, G.C.
McArthur, OH	Billinghurst, C.J.
McConnelsville, OH	Tresize, Wm. C.
Marion, OH	Prentice, T.B.
Massillon, OH	Wertzbaugmer, John G.
Massillon, OH	Fletcher, Mrs. A.
Medina, OH	Snell, M.V.
Middletown, OH	McKecknie, Will E.
Minerva, OH	Conrad, I.N.
Minerva, OH	Hostettler, E.P.
Monroeville, OH	Hoyt, E.C.
Mt. Vernon, OH	Payne
Mt. Vernon, OH	Maxwell
Navarre, OH	Grossclaus & Ricksecker
Newark, OH	Hempstead, C.
Newark, OH	Loveridge, J.
Newark, OH	…, Mrs. J.N.
Newark, OH	Sayre & Chase
Norwalk, OH	Benham
Norwalk, OH	Heath, D.L.

Norwalk, OH	Sackett, L.N.
Oberlin, OH	Alden
Oberlin, OH	Platt, A.C.
Olive Green, OH	Wiley, W.W.
Oxford, OH	Toler, J.C.
Painesville, OH	Clapsadel, F.
Painesville, OH	Marsh, B.F.
Painesville, OH	Quayle Bros.
Painesville, OH	Stinson & Co.
Piqua, OH	Gale, C.A.
Piqua, OH	McNair & Denman
Plymouth, OH	Smith, W.A.
Portsmouth, OH	Janney, L.
Ravenna, OH	Ford, Frank
Ravenna, OH	Stein's Photographic Studio
Ravenna, OH	Stein Bros.
Republic, OH	Bromley, Will V.
Ripley, OH	Adams & Smitson
Salem, OH	Stewart, O.
Sandusky, OH	Frisbie, J.M.
Sandusky, OH	Rhen & Co.
Sandusky, OH	Stelzer, W. & Co.
Sandusky, OH	Weeks & Hodgman
Sandusky, OH	Weeks, R.E.
Shelby, OH	Madden, Mrs. M.
Sidney, OH	McCabe
Springfield, OH	Blackwell, J.G.
Springfield, OH	Capron, Chas. P.
Springfield, OH	Coss, J.
Springfield, OH	Floyd & Co.
Springfield, OH	Floyd & Staley
Springfield, OH	Leffell, Col. Jos.
Steubenville, OH	Elliott & Filson
Steubenville, OH	Weiser, G.W.
Tiffin, OH	Adams, James
Tiffin, OH	Cunningham & Dickens
Tiffin, OH	Dickens, S.
Tiffin, OH	Pennington & Fay
Tiffin, OH	Startsman, T.H.
Tiffin, OH	Tunison & Son
Toledo, OH	Cadwallader, John
Toledo, OH	Fields, Geo.
Troy, OH	Miller, A.C.
Twinsburch, OH	Fessenden, J.W.
Uhrichsville, OH	Golden & Mayer
Upper Sandusky, OH	Merrell, A. & A.D.
Urbana, OH	Collins, G.W.
Urbana, OH	Euans & Brother (probably Evans & Brother)
Van Wert, OH	Hartstock, I.S.
Warren, OH	Brooks & Potter
Warren, OH	LeRoy, F.L.
Warren, OH	Rice, L.M.
Warren, OH	Taylor, C.C.
Washington Courthouse, OH	Willett's Gallery
Washington Courthouse, OH	Willett, W.F.
Warsaw, OH	Dunkleberg & Haley
Warsaw, OH	Rodkey & Blackman
Warsaw, OH	Dunkleburg & Haley Angelo Gallery
Waverly, OH	Safford Gallery
Wellington, OH	Mason, C.E.

Wellsville, OH	Lawrence, Mrs.
West Richfield, OH	Carpenter, C.C.
Wilmington, OH	Whitney, B.T
Wilmington, OH	Wolfe, J.G.
Wooster, OH	Baltzly, B.F.
Wooster, OH	Firestone & Correll
Wooster, OH	Greenwald, J.P.
Wooster, OH	Plumer & Krauss
Wooster, OH	Teeple Bros.
Xenia, OH	Jacoby, W.H.
Youngstown, OH	Heasley, Harry
Youngstown, OH	Shafer, A.
Zanesville, OH	Baird's Gallery
Zanesville, OH	Starke & Barton
Zanesville, OH	Tresize, J.Q.A.
Eugene City, OR	Winter, A.
Jacksonville, OR	Britt, P.
Portland, OR	Buchtel & Cardwell
Portland, OR	Dalton, F.
Allegheny City, PA	Dabbs, B.L.H.
Allegheny, PA	Gano
Allentown, PA	Burlow, S.W.
Allentown, PA	Burcaw, S.W.
Allentown, PA	Groves, W.H.S.
Allentown, PA	Heimbach, F.
Allentown, PA	Hembach's, F.
Allentown, PA	Howard, S.B.
Allentown, PA	Banjamin Lochman
Allentown, PA	Sweitzer, B.K. (B.H.?)
Altoona, PA	Bonine, Elias A.
Annville, PA	Smith, C. (Cornelius)
Ashland, PA	Howard, S.B.
Ashland, PA	Slotterback, G.W.
Bellefonte, PA	Moore & Cryder
Bedford, PA	Gettys, T.R.
Belleville, PA	Segar, Wm.
Bethlelem, PA	Kleckner, M.A.
Bethlelem, PA	Osborne, H.P.
Bloomsburg, PA	Brandau, Geo. C.
Bloomsburg, PA	Hempstead & Leonard
Bloomsburg, PA	Hempstead
Boyertown, PA	Schuler, E.M. (Edwin)
Bristol, PA	Bostwick, J.H.
Brownsville, PA	Hunt & Rogers
Brownsville, PA	Rogers, J. H.
Butler, PA	Huselton, B.C.
Carlisle, PA	Grove, H.H. & Son
Carlisle, PA	Lesher, J.C.
Carlisle, PA	McMillen, J.
Carlisle, PA	Smith, Mrs. R.A.
Catasauqua, PA	Kline, T. J.
Chambersburg, PA	Bishop's, H.
Chambersburg, PA	Soule
Chambersburg, PA	Thompson, John A.
Chambersburg, PA	Zimmerman & Hassler
Chester, PA	Edwards, J.W.
Columbia, PA	Hicks', J.R. Art Gallery state uncertain
Columbia, PA	Hyers, Geo. A.
Columbia, PA	Little, R.J.M.
Columbia, PA	Williams, L.W.

Conneautville, PA	Harris & Roddy
Connellsville, PA	Smith & Armstrong
Dillsburg, PA	Lager, J.W.
Dillsburg, PA	Loyer, J.W.
Dunshore, PA	Musselman ...
Durlach, PA	Pannabecker, J.H.
Easton, PA	Brown
Easton, PA	Carey, J.J.
Easton, PA	Knecht, R.
Easton, PA	Skiles & Hoffmeier
Easton, PA	Tyler
Edendoro, PA	Johnson, L.D.
Elizabethtown, PA	Erskine, J. ....
Erie, PA	Dolph Bros.
Erie, PA	Johnson, N.G.
Erie, PA	Pratt
Fleetwood, PA	Hertzog, W.H.
Frankford, PA	Schofield, John
Germantown (Phil.), PA	Hinkle, D.
Gettysburg, PA	Mumper, Levi
Gettysburg, PA	Tyson Bros.
Gettysburg, PA	Tyson, Issac G.
Gibson, PA	Sweet, A.C. & Co.
Greencastle, PA	Dome, S.
Greencastle, PA	Hurlburt & Henne
Greencastle, PA	Jones, Ira. D.
Hanover, PA	Sheaffer, S.B.
Harrisburg, PA	Burnite & Weldon
Harrisburg, PA	Burnit, D.C. (& Co.)
Harrisburg, PA	Clark, Fred
Harrisburg, PA	Ewing & Painter
Harrisburg, PA	Henderson, R.S.
Harrisburg, PA	Jameson, Chas.
Harrisburg, PA	Keet & Gemmill
Harrisburg, PA	Lemer, Le Rue
Hazleton, PA	Smith, W. W.
Hollidaysburgh, PA	Bonine, R.A.
Honesdale, PA	Foedisch, Charles
Honesdale, PA	Stearns & Rhodes
Honesdale, PA	Stearns, E.I.
Hummelstown, PA	Bare, M.E.
Huntington, PA	Birnbaum, A.
Indiana, PA	Lowry & Donnell
Indiana, PA	McIntire & Tiffany
Indiana, PA	Tiffany, B.B.
Johnstown, PA	Green, Wesley
Johnstown, PA	Statler, Geo.
Kittanning, PA	Ames, N.F.
Lancaster, PA	Cummings, Thomas
Lancaster, PA	Dellinger
Lancaster, PA	Eberman, Charles W.
Lancaster, PA	Gill's
Lancaster, PA	Harmany & Eberman
Lancaster, PA	Jamison & Benson
Lancaster, PA	Rupley, J.B.
Lancaster, PA	Stehman, J.
Latrobe, PA	Shadle, A.
Lebanon, PA	Daily Excelsior Gallery
Lebanon, PA	Fowler, E.B.
Lebanon, PA	Smith, J., Sr.

Lebanon, PA	Spengler, J.A.
Lewisburg, PA	Burkholder, C.C.
Lewisburg, PA	Houghton, J.M.
Lewisburg, PA	McEwen's, W.T. & J.S. Excelsior Photograph Car
Lewisburg, PA	Nice, Jno. F. (John F.)
Linglestown, PA	August, Daniel
Lock Haven, PA	Hopkins, J.B.
Lock Haven, PA	Sloan, J.D.
Manheim, PA	Ensminger, S.A.
Mauch Chunk, PA	Brown, J.
Mauch Chunk, PA	Zellner, Jas.
Meadville, PA	Dunn Bros.
Meadville, PA	Dunn's
Meadville, PA	Harris, H.H.
Mechanicsburg, PA	Bates, J.
Mechanicsburg, PA	Carr, H.G.
Mechanicsburg, PA	Boss, D.W.
Mechanicsburg, PA	Cardon, Thomas B.
Mechanicsburg, PA	Myers, A. G.
Middletown, PA	Matteson, B.W.
Mifflintown, PA	Burkholder, C.C. & Co.
Millersburg, PA	Clark, Fred
Millersburg, PA	Jury, E.
Millersburg, PA	Miller, S.L.
Milton, PA	Halstead, J.
Milton, PA	McMahan
Milton, PA	Wheeland & McMahon
Milton, PA	Wheeland, W.P.
Monogahelia City, PA	Vance, William
Montrose, PA	Cobb, George N.
Montrose, PA	Hazleton & Deans
Montrose, PA	Hazleton, J.B.
Montrose, PA	Lyons
Mount Joy, PA	Stauffer, J.E.
Mount Joy, PA	Waltman
Mount Joy, PA	Stauffer, J.E.
Mount Pleasant, PA	Stauffer, A.N.
Myerstown, PA	Keller, William
Myerstown, PA	Murray, C.J.I.
New Brighton, PA	Noss & Mitchell
New Castle, PA	Hawkins, B.E.L.
New Castle, PA	Phipps, A.W.
New Holland, PA	Mentzer's, J.K.
New Holland, PA	Schlauch, D.S.
New Oxford, PA	Hersh, John J.
Newport, PA	Lukenback's, Wm.S.
Newton, PA	Edwards, L.E. & Son
Norristown, PA.	Bechlar, N.
Norristown, PA.	Fisher's, S.R.
Norristown, PA.	Hipple, E. & W.F.
Norristown, PA.	Lenzi or Linzi, Geo. A.
Norristown, PA.	Saurman & Spang
Norristown, PA.	Stroud, Wm.
Orrstown, PA	Lester, H.C.
Oxford, PA	McCormick (A.)
Pennington, PA	Frederick, (E.R.)
Philadelphia, PA	Albertson & Co.
Philadelphia, PA	Applegate
Philadelphia, PA	Black, J.R.
Philadelphia, PA	Bullock, J.

Philadelphia, PA	Cohil, Charles
Philadelphia, PA	Cohocksink Gallery, Maul & Hallowell, Operators
Philadelphia, PA	Crane, Charles G.
Philadelphia, PA	Cremer & Dillon's
Philadelphia, PA	Cremer, J. & Co.
Philadelphia, PA	DeMorat, A.J.
Philadelphia, PA	Demorat, O.B.
Philadelphia, PA	Downing, John R.
Philadelphia, PA	Draper & Husted
Philadelphia, PA	Evans, C.
Philadelphia, PA	Evers', Theo
Philadelphia, PA	Fly, William M.
Philadelphia, PA	Germon's, W.L.
Philadelphia, PA	Gihon, John L.
Philadelphia, PA	Groom's
Philadelphia, PA	Gutekunst, F.
Philadelphia, PA	Hagaman, M.S.
Philadelphia, PA	Haldt, J.
Philadelphia, PA	Harmon, J.C.
Philadelphia, PA	Hendrickson, A.
Philadelphia, PA	Henszey & Co.
Philadelphia, PA	Hillier's, R.J.
Philadelphia, PA	Hipple, Edward P.
Philadelphia, PA	Horning, L.
Philadelphia, PA	Horning & Brother
Philadelphia, PA	Horning & Fritz
Philadelphia, PA	Hurn, J.W.
Philadelphia, PA	Jones & Bro.
Philadelphia, PA	Keeler, F.S.
Philadelphia, PA	Kelly, (R.N.)
Philadelphia, PA	Keenan, J.A.
Philadelphia, PA	Kientzle (A.)
Philadelphia, PA	Krips, Harrison
Philadelphia, PA	Lachman, Issac S.
Philadelphia, PA	Larkin Gallery
Philadelphia, PA	Laughlin's, J.R.
Philadelphia, PA	Lothrop's Ferrotype Gallery
Philadelphia, PA	Lovejoy, C.L.
Philadelphia, PA	McAllister, William W.
Philadelphia, PA	McAllister & Albee
Philadelphia, PA	McClees, J.E.
Philadelphia, PA	McFarland Gallery
Philadelphia, PA	May, George
Philadelphia, PA	May, L.
Philadelphia, PA	Maul, Hallowell, Cohocksink Gallery
Philadelphia, PA	Monroe, N. M.D.
Philadelphia, PA	Morgan & Brusstar
Philadelphia, PA	Morgan, Edward R.
Philadelphia, PA	Odiorne, Jno. W.
Philadelphia, PA	Pahoads, W.H.
Philadelphia, PA	Penrose
Philadelphia, PA	Phillips, H.C.
Philadelphia, PA	Pirrong, & Son
Philadelphia, PA	Reger, T. M.
Philadelphia, PA	Rehn & Sons
Philadelphia, PA	Reimer, B.F.
Philadelphia, PA	Richardson, R.
Philadelphia, PA	Searby, T.W.
Philadelphia, PA	Simons, M.P.
Philadelphia, PA	Smith, Charles T.

Philadelphia, PA	Spieler, C.H.
Philadelphia, PA	Steinman & Richter's
Philadelphia, PA	Taylor & Lamson
Philadelphia, PA	Tolan, C.
Philadelphia, PA	Trask's
Philadelphia, PA	Tudor, R.M.
Philadelphia, PA	United Photographic Co.
Philadelphia, PA	Urilne, J.
Philadelphia, PA	Van Syckel, (H.) C.
Philadelphia, PA	Warren's, E.W.
Philadelphia, PA	Wenderoth & Taylor
Philadelphia, PA	Wenderoth, Taylor & Brown
Philadelphia, PA	Whitaker & Co.
Philadelphia, PA	Willard, C.T.
Philadelphia, PA	Willard, O.H.
Philadelphia, PA	Wilson, S.D.
Philadelphia, PA	Wise, Geo. D.
Philadelphia, PA	Wright, P. Philip Wright's Photograph Gallery
Philadelphia, PA	Zorn, Ph.
Phoenixville, PA	Channell, R.F.
Phoenixville, PA	Yarnall, M.B.
Pittsburgh, PA	Alexander & Hodil or Hoedil
Pittsburgh, PA	Cargo's Photographic Rooms
Pittsburgh, PA	Dabbs, B.L.H.
Pittsburgh, PA	Kneeland
Pittsburgh, PA	McBride, T.H.
Pittsburgh, PA	M'Bride
Pittsburgh, PA	Purviance [Williams, S.A. & W.T.]
Pittsburgh, PA	Stout, P.A.
Pittsburgh, PA	Van Pelt, J.H.
Pittsburgh, PA	Whitehead, W.H.
Pittston, PA	Miller, J.W.
Pottstown, PA	Campbell, J.
Pottsville, PA	Allen, A.M.
Pottsville, PA	Mortimer, W.R.
Quakertown, PA	Benner, P.L.
Quakertown, PA	Keil, J.K.
Reading, PA	Clarke & Wiley
Reading, PA	Clarke, Samuel
Reading, PA	Dietrick, Wm. H.
Reading, PA	Fies, Jer. B.
Reading, PA	Hess, J.
Reading, PA	Maurer, D.D.
Reading, PA	Patton & Lee
Reading, PA	Patton & Sauerbier
Reading, PA	Phillips, James M.
Reading, PA	Sauerbrier, G.M.
Reading, PA	Saylor, Chas. A.
Reading, PA	Yeager, F.M.
Reading, PA	Union Photograph Gallery
S. Bethlehem, PA	Stuber, F.L.
Salem X Roads, PA	Doncaster's, J.
Schuylkill Haven, PA	Deibert, H.S.
Scranton, PA	Brownell, D.K.
Scranton, PA	Chase, G.B.
Scranton, PA	Derman & Heerman
Scranton, PA	Schurch
Scranton, PA	Simpson, F. H.
Selins Grove, PA	Kern & Gaugler
Shamakin, PA	Raker, C.

Sherman's Valley, PA	Segar, Wm.
South Bethlemen, PA.	Stuber, F.L.
Shippensburg, PA	Snoddy, R.F.
Stewartstown, York Co., PA	Warner, E.C.
Stroudsburg, PA	Jacoby, B.A.
Sunbury, PA	Byerly, S.
Sunbury, PA	Erskine, J.B.
Susquehanna Depot, PA	Cobb & Hempstead
Susquehanna Depot, PA	Hazleton, J.B.
Susquehanna Depot, PA	Hempstead
Tamaqua, PA	Baily, David
Taunton, PA	King, H.B.
Titusville, PA	Goetchius Bros.
Titusville, PA	Mather, J.A.
Towanda, PA	Bender, Johann F.
Towanda, PA	Wood, Geo. H.
Troy, PA	Gustin, M.
Tunkhannock, PA	Sturdevant, …
Uniontown, PA	Hare & Newlon
Uniontown, PA	Newlon & Hare
Venango City, PA	Sires, J.W.
Warren, PA	Carpenter, W.
Washington, PA	Young, J.S.
Waterford, PA	Nichols, S.A.
Waynesboro, PA	Hamilton
Waynesburg, PA	Roberts, Joseph P.
West Chester, PA	Anderson, A.A.
West Chester, PA	Garrett, C.A.
West Chester, PA	McCutchen, F.
West Chester, PA	Odiorne, Jno. W.
West Chester, PA	Shrieves & Battin
West Chester, PA	Taylor, T.W.
West Chester, PA	Woodward, E.
West Middlesex, PA	Sheets, F.
Wilkes-Barre, PA	Ward & Cook
Williamsport, PA	Campbell's Fine Art Gallery
Williamsport, PA	Smith, Cride….
Williamsport, PA	Stuart, E.
Williamsport, PA	Trapp, T.J.
Womelsdorf, PA	Weidman, J.
York, PA	Barratt, H.
York, PA	Evans & Prince
York, PA	Evans, F. Jas.
York, PA	Wallin, Charles E. (& Co.)
Bristol, RI	Carlisle, G.M.
Bristol, RI	Liscomb, William C.
Newport, RI	Black & Case
Newport, RI	Fowler, J.D. & Co.
Newport, RI	Fowler, J.D.
Newport, RI	Williams, Joshua Appleby
Pawtucket, RI	Alden, A.E.
Pawtucket, RI	Dana, G.B.
Phenix, RI	Buffington, M.L.
Phenix, RI	Richardson, J.C.
Providence, RI	Alden, A.E.
Providence, RI	Brown, S.B.
Providence, RI	Carpenter & Lord
Providence, RI	Chase, Theo. F.
Providence, RI	Dunshee
Providence, RI	Ghirardini, N.

Location	Name
Providence, RI	Hacker, Francis
Providence, RI	Hurd, (G.L.)
Providence, RI	Manchester Bro. & Angell
Providence, RI	Manchester Bros.
Providence, RI	Mason & Gardner
Providence, RI	Messinger & Drown
Providence, RI	Messinger, A.H.
Providence, RI	Pearce, H.G.
Providence, RI	Piper, H.G.
Providence, RI	Randall & Fessenden
Providence, RI	Thurston, J.B., Westminster Fine Art Gallery
Providence, RI	Windsor, E.G. & Co. Hacker, F.
Providence, RI	Wright, L.
Providence, RI	Wright, N.R. & Sweet, … note: stamp blocks Sweet Co.
Warren, RI	Trott, J.
Westerly, RI	Schofield
Woonsocket, RI	Birtles, Frances C.
Woonsocket, RI	Chatterton, J.T.
Woonsocket, RI	Goddar, E.
Woonsocket, RI	Metcalf, C.H.
Charleston, SC	Cook, George S.
Charleston, SC	Mundy, J.J.
Charleston, SC	Osborn
Charleston, SC	Quinby (Quinby & Co.)
Hilton Head, SC	Haas & Peale
Fort Sumter, SC	Bernard, Geo. N.
Army of The Tennessee, TN	Taylor & Seavey
Clarksville, TN	Armstrong, W.H.
Clarksville, TN	Bell & Sheridan
Greenville, TN	Reiff & Marsh
Jonesboro, TN	Kenne
Knoxville, TN	Schleier, T.M.
Knoxville, TN	Smiley, T.H.
Lookout Mt., TN	Bernard, Geo. N.
Lookout Mt. (Chattanooga), TN	Gallery Point Lookout, J.M. Linn
Memphis, TN	Balch, H.A.
Memphis, TN	Bingham & …..
Memphis, TN	Carr, Y.A.
Memphis, TN	Day, Y.
Memphis, TN	Mitchell
Memphis, TN	Richmond, B.
Memphis, TN	Taft, J.W.
Nashville, TN	Barnard, Geo. N.
Nashville, TN	Giers & Co.
Nashville, TN	Hall, H. M.
Nashville, TN	Hughes
Nashville, TN	Johnson, R.A.
Nashville, TN	Larcombe, A.
Nashville, TN	Merritt, T.J. & Co.
Nashville, TN	Morse's Gallery
Nashville, TN	Prior & Radford (Rock City Gallery)
Nashville, TN	Saltsman, T.F.
Nashville, TN	Schleier, T.M.
Nashville, TN	Van Stavoren, J.H.
Nashville, TN	Van Stavoren, J. H., Metropolitan Gallery H. Hall Photography
Nashville, TN	Woodward, J. Fletcher
Point Lookout, TN	Linn, R.M.
Trenton, TN	Pittman & Wolfe (studio also at St. Louis, MO)
El Paso, TX	Parker, F.
Galveston, TX	Galveston Photgraph Co.

Houston, TX	Blessing & Bros. Gallery
Houston, TX	Marks' Photographic Gallery
Great Salt Lake City, UT	Savage & Ottinger
Alexandria, VA	Beckwith, E.W.
Alexandria, VA	Bowdoin, Taylor & Co.
Alexandria, VA	Haas, D.
Alexandria, VA	McAdams, [Peter]
Alexandria, VA	Opperman, August & J.C.
Alexandria, VA	Wolff's
Camp Hamilton, VA	Harris & Larabee
Charlestown, VA	Smith, A.F.
Charlestown, VA	Venner, G.W.
Lynchburg, VA	Tanner & Van Ness
Martinsburg, VA	Rankin, R.J.
Mount Vernon, VA	Cancel MVLA (Mount Vernon Ladies Assoc.)
Norfolk, VA	Burwell, F.W.
Norfolk, VA	Clark, T.W. & Co.
Norfolk, VA	Evans, B.F.
Norfolk, VA	Holiday, A. & Co.
Norfolk, VA	Smith, Charles S. Gallery, Thomas
Norfolk, VA	Walter, Thomas
Petersburg, VA	Lazelle & McMullin
Petersburg, VA	Rockwell & Cowell
Portsmouth, VA	Whilloughby, Emm.....
Portsmouth, VA	Holiday, J.
Portsmouth, VA	Howlett, W.L.
Richmond, VA	Anderson & Co.
Richmond, VA	Harris & Bancroft
Richmond, VA	Levy & Cohen
Richmond, VA	Lumpkin & Thomlinson
Richmond, VA	Minnis, G.W.
Richmond, VA	Rees, C.R. & Bro.
Richmond, VA	Vannerson & Jones
Rondezvous of Distribution, VA	Jones, J.
Williamsburgh, VA	Richardson
Barre, VT	Blanchard, A.N.
Bradford, VT	Allen, F.H.
Brandon, VT	Cady, J.
Brattleboro, VT	Houghton's, G.H. Gallery
Brattleboro or Battleboro, VT	Howe, C.L.
Burlington, VT	Davis, Guy B.
Burlington, VT	Mears, A.S.
Burlington, VT	Miller, C.
Burlington, VT	Read, C.D.
Burlington, VT	Styles, A.F.
Chelsea, VT	Stevens, F.A.
Chester, VT	Hayward, A.S.
Craftsbury, VT	Stevens, J.W.
Craftsbury, VT	Stephens, J.W.
Fairhaven, VT	Myers, S.H.
Johnson, VT	Merrill, (N.L.)
Lunenburg, VT	Snow, B.B.
Ludlow, VT	Cox, L.D.
Middlebury, VT	Taft, O.A.
Montpelier, VT	Davis & Barker
Montpelier, VT	Hersey (S.O.)
Montpelier, VT	Watson & Currier
Montpelier, VT	Watson, George
Northfield, VT	McIntosh & Vose
Northfield, VT	McIntosh, R.M.

Poultney, VT	Alexander, David
Proctorville, VT	Conant, F.C.
Proctorville, VT	Hayward, A.S.
Rutland, VT	Merrell, J.O.
Rutland, VT	Mowrey, F.
Rutland, VT	Merrill, J.O.
South Royalton, VT	Hall's
South Stafford, VT	Burnham, S.P.
Springfield, VT	Merrill's
Springfield, VT	Powers, J.D. (James D.)
St. Albans, VT	Carey, E.M.
St. Albans, VT	Richardson, T.G.
St. Albans, VT	Styles' Photograph Gallery
St. Albans, VT	Styles R.H. Smith Co.
St. Johnsbury, VT	Gage, F.B.
Stowe, VT	Barnes, O.C.
West Randolph, VT	Sparhawk
Weston, VT	Hosely, William H.
Weston, VT	Myers, S.H.
Wilmington, VT	Crossier, Frank
Windsor, VT	Cathan, Lucius, H. or L.H.
Windsor, VT	Cushing, H.
Windsor, VT	Stiles & King
Woodstock, VT	Cushing, Henry
Woodstock, VT	Sterlin, S.F.
Baraboo, WI	Mould, M.
Beaver, WI	Kellogg, E.S.
Beloit, WI	Dunshee, H.S.
Beloit, WI	Jones, M.
Berlin, WI	Tripp's, James
Burlington, WI	Kesler, R.O.
Columbus, WI	Dunn, J.H.
Columbus, WI	Francis, F.C.
Columbus, WI	Howard, J.B.
Delaban, WI	Doane, H.R.
Dodgeville, WI	Cornish, J.J.
Fond du Lac, WI	Boorbach, J.O.
Fond du Lac, WI	Byam, G.W.
Fox Lake, WI	Crowns, J.H.
Green Bay, WI	Clark, H.S.
Hartford, WI	Thomas, H.W.
Janesville, WI	Shaw, E.N.
Janesville, WI	Stevens, G.W.
Janesville, WI	Porter
Janesville, WI	Tice, J.A.
Kenosha, WI	Schwartz
Kenosha, WI	Truesdell (S.W.)
Kilbourne City, WI	Bennett Brothers
LaCrosse, WI	Heath, H.C.
Madison, WI	Bodtker, Jas. Fr.
Madison, WI	Curtiss, E.R.
Madison, WI	Fuller
Madison, WI	Roberts, H.N.
Madison, WI	Roberts, H.W.
Manitowoc, WI	Gibson, J.S.
Mauston, WI	Sprauge & Sev......
Milton, WI	Burdick, E.H.
Milwaukee, WI	Broich, Hugo
Milwaukee, WI	Canfield, E.H.
Milwaukee, WI	Clifford & Hawkins

Milwaukee, WI	Lydston
Milwaukee, WI	Sherman, W.H.
Milwaukee, WI	Ten Eyck, Mrs.
Mineral Point, WI	Kendall Bros.
Monroe, WI	Cross, E.B.
Neenah & Menasha, WI	Manville, C….
Oshkosh, WI	Webster & Walker
Plattesville, WI	Vanderbie, L.
Portage City, WI	Jolley's
Portage City, WI	Love, J.W.
Racine, WI	Anderson, J.S.
Racine, WI	Patterson & Johnson
Ripon, WI	Callender, J.H. Photographer & Dentist
Sheboygan, WI	Morgeneier, W.
Sheboygan Falls, WI	Littlefield, H.B. P., Mrs.
Waukesha, WI	Harlacher, G.H.
Watertown, WI	Bishop, F. & Son
Watertown, WI	Griffith, G.W.
Whitetown, WI	Hart, Miss L.A.
Charles Town, WV	Smith, A.F.
Clarksburg, WV	Knight, F.M.
Martinsburg, WV	Abell, Jno,. N.
Martinsburg, WV	Kaufman & Abel
martinsburg, WV	Rankin, R.J.
Morgantown, WV	Shafer & Lingo
Morgantown, WV	Shafer, J.P.
Parkersburg, WV	Hull, H.B.
Parkersburg, WV	Hull, H.B. & Co.
Wheeling, WV	Brown, John
Wheeling, WV	Higgins' Gallery (Higgins, Thomas H.)
Wheeling, WV	Myles, William
Wheeling, WV	Partridge, A.C.
Wheeling, WV	Wykes & Brown
?	Albright
147 & 149 S. Clark Street	Aldridge, Mrs. J.E.
?	Alexander
?	Aylsworth, J.H.
Kelley's Island	Benedict,
?	Bennett, J.C.
?	Benedict, T.A.
?	Bullock, J.
?	Burke
?	Clark, W.W.
?	Cole, H.H.
Holmes Hole	Conant, J.F.,
Warren Village	Conklin, J.A.,
?	Copeland, I.W.
?	Crooks
?	Crowder, J.A.
?	Davis, S.P. (Traveling Artist)
?	Day, E.
?	Dodge, A.H. & Co.
?	Dunbar & P……
?	Fish
?	Gates
?	Gerould, E.P.
?	Goodwin, D.
?	Hall & Judkins
?	Hart, Murry L.

?	House, A.B.
?	Howe, A.C.
?	Jewell, J. Byron
3 Mile Bay	Johnson, W.P.
?	Jones, T.R.
?	Knect
?	Knect, Josiah Travelling Artist
Springville	Lewis, J.S. --
?	Marquis, A. Jr.
?	McDonald, J.C.D.
?	McElhiney
?	McIntosh, A.
?	Miaz, L.M.
?	Miller, S.R.
?	Moore, N.A. & R.A.
?	Morse & Collins, Traveling .....
?	Mosman, J.
?	Nest & Co.
?	Nichols, W.L.
?	Nick & Knecht
?	Nick, William The "Excelsior Travelling Artist"
?	Pardee
?	Palmer, T.
?	Pearson, W.P.
?	Peter, Lewis P.
?	Peters & Brother, Travelling Artist
?	Pleckers, H., Travelling Artist
?	Pollock
?	Priest, J.
?	Pulaifor, C.A.
?	Reed
?	Richardson, L.A., Travelling Artist
?	Russell, O.F. Wolfborough
?	Sargent, H.E.
?	Saunders
?	Sharp,.......
?	Smith
?	Sweet & Morgan
?	Snow, M.W.D.
?	Southbudy, Morton L.
?	Thomas & Pearson
?	Townsend, O.P.
Charleston	Venner, G.W.
?	Warner, T.B.
?	Warren Village,Conklin, J.A.
?	Webster
?	Weedon, 13 E. Broadway
?	Weider
?	Wheeler, A.
?	Wheeler, G.H.
?	Woodard, Philo
NY	Duchochois
NY	Greer, Henry
NY	Jordan

Stamps Found on Photographs

Perforated	Horz	Vert	Imperf	DT	Bisect	Rate	Description
Y	HY	VN	Y	N		1 Cent	Express
Y	HN		N			1 Cent	Playing Cards
Y	HN	VN	N		Y	1 Cent	Proprietary
Y			N			1 Cent	Telegraph
Y	HY	VN	Y	Y		2 Cent	Bank Check (B)
Y	HY	VN		Y	Y	2 Cent	Bank Check (O)
Y			N	N		2 Cent	Certificate (B)
Y				N		2 Cent	Certificate (O)
Y	HY	VY	Y	N		2 Cent	Express (B)
Y				N		2 Cent	Express (O)
Y	HY				Y	2 Cent	Playing Cards (B)
Y						2 Cent	Playing Cards (O)
Y	HY	VY		Y	Y	2 Cent	Proprietary (B)
Y				Y	Y	2 Cent	Proprietary (O)
Y				N	Y	2 Cent	USIR
Y	HY			N		3 Cent	Foreign Exchange
Y			N			3 Cent	Playing Cards
Y	HY			N	Y	3 Cent	Proprietary
Y	HY		Y			3 Cent	Telegraph
Y				N		4 Cent	Inland Exchange
Y						4 Cent	Playing Cards
Y	HN			N	Y	4 Cent	Proprietary
Y				N		5 Cent	Agreement
Y	HN		N	N		5 Cent	Certificate
Y	HN	VN	N	N	Y	5 Cent	Express
Y	HN			N		5 Cent	Foreign Exchange
Y	HY		N	N	Y	5 Cent	Inland Exchange
Y					Y	5 Cent	Playing Cards
Y						5 Cent	Proprietary

Y						Y	6 Cent	Inland Exchange
Y	HN		N	N			10 Cent	Bill of Lading
Y	HN	VN	N	N			10 Cent	Certificate
N	HN			N			10 Cent	Contract
N							10 Cent	Foreign Exchange
Y	HN	VN	N				10 Cent	Inland Exchange
Y	HN		N				10 Cent	Power of Attorney
Y							10 Cent	Proprietary
N							15 Cent	Foreign Exchange
Y	HN		N	N			15 Cent	Inland Exchange
Y	HN		N	N			25 Cent	Power of Attorney
Y			N				$1.00	Probate of Will
Y							1 Cent	Postage
Y							3 Cent	Postage
Y							2 Cent	Postage
Y							1 Cent	Matches
Y							1 Cent	Matches, Powell
Y							5 Cent	Center of Postal Note
Y							1/4 Cent	Revenue

Bibliography

Books

Adjutant General's Office. *Official Army Register of the Volunteer Force of the United States Army for the years of '61. '62, '63, '64, '65.* United States Army Publications, 1865. Ron R. Van Sickle Military Books, 1987 Reprint.

Darrah, William C. *Cartes de Visite: In Nineteenth Century Photography.* W. C. Darrah, Gettysburg, Pennsylvania, 1981.

Darrah, William C. *The World of Stereographs.* W. D. Darrah, Gettysburg, Pennsylvania, 1977.

Georgi, Carl W. *The United States First Issue Revenue Stamps (1862-1871).* Carl W. Georgi, Buffalo, New York, 1962.

Gernsheim, H. and A. *The History of Photography.* McGraw Hill, New York. 1969.

Hamilton, Charles and Lloyd Ostendorf. *Lincoln in Photographs: An Album of Every Known Pose.* University of Oklahoma Press, Norman, Oklahoma. 1963.

Hatcher, James B., Editor. *Scott Specialized Catalogue of United States Stamps*, Scott Publishing Company, New York, New York, 1977.

Hill, R. and George Birbeck Hill. *The Life of Sir Roland Hill and the Penny Postage.* T. De La Rue and Company, Paris, 2 vols. 1880.

Katz, D. Mark. *Witness to an Era: The Life and Photographs of Alexander Gardner.* Viking Penguin a division of Penguin Books, New York, New York, 1991.

Kunhardt, Philip B., Jr., Philip Kunhardt, III, and Peter W. Kunhardt. *P. T. Barnum: America's Greatest Showman, An Illustrated Biography*, Alfred A. Knopf, New York, New York, 1995.

Lane, Maryette B. *The Harry F. Allen Collection of Black Jacks: A Study of the Stamp and Its Use.* The American Philatelic Society, Inc. 1969.

Sargent, Roger W., Editor. *Revenue Stamps of the United States 1862-1899.* "The New

Boston Revenue Book." Rich Lithographing Company, Chicopee Falls, MA. 1942.

Studenski, Paul and H. E. Kroos. *Financial History of the United States*, Second Edition. McGraw Hill Book Company, New York. 1963.

U. S. Office of Internal Revenue. *Report of the Commissioner of Internal Revenue on the Operations of the Internal Revenue System for the Year Ending June 30, 1865*. Government Printing Office, Washington, 1865.

U. S. Office of Internal Revenue. *Report of the Commissioner of Internal Revenue on the Operations of the Internal Revenue System for the Year Ending June 30, 1866*. Government Printing Office, Washington, 1866.

Warner, Ezra J., 1964. *Generals in Blue: Lives of the Union Commanders*, Louisiana State University Press, Baton Rouge, Louisiana, 1964. 1984 Printing.

Warner, Ezra J.. *Generals in Gray: Lives of the Confederate Commanders*, Louisiana State University Press, Baton Rouge, Louisiana, 1959, 1981 Printing.

Welling, William. *Photography in America: The Formative Years, 1839 - 1900*. The Thomas Crowell Company, New York. 1978.

Wilson, James Grant and John Fiske, editors. *Appleton's Cyclopaedia of American Biography*, 6 vols, D. Appleton and Company, New York, New York, 1888.

Articles

Carrick, Will. "Civil War-Era Photographer's Cancels." *The American Revenuer*, pp. 144-146, 172-175, 188-190 September, 1984.

Carrick, Will. "Photographer's Cancels Revisited." *The American Revenuer*, pp. 2-6, January, 1987.

Fuller, Kathleen. "Civil War Stamp Duty; Photography as a Revenue Source." *History of Photography*, Volume 4, Number 4, pp. 263-282, October, 1980.

Morse, Samuel Finley Breese. "Letter." *The Democratic Review*, May 1839.

Exhibit

Baryla, Bruce. "Taxed Photographs 1864-1866." Selected pages from Finlandia '88 Exhibit.

Glossary

Ad Valorem—Literally means, according to the value. This term refers to a tax on gross receipts.

Black Jack—The U. S. two cent postage stamp. The head of President Andrew Jackson was deigned by Joseph P. Ourdan, a national bank note engraver. The head was used on the $1000 bank note used for the Confederacy. Done after a miniature painting of Jackson by John Wood Dodge. The need for this was by the Postal Act of 1863 which abolished the one cent carrier fee and established the postal rate for local or drop letter.

Cancels/cancellations—A mark found on a revenue stamp to prevent re-use. On photographs, stamps were to be cancelled with the name of the photographer and the date of the sale of the photograph.

CDC—Circular Date Cancel

CDV (Carte de Visite)—French for Card of Visitation. The CDV measures 2 1/2" by 4 1/8". This was a convenient size for the photographer to divide a whole plate.

Circassian— The term Circassian is derived from the Turkic Cherkess, and is not the self-designation of any people. It has sometimes been applied indiscriminately to all the peoples of the North Caucasus. Most specifically, the term can apply only to the Adyghe.

Cork Cancel—A cancellation typically used by U. S. Post Office employees to cancel stamps. A variety of hand-carved cork cancels is known.

Frank— The marking of mail relating to postage by a company or government. It can offer the privileges of free or reduced cost postage, or simply the convience of sending large amounts of mail without the need to visit a post office, or have large amounts of stamps on the premises.

Dual Frank—Two stamps used to pay a tax. Refer to Frank.

From Life—Relating to photography, an image that is printed from an original negative.

Gutta Percha—Substance used to make photographic cases. Western inventors discovered the properties of gutta-percha latex in 1842, although the local population in its Malayan habitat had used it for a variety of applications for centuries. Allowing this fluid to evaporate and coagulate in the sun produced a latex which could be made flexible again with hot water, but which did not become brittle, unlike unvulcanized rubber already in use.

Killer— Lines, bars, grid, etc. applied to stamps to prevent their reuse (see also cancels)

Scarce, Very Scarce, Rare—Terms used in this book to explain the relative scarcity of compared data such as geographic area, stamps, photographers and images.

Sun-fixing—A nineteenth century term for photographs.

Sutler — A civilian who sells provisions to an army in the field, in camp or in quarters.

Vignette— In photography and optics, vignetting refers to a reduction in image brightness in the image periphery compared to the image center. Vignetting is sometimes used for creative effect (e.g. to draw attention to the center of the frame). A photographer may deliberately choose a lens which is known to produce vignetting. It can also be produced with the use of special filters or post-processing procedures.

Afterward

Life is, occasionally, sweet. When fate hands a project like this one to a writer, that has to be one of those times. We frequently talk about being in the right place at the right time. Thankfully, I was.

I can never thank David Horton enough for allowing me to participate in this project for several reasons, the first of which is the images. What a joy it was to handle these 140 year old photographs. When I first started working on *Exposing America*, I suppose I thought of it as a photography book, a period photography book at best. How wrong I was. Each of the images included here has become important to me. For the portraits lacking names of sitters or buildings lacking identification, I'm sorry. I wish we could know who or what they were and relate to you their history, but in some cases we must enjoy the image on its own. As I go through them, I feel almost like I'm looking at a family album. In some respects, I am.

The second reason is the education I've received because of my association with the project. When we started talking about the book, all I knew was that we were doing a book based on photographs that were sold between August 1, 1864 and July 31, 1866. I love history, so I was drawn to the project because of that. As we began to place images and describe them, as we placed the stamps and identified them, and as we examined each photograph in detail for backmarks, subject or place identifiers, or other information sometimes noted there, I began a journey which I've loved. We've included rich detail and fascinating information with some of the pictures. But beyond that, I've learned about the history of photography, the photographers, stamp tax laws and stamps.

The third reason is David Horton himself. Working with him has been a dream. His dedication to and knowledge of the subject has borne us through many long hours, lots of laughter, some frustration and hundreds of pots of coffee when we were ready to fall asleep at the keyboard. His excitement is positively infectious. He is truly a pleasure to work with.

There were times when David was expecting to receive a CDV that made *me* eager for the mail carrier to arrive. Peeling away the protective wrapping on some of the images was almost nerve-wracking. I felt, many times, like a child at Christmas, anxiously awaiting the opening of presents. When he revealed the image, I was almost always pleased. And, I was disappointed occasionally when he told me about a photo he was trying to acquire that didn't work out. There was one image in particular that still makes me sad when I realize how close he was to obtaining it and didn't.

Photographs are intended to evoke an emotion from the viewer. Of course, that intention is usually limited to the original owners of the photographs, For me, looking at some of them actually made me laugh out loud, some made me cry. The joy of discovering something unique hidden in a photograph was unbelievable, as was my grief when I viewed the woman holding her deceased child. When I think of how women today take for granted that first baby picture and compare it to that poor woman, I can't help but feel her emotion. By the same token, when we discovered the feather fan in the bride's hand, I laughed joyfully. This woman married 140 years ago . . . and was little different from today's brides. The dog under the chair, the trick photographs, the trainer with the bear, the spotted pony—so many images that are bound to make you smile—those first discoveries will be with me forever.

Though David's collection is vast, there are still great images out there waiting to be interpreted. Why not start searching for them now? You may surprise yourself when your collection begins to grow with new discoveries and new information.

I'm starting my collection with this book. which is very much like a family album of people and places I've grown to love just as the original owners did. I've set my screensaver to pick up these images at random. Sometimes, I just sit and watch the screensaver, awed by the richness and diversity of what I see.

So, we present to you: *Exposing America: Photographs from August 1, 1864 through July 31, 1866.* I expect many others will find the fascination and love for this book that I found, and I hope you enjoy what you see and read.

Sincerely,

N. C. Knight

Index

Symbols
10th Michigan Cavalry— 60

136th USCT— 59, 60

8th Wisconsin— 35

A
Actors— ix, 32

ad valorem— 112, 113

albino— 42

albumen— iv, vi, 4, 13, 14, 24, 93

ambrotype— iv, v, vi, vii, 7,

American Indian— 44, 46

Angel— 162

apple— 73

Arkansas— 55

Art— x, 98, 138, 183, 186, 187, 189, 196, 199, 205, 206, 209, 214, 215

assassination— 95, 172

assistant— 71, 76

Atlanta, GA— 59, 185

author— 73

B
Baker— 70, 196, 201, 205, 206

J. P. Ball— 151, 163

balloon— 152

band— 65, 66

barn— 92

Barnum— ix, 38, 39, 40, 47, 135, 183, 202, 203

Bastille— 92

Battle of Atlanta— 35, 57

bear— 37

Bennett Brothers— 152, 217

bird— 109

Black Friday— 20

blind— 43

Borneo— 47

Boston, MA— 76, 191, 192, 193

George S. Boutwell— ix, 19

Eli Bowen— 47

Matthew Brady— 18, 19, 58, 61, 95, 136, 184, 202

Brewster— 106

bride— 110, 111

bridge— 77, 78, 90

Brownsville, TX— 78

Burman— 144

Butler and Carpenter— 20

button— 56

C
cabinet card— 16, 21

California— 22, 65

camera— iii, vi, 28, 156, 159

capitol— 88

Carpenter— 20, 72, 190, 196, 201, 209, 214

Carte de Visite— iv

CDC— 18, 19, 58, 61, 95, 136, 184, 202

CDV— iv, 16, 22, 24, 26, 27, 40, 42, 60, 75, 77, 88, 93, 94, 95, 96, 97, 98, 105, 107, 109, 111, 148

Charleston, SC— 82, 215

Salmon P. Chase— 20

Chattanooga, TN— 88

Chicago, IL— 64, 79, 90, 186, 187

church— 78, 79, 81, 83

circular date cancel— 18, 19, 58, 61, 95, 136, 184, 202

Circus— 47

Civil War— iv, v, 2, 8, 20, 31, 32, 36, 39, 43, 54, 57, 61, 67, 78, 101, 115

Clarksville, TN— 172, 215

counterfeit— 112

Courthouse— 83, 207, 208

crutch— 42

Ann Pamela Cunningham— 91

Caly Curtiss— 72

D
Louis G. D'Russy— 170

Daguerreotype— vi, vii, ix, 6, 18,

death— 143

Denver, Colorado Territory— 80, 81

Charles Dickens— 73

dog— 142

doll— 37, 108

Double Transfer— 117, 120, 126

drum— 65, 167

Dual Frank— 1

E
E & H. T. Anthony— iv, vi

eagle— 164, 165, 166

229

Elmira, NY— 164, 201

Ralph Waldo Emerson— 16

F
Fancy Cancel— 134, 135

Ferry— 86

fiddle— 67

fireman— 69, 70

First National Bank— 81

flag— 93, 165

E. J. Ford— 63

Ford's Theatre— 32

Fort Marion, FL— 82

Fort Snelling, MN— 86

John Wells Foster— 95

Benjamin Franklin— 115

C. D. Fredricks— 23, 27

G
Galveston TX.— 173

Alexander Gardner— 14, 92, 94, 136

General James Garfield— 54

George S. Boutwell— 19

George Washington— 52, 115

ghost rates— 113

General Q. A. Gilmore— 173

gold— vii, 12, 20, 80, 167

Ulysses S. Grant— 20, 64

gratis— 125

Gray Eyes— 46

Great Salt Lake City, UT— 177

Horace Greely— 94

guitar— 66, 67, 68

gutta percha— 5, 6

H
hammer— 72

Zaruby Hannum— 40

O. A. Hansen— 40

Sir Rowland Hill— ix, 17, 180

Holy Trinity— 49

Honolulu, HI— 57

hook— 43

horse— 75, 76, 108, 109, 168

Jean-Antoine Houdon— 92

Houston, TX— 97, 174, 216

Huntsville, AL— 57, 182

General Stephen Augustus Hurlburt— 56

I
ice skating— 72

Indian mound— 88

Indian Territory— 44

Itasca— 13

J
Jackson, MS— 170, 197

Thomas Jefferson— 115

President Andrew Jackson— 95

K
Kansas City, MO— 65

Key West, FL— 168, 185

J. H. King— 56

S. A. King— 152

L
Lafayette— 92, 189

Lake Tahoe, NV— 176

Lancaster PA— 49

Anne E Leak— 41

letter— 20, 91, 143

Abraham Lincoln— 4, 14, 20, 32, 35, 160

R. M. Linn— 11, 80

Little Rock, Arkansas— 55

London Stereograph and Photographic Co.— 9

Lookout Mountain, TN— 11, 80, 90

lumber mill— 75

M
Madame Sherwood— 48

Magenta— 86

Mammoth Cave, KY— 150, 190

Masonic— ix, 52, 53, 177

Matches— 107, 115, 125, 221

Mexican Revenue— 115, 127

midget— 48

Mississippi River— 77

Maggie Mitchell— 32

James Monroe— 175

Samuel Morse— 18

Mount Vernon— x, 91, 92, 186, 189, 216

Mount Vernon Ladies Association— 91

mulatto— 170

231

James Murphy— 38

MVLA— 91, 92, 216

N
Nashville, TN— 37, 78, 88, 173, 215

Native American— 44, 45

Neff— 87, 186

Negro— 46

Nevada, CA— 137, 182

New Bern, NC— 57, 197

New Haven, CT— 77, 184

New Orleans, LA— 55, 66, 190, 191

Norman Museum— 47

O
obesity— 48

Odd Fellow— 52

Oil City, PA— 85

oil well— 87

Old Abe— 35

P
Palmetto (Palmitto) Ranch, TX— 78

parrot— 37

patriotic— x, 65, 93, 165, 166, 167

Perry and Loveridge— 81, 82

Philadelphia, PA— 85

piano— 68

Plate Imprint— 127

G. Polhamus— 61

Portage, WI— 83, 84

Portland, OR— 62, 209

Postal Note— 125, 221

postmortem— x, 96

Pre-Cancel— 135, 136

Mrs. J. J. Prior— 39

projection— x, 181

proof— 134, 135

Pulaski— 168, 169, 204

Punch Cancel— 134, 137

Q
R
Raleigh, NC— 43

Mademoiselle Ravel— 34

Lizzie A. Reed— 48

Revolutionary War— 33

Richmond, VA— 175, 216

rocking horse— 108, 109

232

John Rogers— 101

Roswell, GA— 56

S
Salem, NC— 79

Salt Lake City , UT— 177

sandstone— 89

San Francisco— 44, 98, 182, 183

sash— 53

Savannah, GA— 54, 168, 169, 185

Scarcity Charts— x, 128

General Winfield Scott— 91

scout— 46

Selma, AL— 171, 182

sewing— 51

General Phil Sheridan— 181

General William Tecumseh Sherman— 64

Shiloh— 57, 182

sidewheeler— 13, 100

Silver Cascade— 74

John Simpson— 43

General Morgan Lewis Smith— 56

Southworth and Hawes— 150

St. Anthony, MN— 84, 196

St. Louis, MO— 86, 89, 196, 197, 215

St. Paul, MN— 77, 89, 196

Stamp Law— x, 112

steam— 50, 51

stereo view— 8, 11, 41, 105

Sutler— 60

T
taxation— v, 20, 113

telegrapher— 71

Thomas Shaw— 3

tin-type— v, vi, 3, 6, 12, 87, 138, 139

tissue— 9

tomb— 92, 175

toys— 107

J. Q. A. Tresize— 4

Trinity Church— 77

Master Allie Turner— 39

U
U. S. Mint— 80, 85

U.S.S. Constitution— 76

233

V
Vatican— 9

Vermont— 46

vice-president— 95

Virginia City, NV— 177

Virginia City, NV, Nevada Territory— 177

vocalist— 39, 68

W
Alfred Wade— 44

General Wadsworth— 61

wagon— 66, 76, 80

Waino and Plutanor— 47

Charles Waldack— 150

Lester Wallach— 33

Artemis Ward— 161

Henry F. Warren— 160

Washington, DC— 44, 94, 184, 185

Jacob Weatherwax— 60

W. W. Weatherwax— 60

weddings— 110

Wheeling, WV— 64, 218

Williams College— 87

X
Y
Z

Notes